Fighting Women

Fighting Women

Anger and Aggression in Aboriginal Australia

Victoria Katherine Burbank

UNIVERSITY OF CALIFORNIA PRESS

Berkeley / *Los Angeles* / *London*

University of California Press
Berkeley and Los Angeles, California

University of California Press
London, England

Copyright © 1994 by The Regents of the University of California

Library of Congress Cataloging-in-Publication Data
Burbank, Victoria Katherine.
   Fighting women : anger and aggression in Aboriginal Australia /
Victoria Katherine Burbank.
      p.   cm.
   Includes bibliographical references and index.
   ISBN 0-520-08307-5 (alk. paper).—ISBN 0-520-08308-3 (pbk. :
alk. paper)
   1. Women, Australian (Aboriginal)—Australia—Arnhem Land
(N.T.)—Social conditions.   2. Women, Australian—Australia—Arn-
hem Land (N.T.)—Psychology.   3. Aggressiveness (Psychology)—
Australia—Arnhem Land (N.T.)   4. Sex role—Australia—Arnhem
Land (N.T.)   5. Interpersonal relations.   6. Feminist criticism—
Australia—Arnhem Land (N.T.)   I. Title.
GN667.N6B87   1994
305.48'89915—dc20   93-20568
                                                              CIP

Printed in the United States of America

1   2   3   4   5   6   7   8   9

The paper used in this publication meets the minimum requirements of
American National Standard for Information Sciences—Permanence of
Paper for Printed Library Materials, ANSI Z39.48-1984 ∞

To Theodore Nadelson

Contents

Foreword

The title of this book might lead the reader to construe it to be about women and aggression—a topic, or topics, that are nothing if not trendy. An anthropologist more opportunistic and less gifted than Victoria Burbank might have capitalized on this trendiness, as Diane Bell does in her *Daughters of the Dreaming* (1983), the regnant devotional tract on Aboriginal Australian women, or as that group of writers did which peaked circa 1970 and which Ashley Montagu (1976) called "innate aggressionists." But as with *Aboriginal Adolescence* (Burbank 1988), her previous book, Dr. Burbank takes a more modest option. The result is the most elegant emic analysis we have of Aboriginal women and of Aboriginal aggression.

There is a further—and related—contrast. *Daughters of the Dreaming* and the innate aggressionists are engaged in purity quests, wherein more immediate data are viewed primarily as flawed reflections of rhetorically prior (masqueraded as ontologically and historically prior) forms, that is, as archetypes (Eliade 1959). Bell's subject is pre-European Central Australian society, a point already made by Francesca Merlan (1988) in her fine review of gender research in Aboriginal Australia. Robert Ardrey (1961) and many others have opted for the savanna baboon. Robin Fox (1967) employs several archetypes, among them, the (allegedly) Aboriginal "patrilocal band," bequeathed to us by A. R. Radcliffe-Brown (1931), Elman Service (1962), and other writers whose main source of theory is the content of their own heads. I have argued elsewhere (e.g., Shapiro 1990, n.d.*a*, n.d.*b*) that much of the history of Aboriginal anthropology is pervaded by archetypical thought and that such thought is intellectually effective largely because it carries what Mircea Eliade (1963) calls "the prestige of origins." The contrast is as before: Dr. Burbank explicitly embraces the mundane affairs of present-day Aboriginal settlement life.

Which is to say that *Fighting Women* is about Aboriginal sociality. In fact, it might be said to be about "Aboriginal social organization." But this expression brings to mind "patrilocal bands," patri- (and matri-) clans, moieties, semimoieties, "sections" (and "subsections"), and kin classification—in other words, schemes of social categories that have attracted (or repelled) students of Aboriginal life for well over a century, that not too long ago held immense prestige in anthropological theory but that in fact come not even close to penetrating the depths of Aboriginal life and thought. Dr. Burbank steers well clear of such purity quests as Kenneth Maddock's *The Australian Aborigines: A Portrait of Their Society* (1972) and David Turner's *Australian Aboriginal Social Organization* (1980), which bypass the analytical advances of the past three decades in reactionary restatement of the alleged importance of Radcliffe-Brown's "local patrilineal clan." Her book takes its proper place beside such brilliant structural analyses of the current Aboriginal situation as Kenneth Liberman's *Understanding Interaction in Central Australia* (1985) and Basil Sansom's *The Camp at Wallaby Cross* (1980). It is from such works as these that an appreciation of Aboriginal social organization richer than anything Radcliffe-Brown could have imagined will emerge.

Warren Shapiro

REFERENCES

Ardrey, R.
   1961   *African Genesis*. New York: Atheneum.
Bell, D.
   1983   *Daughters of the Dreaming*. Melbourne: McPhee Gribble.
Burbank, V.
   1988   *Aboriginal Adolescence: Maidenhood in an Australian Community*. New Brunswick: Rutgers University Press.
Eliade, M.
   1959   *Cosmos and History*. New York: Harper.
   1963   *Myth and Reality*. New York: Harper.
Fox, R.
   1967   *Kinship and Marriage*. Baltimore: Penguin.

Liberman, K.
   1985   *Understanding Interaction in Central Australia*. Boston: Routledge
           and Kegan Paul.
Maddock, K.
   1972   *The Australian Aborigines*. London: Penguin.
Merlan, F.
   1988   Gender in Aboriginal Social Life. In *Social Anthropology and Aus-
           tralian Aboriginal Studies*, ed. R. Berndt and R. Tonkinson,
           15–76. Canberra: Australian Institute of Aboriginal Studies.
Montagu, A. M.
   1976   *The Nature of Human Aggression*. New York: Oxford University
           Press.
Radcliffe-Brown, A.
   1931   *The Social Organization of Australian Tribes*. Sydney: Oceania
           Monographs.
Sansom, B.
   1980   *The Camp at Wallaby Cross*. Canberra: Australian Institute of Ab-
           original Studies.
Service, E.
   1962   *Primitive Social Organization*. New York: Random House.
Shapiro, W.
   1990   Of "Origins" and "Essences": Aboriginal Conception Ideology
           and Anthropological Conceptions of Aboriginal "Local Organiza-
           tion." In *Australian Journal of Anthropology, Special Issue no. 1, On
           the Generation and Maintenance of the Person: Essays in Honour of
           John Barnes*, ed. W. Shapiro, 208–221. Sydney: University of Syd-
           ney Press.
   n.d.*a* Dr. Hiatt and Mr. Brown: Gidjingali Sociality and Culture The-
           ory. In *Festschrift for L. R. Hiatt*, ed. J. Morton, F. Merlan, and A.
           Rumsey. Canberra: Aboriginal Studies Press.
   n.d.*b* The Quest for Purity in Anthropological Inquiry. In *Pseudo-Procre-
           ative Symbolism*, ed. W. Shapiro and U. Linke. Cambridge: Cam-
           bridge University Press.
Turner, D.
   1980   *Australian Aboriginal Social Organization*. Canberra: Australian In-
           stitute of Aboriginal Studies.

Acknowledgments

This book represents many years of fieldwork, data analysis, and writing. During these years, there have been many people and institutions whose support and encouragement have made all the difference.

First, I want to express my gratitude to the Aboriginal people of Mangrove who have allowed me to live in their community, participate in their lives, and share what I have learned with others. I also want to thank the "European" residents of Mangrove who have helped me with my work. Access to the mission's records and permission to use them in this work are very much appreciated.

The generous hospitality and assistance of so many people in Sydney, Canberra, Katherine, and Darwin have made my travels in Australia a memorable and pleasurable adventure. I especially want to thank Janice Reid, David Riches, and Bill, Rita, and Maree Henry for their many acts of kindness during my visits to their country.

Very necessary material support has been provided by the Australian Institute of Aboriginal and Torres Strait Islander Studies, the Harry Frank Guggenheim Foundation, the National Institute of Mental Health, and the National Science Foundation (Visiting Professorships for Women Program). I also wish to thank Barbara Webster for obtaining a computer and David Glenn Smith for obtaining money for computer services at the University of California, Davis.

This book represents only a fraction of the pages I have written on the topic of women, gender, and aggression. Preceding it are numerous research proposals, working papers, and chapter drafts. I am indebted to the many people who have read and critiqued these: Judith Brown, Karen Colvard, H. Kimberly Cook, Gillian Cowlishaw, Irven DeVore, Patricia Draper, Robin Fox, Jane Lancaster, Francesca Merlan, Nadine Peacock, Harold Scheffler, Janet Smith, and Karen Watson-Gegeo. Here I also want to tell Lila Abu-Lughod how very important and affirming I found her suggestion that, among other things, I be myself. For their very detailed and constructive criticisms of the book manuscript, I want to acknowledge and thank Gilbert Herdt, Annette Hamilton, and Judith Stacey. Thanks are due to Warren Shapiro for writing the foreword, a reflection of our long and stimulating association. I also wish to thank my mother, Katherine Burbank, for her help with the proofs of this book and to say that it has been a pleasure to work with the staff at the University of California Press.

A portion of the material in this book has been published in *Human Nature* (Burbank 1992*a*) and in *Sanctions and Sanctuary: Cultural Perspectives on the Beating of Wives,* edited by Dorothy Counts, Judith Brown, and Jacquelyn Campbell (Burbank 1992*b*). I thank Walter de Gruyter, Inc., and Westview Press, respectively, for permission to use this material.

My interest in women's aggression as competition began years ago in a series of fascinating and enjoyable conversations with Barbara C. Ayres and continued later with Barbara Smuts. My treatment of this topic here was greatly aided by conversations with Sarah Hrdy and Debra Judge. Statistical treatment of women's and men's aggression was facilitated by the assistance of Brenda Gunn and Neil Pelkey of the Social Science Data Services.

During the sometimes disheartening and isolated years in which this book was written, two friends stand out, Sally Cole, whose sojourn from Canada in 1991–1992 seemed at times like an angelic visitation, and Belinda Robnett, whose unconditional friendship has meant so much.

And I must finally acknowledge the great debt I owe to my husband, James Stewart Chisholm. His material support, his counsel, and his belief in me have been unparalleled.

1

Introduction

This is a book about women, aggression, and anger. But it is not a book that focuses on women as victims of male aggression; instead, it focuses on women as aggressors and only secondarily considers them as victims. In these pages I shall argue that women's overt aggression is, in some circumstances, a positive, enhancing act. I shall also argue that when we deny women their aggressive possibilities, we potentially diminish their being.

At odds with much of the contemporary literature on violence and aggression in which women are cast as men's victims, this perspective is a result of my experiences in an Australian Aboriginal community where women's initiation of aggressive acts was conspicuous. In 1977, I began an eighteen-month period of dissertation research in the Arnhem Land community that I call Mangrove.[1] I intended to look at the ways that men and women structured their social universe, expecting to find that male and female conceptualizations varied in ways significant for understanding what we call today "gender relations." Instead I came away with material for a dissertation that was eventually entitled "Expressions of Anger and Aggression in an Australian Aboriginal Community" (Burbank 1980*a*). This dissertation presents an ethnotheory of aggressive behavior from the perspective of Aboriginal women, and it is in the roots of this dissertation that this book begins.

I had not intended to study "aggression" when I first went to Mangrove; the material I collected was not structured according to any specific research plan. Indeed, my interest in aggressive behavior at Mangrove was precipitated by my realization that events called "fights" provided a center for women's conversations with me and with others and thus were a major part of my field notes. Their interest in aggressive behavior was the spark for mine and became a primary vehicle for exploring my guiding question, "What is it like to be an Aboriginal woman in this community?"

Returning to the United States early in 1979, knowing that I would be writing about women and aggression, I began to look for a theoretical framework that would allow me to use my "data" to address questions of significance in anthropology. I found, however, that theories of aggression that even mentioned women as aggressors dismissed their aggression as minimal and insignificant, behavior not worth theorizing (e.g., Tiger and Fox 1971). With women "stereotyped" as the "peaceful" sex (Glazer 1992; Schuster 1983, 1985), how was I to present women's aggressive actions? This dearth of theory on women aggressors was thought-provoking but not disheartening; it allowed me to describe aggressive acts within the framework of what I have termed an "ethnotheory of aggressive behavior"; that is, in terms of the concepts, categories, connections, and rules articulated by the Aboriginal women who discussed this topic with me. Although I have come, along with so many others (e.g., Gergen 1990; Lutz 1988; Marcus and Fisher 1986; Michaels 1987; Rosenberg 1990), to see anthropological description as a far more difficult endeavor than I once thought it to be (a topic I return to in chap. 3), at the time I thought that the presentation of an ethnotheory allowed me to describe aspects of Aboriginal experience without the distorting lenses that Western frameworks invariably impose on non-Western people.

But my experience of aggression at Mangrove can be put to further use. In writing this book, I have three goals. First, I want to further explore Aboriginal women's experience of aggression and to explore the manner in which I have come to understand this experience. Second, I want to explore Western women's experience of aggression, or lack thereof, in light of Aboriginal women's experience. And finally, I want to explore the manner in which Western theories, metaphors, and stereotypes of female aggression and victimization frame our understanding of human aggression and gender relations.

In this chapter, I address several issues of theory, method, and ethics of importance to a study of aggression; in chapter 2, I introduce the reader to aggression at Mangrove. Chapters 3 and 4 focus on Aboriginal women's constructions of aggressive acts. These discussions incorporate material both from my dissertation and from subsequent field trips to Mangrove—one, of nine months duration, in 1981 and one, of seven months duration, in 1988. In chapters 5 and 6, I interpret intragender and intergender acts of aggression in light of both Western and Aboriginal theories. In the concluding chapter, I summarize the lessons we can learn from the women who fight at Mangrove.

Feminism and Aggression

Aggression has long been a feminist concern. On the one hand, feminists see "aggression" as a central concept in an ideology of male domination. Michele Rosaldo (1980a:416) says, for example, "What I would suggest is that in our society talk of natural aggressive and assertive drives is one way that sexism and other forms of social inequality are interlinked." On the other hand, the concept of "aggression" has been used by feminists for their own ideological ends. Jane Flax, for example, calling for a feminist "transvaluation of values—a rethinking of our ideas about what is humanly excellent, worthy of praise, or moral" uses "aggression" to warn us of the pitfalls of a singular focus on the "superiority of the opposite."

Our upbringing as women in this culture often encourages us to deny the many subtle forms of aggression that intimate relations with others can evoke and entail. For example, much of the discussion of mothering and the distinctively female tends to avoid discussing women's anger and aggression—how we internalize them and express them, for example, in relation to children or our own internal selves. (1987a:641)

Feminists have idealized women as both "moral mothers," that is, as "nurturant," "compassionate," and "innately pacifist," and as "individually violent in self-defense or vengeance" (di Leonardo 1985: 602–603). They have identified male violence against women as a major social problem (e.g., Hanmer and Maynard 1987a; Hirsch 1981; Yllo and Bograd 1988) but insofar as it is "seen as a socially produced and often socially legitimated cultural phenomenon," not necessarily as an indicator of innate or immutable male aggressiveness. Instead, it is cast as an instrument used by men to dominate women (Edwards 1987:26; see also Frost and Averill 1982; Liddle 1989). Feminists have also wondered, as I do, if "Perhaps women are not any less aggressive than men; we may just express our aggression in different, culturally sanctioned (and partially disguised or denied) ways" (Flax 1987*a*:641). Further discussions of the various ways in which feminists have conceptualized links between gender relations and aggression and the influence of these theories on my thinking are presented throughout this work.

Aggression Defined

What do I mean when I talk about "aggression"? "Aggression" and "aggressive" are, as *Aggression: The Myth of the Beast Within* (Klama 1988) tells us, terms used to signify a multiplicity of perceived dispositions (or personality characteristics) and actions (see also Brown and Schuster 1986). War, in the Western scheme of things, is aggression; so is football. Children who fight over toys might be described as aggressive; so might the behavior of a "pushy" salesman. But it is our use of the word "aggression" that makes us think that all the things we label "aggression" are unitary (Klama 1988; cf. Gergen 1984); indeed, on only a little reflection we can see the utility of a perspective that takes into account motive and separates, at least initially, the actions of a man beating his wife from those of a serial killer, a pilot dropping bombs over Baghdad, or the operator of a Nazi gas chamber (see also Attili and Hinde 1986). This discussion will focus on acts that I think of as emotion-based, interpersonal aggression. That is, it will focus on individual behavior that is perceived to be motivated at least in part by "anger," or similarly described emotions.

A failure of the social to control is a common theme in Western discourse on aggression; a common image is "nature red in tooth and claw," bursting through a civilized facade. It has, however, almost from the beginning of my work on this topic, been apparent that aggressive acts at Mangrove are not examples of cultural disintegration but rather examples of culture at work. The fights and arguments that I describe are clearly structured activities, patterned and predicted by cultural rules. Indeed, a number of observers have commented on the almost stereotyped quality of aggression in Aboriginal communities (e.g., Hart, Pilling, and Goodale 1988; Langton 1988; Macdonald 1988; McKnight 1986; Sansom 1980; Stanner 1968; Tonkinson 1978; Warner 1937).

Similarly, my focus on motive and emotion should not be confused with an approach that assumes aggressive behavior is best explained with reference to instincts or drives, though I find little empirical reason to reject the possibility of pan-human behavioral propensities with respect to aggressive behavior. But as I illustrate throughout this work, frameworks derived from sociocultural anthropology provide the most interesting treatments of the questions I pose about Aboriginal and Western experiences of aggression. Thus I choose here to focus on aggression in sociocultural context, and assumptions about the cultural construction of aggressive feelings and behavior are central to my discussion.

My thinking on women and violence at Mangrove has been facilitated, in particular, by two developments in sociocultural anthropology. One is the move away from a view of emotions as universal, interior "feelings" to a view of emotions as socially produced, socially relevant experience (see Lutz and White 1986 for overview; Lutz 1988; Lutz and Abu-Lughod 1990; White and Watson-Gegeo 1990). For example, following Fred Myers's (1979, 1986, 1988) reworking of emotions as judgments on the person's relationships to the world, I have come to understand anger as a form of perception that "tells" an actor certain things about his universe. I discuss my understanding of the relationship between culture and perception in chapter 3.

A second development is the explicit concern in anthropology with the relationship between "the system" (a familiar term for those whose political initiation occurred in the 1960s) and "action," or when the context is one of asymmetry or inequality, "practice" (Collier and Yanagisako 1989; Ortner 1984, 1989; Yanagisako and Collier 1987). Here Lila Abu-Lughod's and Catherine Lutz's (1990; see also Abu-Lughod 1990a) interpretation of "discourse" as social practice producing both reality and our experiences of it is of particular importance, for it allows me to pursue an intuition that aggression, at least at Mangrove, is an act in which people try to both communicate about and reconstruct aspects of the world that displease them (see also Macdonald 1988; Riches 1986; Sansom 1980). This interpretation of aggression as discourse or practice is particularly relevant to discussions of gender relations and aggression in chapters 5 and 6.

In this book I do not address questions of disposition or temperament signaled by the word "aggressive"; instead, I focus on acts that might be labeled "aggressive" insofar as they result in physical or psychological harm. In conformity with much of today's current usage, I use "violence" to mean acts of physical aggression (e.g., Gelles and

Straus 1979). Intention and consequence are not, of course, the same thing, and we must question whether or not an act that results in the harm of another was indeed intended to do so. In some instances this is a determination we feel we can make with confidence. We "know," for example, that neither the nurse giving an injection nor a mother struggling to quiet the crying, squirming child intend any harm. On the contrary. But what of the mother who spanks a child who has wandered into the street? Is the motivation for this act concern that the child learn that the street is a dangerous place? Or is this mother expressing anger engendered by fear for her child? Is this spanking "punishment" or "aggression"? Indeed, this last example suggests that like any human action, "aggressive behavior" may be multidetermined, motivated by a variety of perceptions, emotions, and needs (cf. Brown and Schuster 1986; Simmel 1955). Furthermore, the determination that an act is aggressive may vary with perspective (Heelas 1982; Riches 1986). The rape victim feels attacked; but the rapist may feel he has only acted "forcefully." Victims, aggressors, and observers may all understand the hurt of another in different ways.

How, then, can I be sure that what I call "aggression" in Western society bears resemblance to what I understand as "aggression" at Mangrove? Speaking of "violence," Paul Heelas (1982:47) has argued that it is "impossible to devise an objective measure or definition that can be applied cross-culturally." He does concede, however, that acts may be described as "violent" with "the permission of participants" (ibid.: 53). As will be seen, acts women describe as "trouble" bear great resemblance to action we label "aggressive." Similarly, as we commonly conceptualize a link between anger and aggression, so do women at Mangrove posit a relationship between certain emotions like "anger" and "jealousy" and "fights." My definition of aggression is derived, in large part, from my understanding of Aboriginal women's experience and conceptualization of "trouble" at Mangrove. Henceforth, when I use the labels "aggressive behavior" or "aggressive acts,"[2] these can be understood as designations with which I think Aboriginal women would generally agree.

Stories of Aggression

Method, it is said these days, is theory. Our methods reflect our assumptions and values; they limit what we study and what we learn (Crawford and Marecek 1989). But fieldwork is like daily life itself. Our experiences, though routine, vary. Our consciousness is fragmented—by physical sensations, by psychic needs, by our own acts, by the acts of others. We are distracted by sounds and smells and sensations. Our interaction with other people is filled with nuance—some just on the edge of experience, some, no doubt, beyond our conscious experience. And, over time, our relationships, our expectations of our friends and acquaintances, and theirs of us, change. A diary of fieldwork written by someone trained in or with a genius for self-consciousness might begin to capture the method of sociocultural anthropology. But that is another kind of book.[3]

Perhaps the best way for me to describe what I do at Mangrove is to describe assumptions about my interactions with Aboriginal people and how I think these affect what I learn in consequence. I present this brief description with the qualification that it captures, at best, the intended spirit, not the substance, of my method in the field.

Early in my fieldwork, I sensed, on the basis of interactions with Aboriginal people and "European" residents on the settlement, that a primary—and negative—Aboriginal experience with Westerners was one of being judged and, often, found wanting. Most Westerners were there to "convert," "civilize," and "educate." In the final analysis, commitment and friendship aside, Aboriginal people were not acceptable as they were. I think it a fair generalization to say that anthropologists are different in this regard (see Marcus and Fisher 1986). I perceived myself as a different kind of Westerner; I was not there to judge or change but to accept and learn. Over the years and by various means (some undoubtedly more successful than others), I have tried to communicate this stance to the people I know at Mangrove.

Now, whether or not Aboriginal people at Mangrove distinguish me in the same terms that I distinguish myself from the many missionaries, schoolteachers, and bureaucrats they have known is an open question. I know from conversations with other Westerners at Mangrove that they too become friends and "kin," receive visits, requests, gifts, and confidences. I also know that Aboriginal people visit me and do the same kinds of things that they do when they visit each other: ask for or bring something, including news; talk about past, current, or future events; or just be there.

From the beginning of my first field trip to Mangrove, Aboriginal conversation (both directed at me and at others in my hearing) has included accounts of aggressive incidents. Why some Aboriginal people talk so often of aggression I do not really know. They seem to like to talk about current events on the settlement, and fights and other forms of aggression are often current events. However, they also often speak of aggressive events that have occurred in the past. Others have commented on this aspect of Aboriginal discourse. Speaking of Wiradjuri stories of "real characters and events," Gaynor Macdonald says,

Most stories carry basic messages, highlight concerns, and reveal features of Koori life and values which have persisted over time. In this sense, the story is like a myth. Stories are not told to inform or illuminate but, rather, to illustrate and to emphasise. (1988:180)

Of fight stories, in particular, she says,

Fights have a symbolic significance of which Kooris are well aware. In the fight, as in the fight story, there is a transformation of the basic themes which can be discerned in social relations generally. The fight becomes the anecdotal expression of life, the ordering of reality into one symbolic event which expresses the various tensions, oppositions, contradictions and values with which people live day by day. These are relived in the stories which thus take on their timeless quality. (ibid.)

Jeff Collmann discerns in the telling of an Aboriginal life story the importance of fighting in a woman's self-image.

Kathy's image of herself as a "proper number one fighter" embodies her entire social being and that of her women peers. As fighters they most clearly confront the world, its white people, its men, and other women outside their own camps. In this guise they become protectors of their domestic groups as well as their autonomous providers. (1988a:15)

Whatever people's motives for talking about aggression and for talking about aggression to me, I think it reasonable to say that aggressive interactions generate great interest, bespeaking the importance of these events for people at Mangrove. What this importance might be is explored in this book.

I use these stories to explore Aboriginal women's conceptualization of aggression in their community. As a cultural anthropologist I am especially interested in how people see their worlds, how their categories, rules, theories, and perceptions structure and generate their experience (e.g., Agar 1973; D'Andrade 1984; Goodenough 1970; Holland and Quinn 1987; Shweder 1990). As Joseph Reser (1991) has pointed out, a social constructionist approach is particularly useful to the study of violence in Aboriginal Australia. These stories provide a major basis for my analysis of anger and aggression at Mangrove, presented in chapters 3 and 4.

Most of these stories were volunteered in informal conversation, often in my home at Mangrove. I did not take notes or otherwise record them; instead, I remembered the stories and wrote them down as soon as possible afterward. Just as Aboriginal people find aggression very interesting, so do we, at least to judge from its presence in our media. I have certainly been exposed to Western art's reworking of aggressive phenomena. I am a widely read fan of mystery and detective fiction. "Police Woman" was the only television show I regularly watched as a graduate student; I thought at the time that it displayed a certain feminist sensibility. And since the days of *Taxi Driver,* I have become accustomed to graphic portrayals of aggression in the movies. So I have my own ideas of how a "fight story" should go. The question is, to what extent do my ideas filter and distort Aboriginal ideas in the process of remembering and writing them up in my field notes and in these pages? I discuss this issue in detail in chapter 3. Here I want to talk briefly about one aspect of "method" that has, I believe, served to protect, at least to some extent, the "authenticity" of Aboriginal fight stories.

In the early months of my first trip to Mangrove I learned at least one very important lesson about differences between my communication style and that of Aboriginal women. Asking questions in white middle-class society is often regarded as polite. Note, for example, our greeting, "How are you?" Questions, at least from whites to Aborigines, however, are another matter (see Liberman 1985; Myers 1986; Reid 1983). When being told of a fight, my questions of "who," "when," "where," "why," and "how" did not convey interest (or perhaps conveyed too much). Nor did they lead to clarification, because they usually had the effect of silencing an otherwise animated conversationalist. I learned instead that when someone speaks, it is best to sit back and listen (see Bell 1983).

In Basil Sansom's experience, the "recounting" of events is subject to restraint. As a general rule, one should not give a blow-by-blow description of an event; one can, however, present a "communal verdict," "to tell interested people that, as a result of a chain of uncounted events, there is a new state of affairs in social relationships." For example, "Big Jack bin bash Olive [his wife] for no reason. She sick now" (1980:84). While I find that some of my notes of aggressive events read somewhat like "verdicts," they usually contain more detail.

Here, for example, is an entry in my field notes made during my dissertation field trip:

May 20, 1978
[Woman]: Said had been a fight with *nulla nulla* [fighting stick] between [first woman] and [second woman]. Latter has left husband, and [first woman's husband] has been *mangumangu* [eloped] with her. "That boy causing trouble." Regarding [second woman], [speaker] said her mother and father were too much gone fishing so she helped her and they will *gula* [verbal or minor physical aggression] for her when they get back.

This account tells us that two women fought with women's fighting sticks because one of them had run off with the other's husband. The account does not mention that the speaker is a close classificatory mother to the second woman. But it does tell us that knowing the second woman's mother and father (people who might step into a fight on a daughter's behalf) to be away, the speaker intervened in their place. The speaker also predicts that the second woman's mother and father will respond with further aggression when they hear about the event. In other words, it tells us much more than the fact that two women have interacted in such a manner that a change in their relationship might be expected.

Communities differ, of course, and Sansom was working in a fringe camp in Darwin, not in an isolated community in the Arnhem Land Reserve. Perceiving themselves to be surrounded by a sea of potentially hostile and powerful whites (like the police), Aborigines in Darwin might well be more sensitive about the dissemination of certain kinds of information. While it is not clear to what extent Sansom worked with men as opposed to women, the difference between stories that detail aggressive happenings and stories that present verdicts might also reflect the different ways that men and women talk about violence. I pursue this topic elsewhere (see Burbank 1992*a*).

I have observed relatively little of the aggressive behavior that I write about in these pages; in terms of my goal of describing an ethnotheory of aggressive behavior, this fact holds little importance. But I also want to address questions that would normally benefit from observational data. To do so, I have assumed that fight stories are representations of reality, that is, that Aboriginal constructions of fights represent "what really happens" with no more systematic bias other than that imposed by any specific body of culture.

There are a number of reasons to believe that these accounts are no less reliable than many of the crime reports used by other investigators (e.g., Daly and Wilson 1988).[4] Among these reasons are (1) the number of different people who talked to me about aggressive acts during the three periods of fieldwork; (2) the fact that usually when two accounts of the same event differ, they are additive rather than contradictory; (3) my observation that accounts of aggressive acts offered to other Aborigines did not differ from accounts offered to me; and (4) when only one woman told me about an aggressive event, she was likely to be among the women I knew best, and on many other occasions such women had offered accounts that were verified by my observations or the accounts of others.

This reliance on Aboriginal accounts of aggressive behavior bears some resemblance to the "peer nomination" technique first used for measuring the aggressive behavior of schoolchildren. It also shares a strength of this approach: who knows better about the uses of aggression than its perpetrators, victims, and witnesses (Björkqvist, Österman, and Kaukiainen 1992). This exploration of aggressive behavior may be described as an example of "use of the situation-at-hand" (Cook and Fonow 1990:86); in this case, the willingness of Aboriginal people to talk about aggressive events has provided a unique corpus of naturalistic data on aggressive human interaction.

Ethnography and Ethics

In my experience, which first took place among anthropologists working in Australia, there has long been an undertone of worry about the kinds of things we do as fieldworkers. This worry is expressed, for example, in conversations in which the words "colonialism" and "exploitation" are juxtaposed to the words "fieldwork" and "ethnography." Thus, it was with considerable interest and a sense of recognition that I read a paper by the feminist sociologist Judith Stacey in which many of these concerns were expressed. Stacey (1988:22) sums up her mistrust of the ethnographic endeavor when she says, "I find myself wondering whether the appearance of greater respect for and equality with research subjects in the ethnographic approach masks a deeper, more dangerous form of exploitation." And, "Precisely because ethnographic research depends upon human relationship, engagement, and attachment, it places research subjects at grave risk of manipulation and betrayal by the ethnographer" (ibid.:22–23).

Stacey finds two areas of contradiction between the ethnographic enterprise and feminist principles: first, what she calls "the conflicts of interest and emotions between the ethnographer as authentic, related person (i.e., participant), and as exploiting researcher (i.e., observer)," and second, "the dissonance between fieldwork practice and ethnographic product" (ibid.:23). I use her distinction between fieldwork practice and product and her conceptualization of their contradictory interrelatedness to organize this discussion.

It seems to me that our perception of the process of ethnography and the product of ethnography as ultimately "exploitative" is based on the perception that "research" is in opposition to "relationship" and therefore ultimately or inherently antihuman. I would also suggest that our opposition of relationship and research is based on our concept of "use" and the fear that we are turning our subjects into objects. Donna Haraway identifies this "inherited analytical tradition."

As "resource" an object of knowledge is finally only matter for the seminal power, the act, of the knower. Here, the object both guarantees and refreshes the power of the knower, but any status as *agent* in the productions of knowledge must be denied the object. (1989:13)

It is no accident that feminist scientists have made ethical concerns so explicit in their methodology. It is, after all, women who have most dramatically been cast as "other" and who have so directly experienced the "political domination of women through their objectification in research" (Cook and Fonow 1990:76; see also Abu-Lughod 1991; Flax 1990; Mascia-Lees, Sharpe, and Cohen 1989).

But fieldwork need not be predicated on the assumption that research must be opposed to relationship. To examine this point, I return to the concept of "use." Stacey illustrates the "exploitative aspect of ethnography" with her experience of being both "friend" and "researcher" on the death of a key informant. She is uncomfortably aware, for example, that "the funeral and family grieving process [would] serve as further research 'opportunity'" (1988:23). I argue that the ethnographic experience is not unique; humans, not just fieldworkers, put their experiences to other use. I doubt that Stacey was the only mourner at the funeral with a "hidden agenda" (a phrase that belies the positive use to which our experiences are often, if not usually, put). Think, for example, of the comfort we attempt to bestow on a friend in pain when we tell stories of similar suffering. Or, to present the negative face of this aspect of human relations, think of the times we have felt "used" by a friend. Research and relationship are not inherently contradictions. What is critical—but variable—is the quality of the relationship and the content of the research.

Nor need fieldwork be predicated on the assumption that the subject is a passive exploited object. In fact, much of anthropology teaches us that, to the contrary, we should strive for the active participation of the people we engage in our fieldwork endeavors (e.g., Marcus and Fisher 1986). In the field of Aboriginal Australia, for example, William Stanner made this comment about the study of religion: "The first duty of anthropology in dealing with aboriginal religion is to try to elicit the kind of reality the facts of study have for the people responsible for them" (Stanner 1966:25 in Merlan 1989:xiv).

There is currently a concern with the "power relations in the ethnographic encounter"; the ethnographer is cast as "privileged" and "powerful," her subjects as "powerless" and "oppressed" (e.g., Jennaway 1991; Larbalestier 1991; Mascia-Lees, Sharpe, and Cohen 1989; Moore 1988; Patai 1991; Stacey 1988). There is no doubt that Westerners are citizens of the more privileged nations, and their positions in academia bespeak a level of physical comfort that compares favorably with most of the world's experience. There is also no doubt that a legacy of colonialism and continuing relations of inequality characterize many of the communities in which we do fieldwork. But do these inequalities of prior experience translate into unequal relationships in the field? Are ethnographic subjects really without power (see Bell 1990)?[5] Did women and men at Mangrove work with me because, as an American, I was seen as a representative of the world's most powerful nation? In my experience, they did not. People spent time with me, initially, I suspect, largely because of compassion for a solitary stranger (see Myers 1979, 1986). Later, people spent time with me and helped me with my work for a variety of reasons, no doubt, but these included, I think, the fact that I tried to make their work with me an attractive pastime.[6] My attempts to conduct myself according to Aboriginal etiquette was a facet of this. So were my attempts to be sensitive to the mood and feelings of others. My other attempts took a more material form. Usually when I asked questions and took notes, people were paid. Over the years, the amount I have paid for interviews has varied, but generally it has been small—not enough, I think, to induce a person to work with me if she did not wish to do so. Indeed, my requests to work with women (usually made through a third party) have been turned down on more than one occasion. To reciprocate for information that I received as a participant-observer, I gave rides (when I had a vehicle), helped feed and care for children, cooked, gathered wood and carried water, wrote letters, made my living quarters and furnishings available to people, and gave gifts of money, food, tobacco, clothing, and other miscellaneous items.[7] I do not think I would have had to work so hard at being a "good" friend, kinswoman, or neighbor if I was indeed perceived as a powerful figure.

But here I must begin to talk about the ethnographic product. There is one way in which the ethnographer is more powerful than the subject, and this is as a writer (Abu-Lughod 1991). Kitty Kelly (1991), in this instance (and in this instant), is more powerful than former First Lady Nancy Reagan. And there can be no doubt that this book, in particular, is (as are ethnographies in general) a Western product, designed to serve a series of very Western purposes.

Given that it is primarily writing and publishing (as opposed to teaching, counseling, socializing, or political activism) that garners rewards in academia today, I have chosen a book as a vehicle for exploring my experiences with Aboriginal people and the interactions of these experiences with the texts of my discipline. This is not to say that Aboriginal people might reap no benefit from this product; my intentions are that they shall. But, to use Stacey's words, "In the last instance an ethnography is a written document structured primarily by a researcher's purposes, offering a researcher's interpretations, registered in a researcher's voice" (1988:23).

What I strive for in this book is a construction of Aboriginal culture that both addresses my questions and concerns and yet communicates some of the complexity of Aboriginal lives (see Bell and Nelson 1989). My goal is to use my experiences with Aboriginal people but not in a manner that renders them as passive, objectified subjects. To borrow Abu-Lughod's (1991:150) words, I strive here to convey that "the effect of extra local and long-term processes are only manifested locally and specifically, produced in the actions of individuals living their particular lives, inscribed in their bodies and in their words." I believe that I achieve this goal insofar as I am able to portray Aboriginal social life, particularly that related to aggressive interactions, within the context of Aboriginal understanding.

This book is an example of what Richard Shweder (1990:33) has called "thinking through the other," as I use the self-consciousness of others to help me discover what is less conscious, or absent, in my own thinking. But I would argue that this analytic technique represents the use of experience, not the expropriation of experience, as it does not preclude other views of women (whether Aboriginal or Western), aggression, and violence. While this quality of a text ultimately depends on the circumspection of the reader, it is encouraged in today's fashions in ethnography by a postmodern reworking of the traditionally "feminine" virtue of modesty—now transformed into the "masculine" peacock displays that challenge textual "authority" (e.g., Clifford and Marcus 1986). Qualifications that should suggest the limits of my authority may be found throughout this work.

The Romance of Fieldwork and Violence Toward Women

Why does this exploration of women, anger, and aggression begin in an obscure community of former hunter-gatherers, a small group of people who are, from the Western perspective, on the periphery of world affairs? A partial answer to this question is provided with reference to a romantic vision of hunters and gatherers.

In the early 1970s, when I became acutely aware of a feminine status defined as inferior in my own society, I was an undergraduate anthropology major beginning to view social issues through the lenses of evolutionary and cross-cultural perspectives. "Have women always and everywhere been dominated by men?" I asked, along with many others (e.g., Reiter 1975; Rosaldo and Lamphere 1974). Hunting and gathering societies held a special place in my search. The day's wisdom was that hunting and gathering societies could provide critical "exceptional cases." If men and women were found living in harmony and equality in these societies, it would be of particular scientific and political significance, for they were then regarded as contemporary examples of the vast stretches of early human history. They were groups of people more "essentially" human, their relationships expressing human needs and qualities rather than the distortions of rank, caste, or class (e.g., Begler 1978; Collier and Rosaldo 1981; Leacock 1978; Lee and DeVore 1968; Rosaldo 1980a).

By the time I first visited Mangrove, however, I had set aside my interest in women's status, defining it as "our problem," one so compelling that it might blind me to other possibilities in the realm of "gender relations." In place of my romantic hopes for a historic vision of human equality, I found a contemporary community of former hunter-gatherers that was nevertheless filled with lessons for the Westerner seeking humane examples of the current human condition. The expression and control of anger and aggression was one of these lessons. I expressed this sentiment when I discussed my intentions "to write a book about fighting" with people at Mangrove. This admiration is truly felt and is, no doubt, reflected in my treatment of the topic of aggression at Mangrove. But I must ask here to what extent does my belief in the goodness of "hunter-gatherers" deflect my vision from a less appealing reality (see Counts 1990*a;* Erchak 1984).

This question is particularly significant in light of a current literature that highlights the victimization of Aboriginal women, casting violence against Aboriginal women as a problem of increasing proportions (e.g., Atkinson 1990*a,* 1990*b;* Bell and Nelson 1989; Bligh 1983; Bolger 1991; Daylight and Johnstone 1986; Gerrard n.d.; Hunter 1991). Using clinic records and observations in two Arnhem Land communities, Grayson Gerrard (n.d.:9) has estimated that up to 67 percent of the women have been assaulted by a man "at least once in their lifetimes." Audrey Bolger (1991), in a study of violence against Aboriginal women in the Northern Territory, has estimated that each year as many as one-third of Aboriginal females may be the victims of murder, assault, or sexual violence. Using statistics collected by the police, hospitals, community clinics, and women's refuges, Bolger says that most Aboriginal women are attacked by men; in the majority of cases women are attacked with weapons ranging from rocks and sticks to spears, knives, and guns. Women are, according to Bolger's study, also repeatedly harassed into giving up money needed to support themselves and their children or forced into sexual acts they would otherwise refuse (see also Atkinson 1990*a;* Bell and Nelson 1989; Gerrard n.d.).

Bolger shows a healthy skepticism of precollected data and repeatedly questions the extent to which skewed reporting distorts the picture she paints of the distribution of violence in the Northern Territory. She observes, nevertheless, that there is considerable variation between communities. Urban areas, for example, report more violence against women. Within the more isolated communities, she also found variation. In some, many cases of violence against women were reported; in

others, none. Though Bolger says there are no patterns to this variation, she does identify factors associated with more violence (see also
Wilson 1982).

Alcohol is one of these. As Bolger points out, it is not only intoxicated men who attack women, but drinking and intoxication are associated by Aboriginal women with the increasing violence in their lives.
Police reports in the Northern Territory do not systematically record
whether or not alcohol is implicated in acts of violence against Aboriginal women. Nevertheless, Bolger reports that alcohol is involved in just
under half of all cases; it was clearly absent in only 10 percent. It is of
relevance that Mangrove is a "dry" community that has successfully (for
the most part) enforced its policy regarding alcohol. This aspect of violence and the way it is perceived by people at Mangrove is discussed
further in chapter 3.

Bolger also indicates that protection of women may be limited when
communities are large, crowded, and composed of people from several
language groups. Mangrove, as I have indicated above, is a relatively
small community that grew from about 400 people in 1977 to about
575 in 1988. It is located on an approximately square half mile of
coastal sand dunes just yards from the sea. Most significant, I think it
fair to say that the people of Mangrove regard themselves as a community. Most of the population derives from one language group and ten
interrelated clans.[8] Though it is also home to a minority of people who
speak, or once spoke, five or six other Australian languages, these people do not form an obviously separate subgroup. They are integrated
into the predominant language group through ties of kinship, marriage, and friendship. Thus, Mangrove again departs from the picture
of Aboriginal communities where violence, particularly against women,
is exacerbated by problems of social control.

Finally, Bolger (1991:44) indicates that violence against women
appears to be an increasingly severe problem, one that is associated
with the "cultural breakdown, dislocation, alienation, and poverty"
that increasingly characterizes various Aboriginal communities.
For example, women in some of the town camps that Bolger surveyed reported that drinking and violence had increased in recent
years.

Before people didn't drink much—they used to drink friendly—not like now—
fighting, hitting with tin on head, face—fighting in camps or streets. My
daughter gets really bashed up fighting all the time. She always has her leg, or
hand or head bandaged. (Aboriginal woman; ibid.:33)

Bolger undertook her study from July 1989 to July 1990 and used statistics that clustered in the late 1980s and early 1990s. I have not visited Mangrove since 1988. Given the disturbing trend of increasing violence against Aboriginal women, I must consider the possibility that I am writing about a series of social arrangements that no longer exists. There were indications in 1988 that factors associated with increasing violence toward women are on the increase; significant among these is an increasing use of alcohol on the part of women themselves, though in 1988 it occurred away from the settlement. I might anticipate, however, that ongoing attempts to Aboriginalize the settlement, for example, the school, would counteract "cultural disintegration" and "alienation," states often associated with greater violence against women.

Perhaps the most convincing evidence that the violence I describe for Mangrove is usually of a different order from that associated with the increasing victimization of Aboriginal women is to be found in the nature of the aggression itself and the community's response to it. I describe specific acts of violence and intervention in that violence throughout this work. Here, in preface to these descriptions, I present two cases of aggression. The first is a case from Bolger's study, illustrating what violence at Mangrove is generally not.

A woman in an Aboriginal organisation related an incident where she returned to her workplace to find a half drunk Aboriginal man standing over a woman and kicking her in the ribs with big boots. Three male field officers were standing by watching. She told them to stop him, whereupon they replied: 'You can't interfere, it's Aboriginal Law.' Retorting that it was NOT Aboriginal Law to kick a woman like that with big boots, when drunk, she then told the man to stop and get out. He was so surprised that he did! (1991:51)

In contrast, here is an account of an aggressive incident that I witnessed at Mangrove in 1978.

I am awakened by Lily's sister leaping out of bed and the sound of yelling outside. I hear a woman, swearing, every other word is "fucking" said in a beautiful "proper" English accent. Her husband picks up a stick and goes toward her. She is standing in front of my neighbor's house. The husband's mother steps in her son's path. He swings at her, and she ducks out of the way. A man from the neighbor's house, the husband's "uncle," grabs him. While he is being held, his wife rushes at him. His mother goes after his wife, but she eludes her. The husband breaks out of his "uncle's" grasp. Both he and his wife bash at each other with sticks. The "uncle" grabs the husband again. The wife walks over to the next house (about 30 feet away). Her husband gets a fish spear from Tina's camp and heads toward her. His mother goes up to him and blocks him with her body. He, however, continues toward his wife. He no longer has the spear. The wife remains standing in the next yard. Her husband walks right up to her. A woman from the house where the wife is standing, carrying a board, walks around them at a distance of about 5 feet but does nothing. They tussle. The husband's mother goes over and tries to pull her son off his wife, but the wife is thrown to the ground. Her husband then kicks her. People shout for him to go. After kicking his wife several times, the husband leaves. Tina sticks her head in the caravan a few minutes later to say that the wife threw a stone at her husband because he was going fishing without her.

Observe that at least three people attended this fight, ensuring that neither the woman nor her husband was severely hurt. I made no note of this, but it is probable that the man was kicking his wife with his bare feet; rarely does anyone at Mangrove wear footgear more substantial than plastic thongs, and it is unlikely that anyone would wear shoes to go fishing. I think it is also significant that the woman, a relatively new bride, came from another community some distance from Mangrove and at the time of the fight had no kin in the settlement. Her protection, however, was ensured by her in-laws. I discuss the kinds of rules and expectations that predict such behavior in chapter 4. I discuss the social implications of defense and protection in chapters 6 and 7.

In focusing on Aboriginal women at Mangrove as aggressors rather than as victims of aggression, I do not mean to imply that women at Mangrove are never victims. Nor do I mean to imply that it is more acceptable for Aboriginal women to be beaten or otherwise attacked by Aboriginal men. Indeed, in this work I hope to provide an understanding of what is required if all women are to be protected from violence.[9] Here I propose that where women can take the stance of aggressor, they experience aggression differently than women who experience aggression primarily as victims. I argue that because of the sociocultural circumstances that I discuss in this book, Aboriginal women are more prepared to combat the effects of male aggression.[10] Westerners have something to learn from them in consequence.

Who This Book Is For

I have written this book with several audiences in mind. First, it is for my anthropological colleagues, particularly those interested in issues of gender, anger and aggression, and the ethnography of

Aboriginal Australia. I have also hoped to communicate some of the lessons that I have learned from my experiences at Mangrove to a more general audience, though I realize my engagement with the anthropological literature might deter the casual reader. I have also written this book with the people of Mangrove in mind. In addition to my Aboriginal kin and friends who might soon read what I write, I envision some future Aboriginal historian looking back through the pages of this book for hints within the Western mind of what life was like at Mangrove in the 1980s.

2

Aggression at Mangrove

Aggression and Gender Relations in Aboriginal Australia

Discussions of aggression and gender relations in Aboriginal Australia have focused almost exclusively on male aggression directed against women and how it has changed from past to present. Speaking of hunting and gathering societies in general, Jane Collier and Michele Rosaldo (1981) have asserted that male/female aggression is a function of male/male aggression. They contend that where Western contact has increased male aggression, as they say it has in Australia by touching off intergroup warfare, male aggression against women is most "extreme." Somewhat inconsistently, Eleanor Leacock has interpreted the "spirited" manner in which Aboriginal women attack others as evidence of "a persisting tradition of autonomy" but sees the aggression men direct against women as a postcontact tendency to "turn hostility inward" (1978:250). Diane Bell has taken a position similar to that endorsed by Leacock.

[Men's] new models of marriage and male-female relationships, forged within the violent brutalizing context of colonization in Central Australia, emphasize dominance and control. Their anger has turned toward women and their expression of male solidarity takes the form of interpersonal violence. (1980:265)

Annette Hamilton, in contrast, has wondered if the presence of European authority has not stopped, or reduced, men's "outright violence against women" just as European presence has brought an end to male feuding (1981*a*:75). Robert Tonkinson is sure that it has, at least for some women.

> Traditionally, if wives aroused their husbands' ire, no-one outside the family interposed in domestic contexts unless a woman was being seriously wounded. . . . In their new situation as valued workers and sexual partners of the European boss, housegirls could flee to the sanctuary of the homestead and generally be assured of the boss's protection in the event of physical attack by their husbands or other senior male or female relatives. (1990:129)

I do not want to speculate about gender relations in the precontact period or phrase my discussion of aggression and gender relations in terms of change from past to present. Instead, I want to begin with the understanding that I will be talking about Aboriginal people who have adopted (whether by force or choice) elements of Western culture and Western institutions. In doing so, however, they have made them their own. Myers (1986) speaks for many of us when he says that those who see Aboriginal people as pathetic survivors of colonization see only their material conditions, not their "substance." Men and women of Mangrove may, or may not, be confronting issues generated exclusively by modern circumstances when they behave aggressively. But clearly their responses are a product of their unique cultural background whatever its amalgam of Aboriginal and Western elements. The following excursion into some of the recent history of Mangrove's Aboriginal population is motivated not by a desire to re-create the past but rather to understand the present.

Any such presentation inevitably involves choice; some elements are included, and some are not. My selection of what to include in this partial history of Mangrove is to some extent "theory driven" insofar as I attend to aspects of Aboriginal sociality associated with aggressive behavior in Western and Aboriginal theories. Formulations of aggression as a consequence of stress, crowding, and frustration (e.g., Berkowitz 1969; Dollard et al. 1939; Robarcheck 1977) are pertinent here, as are frameworks that emphasize its social construction (e.g., Klama 1988; Sansom 1980). And certainly ideas about the relationship between change and gender relations in the Aboriginal context (see above) inform my perspective. But this history must also be described as somewhat "opportunistic" or "ad libitum" (Altmann 1974). For example, I rely on mission records rather than those from the District Welfare Office, for I had more access to the former than the latter.

Mangrove

Located in southeastern Arnhem Land in the Northern Territory of Australia, Mangrove was established as a Protestant mission in the early 1950s. Since then it has grown into a "town" with a population that approached six hundred by 1988. Most of its first Aboriginal residents were people who had once lived in the surrounding countryside as hunters and gatherers. By the time of my last visit, only the oldest settlement inhabitants had memories of the nomadic past.

Though Mangrove is segregated from more Westernized parts of Australia by the geographic and political isolation of the Arnhem Land Reserve, Western culture has clearly had a major impact on its Aboriginal population. People on the settlement live in houses, some of which are equipped with stoves, refrigerators, toilets, and washing machines. They purchase food, clothing, and household goods at the local "shop"; drive cars and trucks; and use motorboats, metal fishhooks, crowbars, rifles, and shotguns in their hunting and gathering pursuits. They send their children to school, take their sick to the local health clinic, cash their paychecks or welfare checks in the "office," and go to church or to the movies when the spirit moves them. People play cards and listen to popular country and western and rock and roll music on cassette players. Since the 1980s, some households have acquired televisions and videos. English is taught in the school, and an Aboriginal version of it is spoken by the majority of people, along with an English-based Creole and the indigenous Australian language.

It is difficult to ascertain the extent to which the Aborigines of Mangrove have been "brutalized" by Western contact. For about five years at the beginning of the twentieth century, cattle were run near an area once occupied by some of the clans now represented at Mangrove. This cattle company killed Aboriginal people as a matter of course (Bauer 1964; Merlan 1978). Keith Cole (1982) states that ancestors of Mangrove's people were killed during these exterminations. He does not, however, provide details of these events. One married couple at Mangrove spoke with me of violence against Aboriginal people. "The Welfare," they said, prevented further killing.[1] I asked five other women if they had heard about whites killing Aborigines. Two said yes, but other than saying that the events occurred long ago, before the mission, they did not provide further information. It is possible that because I am white, they did not wish to pursue the topic, but I think this unlikely. On other occasions, women volunteered accounts of contemporary Aboriginal/white clashes (such as attacks on Aboriginal people visiting Darwin).

According to contemporary histories, European settlers viewed the indigenous population as a hindrance to white expansion; at best, Aborigines were seen as an inferior people who needed protection from themselves as well as others (e.g., Cowlishaw 1988). In the early twentieth century, however, it was generally assumed that the "Aboriginal problem" would soon disappear along with the Aboriginal population. From 250,000 or more people in 1788, the year that Europeans first occupied Australia, the number of Aborigines had dwindled to an estimated 66,950. Alienation of Aboriginal land and livelihood, disease, alcoholism, and human predation had all taken their toll (Rowley 1977). "In the course of a generation or two, at the most, the last Australian blackfellow will have turned his face to warm mother earth" (Bishop Frodsham's Report of the Church Congress, 1906, quoted in Cole 1977:181).

According to Cole (1977), the founding of the first mission in the general area (about 75 miles from Mangrove) was largely motivated by Christian charity and compassion, an attempt "to smooth the pillow of a dying race." The first missionaries were exhorted by their church to give their Aboriginal charges proper protection and adequate care. In the 1930s and 1940s, however, it became apparent that Aboriginal people were not dying out. The emphasis in government and mission policies shifted from protection to preparation in anticipation of the work of "assimilation" (Rowley 1977).

Over the years, I have been able to speak with several missionaries who were present in the early decades of the settlement. These conversations and more formal interviews along with access to mission letters, reports, and journals and the work of church historians allow me to paint at least a partial picture of early Aboriginal experiences with Western social forces. On the basis of this picture, it can be argued that settlement living itself fosters interpersonal violence (see also Wilson 1982).

The mission period, particularly during the 1950s and 1960s, can be interpreted as an experience of near-total institutionalization in which the value and autonomy of Aboriginal social practices were severely (if not intentionally) attacked (Morris 1988). At the time that Mangrove was established, Aboriginal people were regarded as "wards" of the Australian government, in the "care, charge, and control" of the mission authorities. In accord with the Australian government's policy of "assimilation," the early mission effort was one of socialization as well as religious conversion; their wards were to be prepared for citizenship in the state. Children were sent to school and adults trained in pursuits like farming, carpentry, and domestic labor. Western ethics and etiquette were taught along with religion and morality; Aboriginal social practices could continue only so long as they did not "fall afoul of the Commonwealth's standards of life."

Meeting for people at Store. Reminder of New Year and Rules. Spoke about Church attendance—expected at 7:30. . . . Bell is work bell. If not present at end of Service then late for work and pay will be reduced. Also emphasized importance of bells—punctuality. No early knock off without permission. Will make out list of Mission Rules for observance in Sales Store. (Superintendent's Journals, Jan. 4, 1960)

I did not uncover records of these early rules, but something of their general spirit, if not their actual content, may be inferred from conditions agreed to by a group of people who began settling at Mangrove in 1958.[2] These conditions of residence on the mission indicate what was also expected of its original inhabitants.

Certain stipulations have been laid down and adopted by the older men of the [incoming people], which include (a) They will give all their shovel spears [spears with metal blades] to the Superintendent of the Mission. (b) When, and if they see trouble coming between them and the [original mission inhabitants], they will not approach any of them as a tribe, but will, and must come immediately to the superintendent, depending upon the Mission authorities for their protection (and not their hot heads and spears). (c) That they will send their children to the Mission school. (d) That they will try to be a help to [the original inhabitants]. (e) That they will be willing to learn the Christian way of life. (Mission Report, June 1959, quoted in Cole 1982:40)

Entries in the superintendents' journals indicate that much of the Aborigines' behavior was not, from the missionaries' perspective, in accord with the "Commonwealth's standards of life." In consequence, they extended their authority over behavior that was sometimes not unlawful even according to white Australian law. As punishment for perceived misbehavior, people were expelled from the mission for various periods of time, denied work or given extra work for no pay, or banned from the shop. On some occasions, the whole population would be punished or threatened with punishment for the offense of one. For example, "Sales store window broken last night—people given to Friday midday to find the culprit. If not so able they will have two weeks walkabout" (Superintendent's Journals, June 4, 1959).

Mission personnel concerned themselves with nearly every aspect of the Aborigines' daily life, to judge, again, from journal entries and mission reports. Control was not limited to the activity, education, diet, and personal hygiene of the children and the economic life of adults. The missionaries also attempted to control what were largely, certainly from the Aboriginal perspective, matters of individual autonomy. They attempted to control the movement and location of people.

Some men went to [another mission] [names listed]. Told to return as did not have permission to go. (Journals, April 25, 1960)

They attempted to control their housekeeping.

Self inspection of camp and toilets. (Journals, March 3, 1961)

Self talk women re wasting of rations. (Journals, November 11, 1961)

They attempted to control recreation and comportment.

Stopped camp dancing at 10:30pm. (Journals, December 5, 1958)

[Male name] came and said he was sorry for giving cheek and so is now allowed to start work. (Journals, February 9, 1959)

Similarly, agents of the Australian government took an interest in the day-to-day affairs of the mission's Aboriginal population. For example, here is a journal record of the district welfare officer's visit in September 1966:

Mr. [district welfare officer] saw:
    [Man's name]—re job at Groote: debt
    [Man's name]—re girl . . . warning
    [Man's name] Family—to return to live at Groote permanently
    [Man's name]—warning about throwing boomerang
    [Name]—tribal marriage
    [Man's name]—re wanting [female name] for wife . . .
    [Woman's name]—re domestic fights must stop
    [Man's name]—re domestic fights must stop
    [Woman's name]—re permission for [her son] to marry
        [woman's name] if old [man's name] agrees.

Over the past three decades, the more direct forms of institutional control over Aboriginal people have diminished as they have gained the same rights and obligations as other Australian citizens. At Mangrove, the mission turned over the management of the settlement to the "station council," a mission-introduced governmental body. Renamed the "town council" by 1981, it consisted of two male representatives from each of the ten resident clans. The town clerk, a "European" employee of the council, regularly attended meetings but only in an advisory capacity. The council received and distributed all government money coming to the settlement—the economic mainstay of its population. It hired (and fired) the majority of Aboriginal and white workers on the settlement and had the right to make and enforce settlement rules. In 1988, the council continued to function as the official governing body of Mangrove. By that year, an Aboriginal convert to Christianity had replaced the mission chaplain, Aboriginal health workers collaborated with doctors and nurses sent to work at Mangrove's clinic by the Northern Territory's Department of Health, and a number of men and women were being trained by the Department of Education to replace the white teachers at Mangrove's school.

But even in these days of relative autonomy, the argument that settlement living itself foments violence still carries force (see Bolger 1991). I have discussed elsewhere how the imposition of Western culture on Mangrove's Aboriginal population has led to a battle between the generations over issues of sexuality and marriage (Burbank 1988). David Biernoff (1974, 1979) has suggested that the physical constraints of settlement living foment conflict. With most people residing on the settlement year-round in European-style houses, it is no longer easy for people to simply leave when conflicts arise. This is an important point, for the relative harmony of hunting and gathering communities has often been attributed to the flexibility of their residential arrangements (e.g., Draper 1978; Lee 1979; Turnbull 1982).

People do leave Mangrove all the time, to visit outstations,[3] other Aboriginal settlements, and towns. They travel so often, in fact, that two private air carriers have apparently found it profitable to maintain aircraft and two pilots at the settlement. Most of the people of Mangrove no longer walk the distances they once traversed as nomads; they travel in airplanes, boats, or vehicles. Access to means of departure is not always easy, however. Most people do not own vehicles (and most women do not know how to drive). During at least five months of the year, the roads are bogged by the rains of the wet season. The difficulty of getting out of Mangrove was underlined one day in 1988 when I was visited by a young married woman who had been in a fight with one of her clan sisters. Her opponent's father, I was told, was looking for her, spear in hand. I had a vehicle and, as requested, drove her out to the airstrip. We located one of the pilots, but, following company policy, he refused to fly as she had no money to charter a plane.

On the basis of what I have said so far, it would be easy to interpret aggressors at Mangrove, and their targets, as the more-or-less passive victims of circumstances beyond their control; as a people trapped in a sociocultural setting that exacerbates conflict, tensions, and frustrations unknown in the past. This picture is, however, incomplete. Another perspective on aggression at Mangrove comes into view if we attend to the meaning it holds for its perpetrators and victims. But a discussion of Aboriginal meaning must be preceded with a discussion of Western meaning.

The Settlement and Aggression

My reading of mission journals and records indicates that aggressive behavior has always been an aspect of settlement life. It also indicates that the missionaries perceived its Aboriginal forms as a violation of civilized behavior requiring Christian attention and guidance.

In the evening I gathered the men together. We covered five things. . . . [A man name]'s conduct whilst I was away. He, in anger over some food, threw a spear at his mother. It would have been easy to expel him for life as the penalty should be. However the men decided that he should have one chance more of proving himself. However, it is on Record that there is to be no "next time" trial but immediate expulsion upon similar circumstances. (Superintendent's Journals, September 23, 1952)

The missionaries' response on this occasion indicates a perspective on aggression that is shared by many in the West: aggression is "wrong." David Gilmore (1987) has observed that even most theorists "take a dim view" of aggressive behavior (see also Hirsch 1981). Our guiding paradigm, he says, frames aggression as "social disruption"; the associated metaphor is aggression as disease. Gilmore, however, following Georg Simmel (1955) and Lewis Coser (1956, 1967), dissents from this view: "Interpersonal aggression, so long as it is directed by culture into non-violent (symbolic) forms of abuse, is not necessarily harmful when viewed from the broad perspective of aggregate social relations" (1987:11). Aboriginal people I know would, as I understand them, take this dissenting view a step farther; even physical aggression is not necessarily a bad thing. As Marcia Langton (1988) and David McKnight (1986) would agree, the words of William Stanner capture the attitude we have learned about aggression from Aboriginal people.

Their lives together certainly had a full share of conflict, of violent affrays between individuals, and of collective blood-letting. But in some ways they were more skillful than we are in limiting the free play of man's combative propensity.

If we judge by their settled customs they admitted to themselves that people simply are aggressive and that it was no bad solution to allow what could not be avoided, and to ritualize—and thus be able to control, approve and enjoy— as much as possible of what has to be allowed. (Stanner 1968:47 in Langton 1988:204-205; see also McKnight 1986)

Physical aggression, however, was of particular concern to the missionaries:

Many social problems . . . are causing concern and tension amongst the Aboriginal people and it is our responsibility to emphasize that physical violence is not the answer to these problems. (Mission Reports, May 1969)

This concern, at times, seems to have motivated mission attempts to control actions that were, from the Aboriginal perspective, legitimate means of reacting to moral breaches.

Sunday, November 23, 1958
[Male name] and [female name] [engaging in coitus]. [Male name] sent walkabout for 12 weeks—[female name] to work 12 weeks without pay in sales store.

Tuesday, November 25, 1958
[Husband of woman named above] belted [wife] and was sent walkabout for one week.

According to mission journals, Aboriginal people were asked to "control bad language." When their aggressive behavior came to the attention of the missionaries, they were sent "walkabout" (sent away from the mission to forage in the surrounding countryside), fined, banned from shopping in the mission store, or denied rations. The missionaries did not rely solely on their own sanctions to control Aboriginal aggression. In cases of murder, manslaughter, and injurious assault, the police stationed about 100 miles south, or in Katherine, a town about 250 miles to the west, were called to remove the offenders. The prisoners would be tried in a court of white Australia and, if found guilty, imprisoned in places like Darwin's Fanny Bay Gaol.

With respect to women, the mission presence appears to have protected them from at least some male violence. Missionaries took the part of women who might otherwise have been the victims of male attack.

[A woman] came for [nursing] Sister at night and said [a man] had a stick to hit her. [Another man] stopped him. I went to village with my wife and [the woman] and warned [the man]. Said leave for Koolatong. (Journals, November 29, 1967)

[A man] tried to force [a woman] to go with him as a second wife. This she refused to do and he gave her a beating. She spent the night with us. (Journals, September 10, 1976)

But it is not clear to what extent the mission presence reduced aggression, particularly that directed at women by men. Elspeth Young has remarked that mission policy encouraged the staff to "remain aloof from the Aborigines" (1981:183). This attitude, along with the residential separation of Europeans and Aborigines (which did not begin to break down until the late 1970s), likely prevented the mission staff from knowing about many conflicts.

On all my visits to Mangrove, physical aggression was controlled, for the most part, by neighbors and kin. The council and a police aide (an Aboriginal representative of the police stationed about 60 miles from Mangrove) might take steps to intervene on some occasions, but these were rare. Both they and the police seemed to accept that aggression, though illegal from the standpoint of federal law,[4] had a certain legitimacy and would be controlled by people in the community. For example, here are notes of a remark made by a Northern Territory policeman whom I interviewed in 1981.

Like maybe an old man of thirty or forty and a young fella are having it out over a girl. They are not out to hurt each other seriously. Maybe the old guy hits the younger with a woomera [spear thrower]. But then the young fella goes off and gets a bunch of spears, well that escalates things. Even when a fight is reported sometimes we turn a blind eye. Especially if it's a community set up, we don't worry about it if it's an old man fighting a young man, it's a form of discipline.

Aggression, Authority, and Law

Mangrove is not unique insofar as its members talk about aggressive behavior both as an instrument of authority and as a violation of authority, as legitimate and illegitimate behavior. Authority in contemporary Aboriginal communities appears to stem from two sources: the "Dreaming" or "Law," on the one hand, and the white polity, on the other (see Williams 1987, 1988). When Aboriginal people at Mangrove have used the word "Law," they have usually done so to explain or justify rules and expectations about social forms and conventions. Associated with the Dreaming, the creation of natural and moral worlds (Stanner 1965), use of the word "Law" signifies what is morally acceptable.

A number of anthropologists (e.g., Langton 1988; McKnight 1986; Pilling 1957; Tonkinson 1985; Williams 1987) have observed that physical aggression has long been a legitimate form of social action in Aboriginal society. Illustrations of this point are easily found scattered throughout the literature. For example:

Men grow angry at the death of a relative and give expression to their sorrow by spearing those who "should have protected" him or her. After the killing in Kanawa's group, a wave of such expressive spearings took place among her relatives. *This was proper.* (Myers 1986:169, my emphasis)

In his paper, "Law and Order in Aboriginal Australia," Ronald Berndt remarks that a man not uncommonly "take[s] the law into his own hands" and that this is regarded as "legitimate" behavior (1965:173). Phyllis Kaberry's (1939) description of formal dispute settling is too long to relate here but should not be missed by anyone interested in the legitimate expression of physical aggression in Aboriginal Australia.

The link between physical violence and the Law in Aboriginal society has similarly been noted by many. John Bern, for instance, describes sorcery and physical aggression as instruments of coercion and says "they are policy decisions often taken in the context of the cults, and are reactions to attacks on the prerogatives of those in control as well as to infringements of the rules of the cults" (1979:128). In a discussion of initiation as an aspect of Aboriginal political life, Les Hiatt (1986:10) quotes T. G. H. Strehlow: "Executions of younger males, especially of those who were considered to be disrespectful to the authority of their own elders, on charges of sacrilege were . . . a feature of the accepted penal system of all . . . tribes in the Centre" (Strehlow 1970:120). Lee Sackett also describes how senior men use initiation to punish disobedience.

> But in this case [of subincision], as punishment for misbehaving, the initiand was given a "low cut," that is, the total process was completed in one drawn-out operation. The expression "drawn-out" is used advisedly for throughout the procedure various men urged first one and then the other initiator to perform the cutting slowly in return for the youth's illicit sexual exploits. Several times during the proceedings the initiand pleaded for the men to "wait." Among the more frequent and unsympathetic replies to this was the statement, "this will teach you to fuck around." When the operation was finally finished . . . the new man was again told his "low cut" was punishment for disregarding his elders' earlier advice. Now perhaps he would settle down and join with them in looking after the law. (1978:122–123)

Aggression, especially aggression as punishment, may have long been associated at Mangrove with violations of the Law. One older man, for example, discussed the use of violence in precontact days. He began by saying that if a young man made "trouble" after participating in a ceremony, he would be speared and killed. He continued, "If you hear the men call out for the ceremony you women call back. If a woman doesn't, an old man gets up with a spear and spears that girl right here [through the chest]. No more pretty young girl. But now because we are afraid of the white law we don't do this."

Even if this is a cautionary tale rather than an account of actual past practices, the conceptual link between Law and aggression is made—at least by this man. This statement also indicates that a primary form of Aboriginal social control, the threat of aggressive retaliation for wrongdoing, has been undermined by the imposition of white laws and authority.

Langton's (1988) argument that swearing and fighting are culturally ordered forms of "dispute processing" and "conflict resolution" that maintain and express "customary law" captures the sense of expectation and approval that accompanies at least some aggressive behavior at Mangrove. Here, for example, are my notes of a woman's remarks on fighting:

> If my daughter and her husband are fighting, I'm not going to interfere. If she is [fooling around with another man], he can strike her.

But it may not have escaped the reader's notice that in all these examples of legitimate physical aggression, women are not mentioned as perpetrators. In chapter 6, I discuss the manner and extent to which Aboriginal men and women share definitions of legitimate aggression.

Aggression in Daily Life

The description that follows derives from a series of annotated excerpts from my journals. I present these to give the reader a sense of how commonly aggressive acts reverberate in the day-to-day life of the settlement. These excerpts are taken from a six-week period, beginning on March 15, 1988, the first day of my last visit to Mangrove. My choice of this period is arbitrary; I believe it represents the rhythm of aggression at Mangrove as well as any other. I include here mention of all the aggressive events that I recorded but do not include all comments made about them for reasons of space. Following some of the journal entries, I make general statements of pattern. Some of these focus on gender differences and similarities. This reflects my theoretical interest in the intersection of gender and aggression (e.g., Burbank 1992a) and serves as prolegomenal material for the argument of this book. These generalizations are based on analyses of the 793 cases that I have abstracted from the fight stories, 656 of which occurred during my stays at Mangrove.[5]

March 20, 1988
I said not much fighting here these days. [Woman A] said, no, sometimes they do, sometimes they don't.

For the first ten days of my last visit to Mangrove, the kinds of aggressive acts I describe in these pages did not come to my attention. I do not usually think of the people at Mangrove in aggressive poses. My memory pictures often center around households, groups of people sitting around a fragrant breakfast fire, the meal long since eaten. Now people talk, sometimes walking from one group to another, bringing and receiving news. A woman sits nursing her baby. Another sits with a toddler in her lap. Older women stitch on the pandanus leaf baskets they will later sell; men fix trident fishing spear heads to the wooden shafts they have previously straightened over hot coals. People of both sexes gather around blankets placed in the shade for a game of cards.

Older children bring younger ones into the circle of adult care as the school bell or the attractions of the nearby beach and bush lure them from the family's hearth. A group of older women, their procession headed by a group of trotting dogs, departs for a day of fishing or an excursion to gather handicraft materials.

At morning teatime, when workers break from their tasks and children from the schoolroom, everyone seems to gather at the shop. Men stand together in front of the council hall. Women make their morning purchases in the store. Money, cigarettes, and food are asked for and given; my ears are filled with the sounds of conversation and laughter. Women visit their children in the shade of the school buildings, bringing snacks of chips, oranges, and soft drinks, departing when the school day resumes. The morning's purchases are taken home in preparation for the midday meal. Women wash and hang clothes. Men and women work around their houses, sweeping porches and raking the surrounding sand clean.

Afternoons are often hot; this is the quiet time of day. Husbands and wives rest in companionable silence, two or three adolescent boys sit listening to taped music, young women delouse each other's hair, an old woman sleeps in the shade. Dogs loll in the dirt and cawing black crows investigate the trash barrels that line the roads of the community. A young couple walks up the red dirt road; a mother takes her ailing child to the clinic. As the day cools, men and women may again be seen leaving the village for the sea. A man stands quietly on one leg in the shallow water, fish spear poised for a strike. Women cast their lines into the deeper channel, then reel in their twisting catch. Laughing groups of adolescent girls walk along the village roads. Older schoolboys practice forward and backward flips, their landings softened by the ubiquitous sand dunes. A married couple arrives in the camp of another, bringing a bag filled with flying fox and the shotgun borrowed for the hunt.

Night falls, and people again gather around fires, to eat, to talk, and to play cards. Children continue to run, play, and shout until they fall asleep. By 10:00 or 11:00 p.m. most adults have joined them, and all is quiet.

But these memories do not represent all of life on the settlement. Periodically, if only briefly, aggressive acts are interspersed in the daily routine. On average, according to my calculations, slightly more than one aggressive event occurred at the settlement every other day. Generally, these are short-lived occurrences. An aggressive event might occupy several minutes in a day otherwise filled with the less spectacular but seemingly more benign business of family and community living. These events varied in severity, ranging from verbal to armed attacks.[6] They were not, therefore, always as dramatic as the following:

March 25, 1998
[Woman S]: Last night [a young man] was in a "fight" with [a boy from another settlement]. This morning or last night. [The young man] had a *galiwanga* [a machete-like knife] and hit the boy while he was sleeping. This morning he had a rifle and was just shooting it at a house. [His father] was trying to stop him. Everybody was "hiding."

[Woman M]: This morning was in village . . . when saw everybody running. That was [the young man] shooting. He and [boy from another settlement] had a fight. [The young man] went into a house where the boy was sleeping. The boy might be only 12 or 13. He doesn't know how to fight. His jaw and face are all swollen.

Men are the preponderant users of the most dangerous weapons employed at Mangrove: guns, spears, and knives. Ninety-seven percent of this use was performed by men ($z = 9.02$, $p < .0001$).[7] However, some male weapon use may be less harmful in intent, as well as in effect, than it first appears. For example, in only a few cases was it reported that a man was really trying to shoot somebody. Note how the young man in this case shot at a house, not at a person. In all of the 793 cases, only two people (both male) were injured by gunfire, neither seriously. Similarly, when men take up spears, more often than not, no one is injured. In play, children dodge the grass spears thrown by their playmates (see Goodale 1971; McKnight 1986; Tonkinson 1978). Dodging is a skill that probably reduces the number of adult spear injuries, and aggressors are undoubtedly aware of this skill. Men, however, have been the murderers in this community. Usually their victims have been other men; I recorded seven cases of male death. To my knowledge, two women have also been murdered on or near the settlement. None of these incidents have taken place during my visits to Mangrove.

March 31, 1988
Meeting today to elect representative for the Aboriginal Commission. . . . [Woman A] said yesterday when there was a meeting there was an "argument."

April 1, 1988
[Woman A]: [A woman's husband] asked her for some money and she wouldn't give it, so he cursed all the beach from the jetty right up to [Sandy Creek]. [People calling the ceremony used in the curse] "gagu" [mother's mother], "abuji" [father's mother] or "mother" can take it off. He put it to the ceremony.

"Cursing" is a supernatural form of attack that may be used by men and women, young and old. About 5 percent of the aggression that occurred during my visits to Mangrove took this form. The use of this aggressive technique is described in chapter 6.

April 5, 1998
[Woman A]: Yesterday [her daughter-in-law] caught some fish. She and [her husband, speaker's son] were cooking it and telling each other story and they forgot to give any to [speaker] and then she saw it just bones. They said sorry, and she said, tomorrow I'm going to catch a fish and eat it myself. I can't give any to you and I won't be sorry. And her mouth had a bad taste because she didn't eat any meat.

Almost one-fourth of the aggression I was aware of during my stays at Mangrove was verbal. Of all such aggression, 61 percent of verbal aggression ($z = -4.2$, $p < .0001$) and 75 percent of verbal restraining ($z = -3.71$, $p = .0002$) were performed by women. Men also attack verbally, but their aggressive interactions are more often characterized by physical acts.[8]

April 5, 1988
[Woman A]: The other morning [a young woman] was coming up to the clinic when [another young woman] started saying things about her and [a man]. She [the second woman] was "jealous." [The first woman] said no, he is my full relation, I wouldn't do that. And then they had a fight. . . . [The first woman] got a knife and a stick and her aunties [two names] got stick and they went to that house. And they said to [the second woman] wake up, somebody is here to fight with you. But [the first woman] didn't use that knife. [The second woman] was standing by the house and [the first woman] swung at her with a stick, but hit a part of the house and then [the second woman] picked up a little baby that was standing beside her and that baby saved her [because her opponent wouldn't risk hurting a child].

Women's aggression is not limited to its verbal manifestations. Of the 174 fights—that is, interactions that involved at least a threat of physical violence—that occurred during my visits, women were aggressors or victims in at least 72 percent. Women's weapons are usually sticks—weapons that can do great injury but not with the ease of men's weapons. Women's use of sticks accounts for 72 percent of the total ($z = -4.05$, $p < .0001$). Men and women use rocks and tin cans as weapons to a similar extent ($z = .58$, $p = .5637$). They also act much like each other with respect to the use of unarmed physical aggression ($z = -.36$, $p = .7127$) and the physical restraining of others ($z =$

.65, p = .5150). I discuss women's physical aggression in chapters 5 and 6.

April 7, 1988

[Woman A]: Last night they stole a truck. [A young man] ran off with [a teenage girl].⁹ They were looking for them and when they found them [a man] hit [the young man] with a boomerang. Then after [the young man] went to the *billabong* [pond] and then he took the power house truck. He was "skidding it" up by the office and then running it by [a woman's] house. It woke [speaker]. . . . They didn't stop until they ran into [a man's] house. [Speaker's daughter's mother-in-law] saw [speaker] at the hospital and said I'm going to take [our mutual grandchild]. Maybe there will be a fight where you live because of that boy taking the girl.

April 8, 1988

[Woman A]: [The girl's father] cursed the shop to [a ceremony]. But [another man] said it could be burned [purified with smoke from burning leaves and thus safe for use]. [The girl's father] calls [the ceremony] "mother," he can put it because he is *Mandharija* [moiety name], he couldn't if he were *Mandhayung* [moiety name] because it would be his. But maybe they haven't burned it yet because they want to know which boys took the ignition switch/key? out of the hospital truck. It's a bit "hard."

[Woman W]: [The girl's father] cursed the shop because [his daughter] had been running off with [the young man]. After work yesterday, [speaker] went looking for [the teenage girl]. [Woman C] also told me [the girl's mother and the mother's sister] were looking for her. They found her. Her mother gave her a "hiding." This for running off with boy. [Woman W's daughter] commented that they should send her to [another settlement] because she and [the young man] were running off too much. [Woman W] said our "uncle" smoked [purified] the shop.

This series of events illustrates several characteristics of aggression at Mangrove that will be discussed in the chapters that follow. Among other things it suggests how "making trouble," like illicit dating (Burbank 1987a, 1988), can lead to "trouble" that is, "a hiding." It also illustrates how people at Mangrove frequently deflect aggression away from human targets (Burbank 1985). The young man who took the power house truck and "skidded" it on the roads of the community did not attack, as he might have, the man who had struck him with a boomerang. This may reflect his perception of the man's right to punish him. He nevertheless expressed his anger through an aggressive display of driving. As the man whose house was run into was in no other way involved in the event, I assume the final collision was accidental, or at least not revengeful. While both men and women perform these "displays," as I call them, men are more likely to do so ($z = 6.14$, $p < .0001$). Displays account for about 13 percent of the cases that occurred at Mangrove during my visits.

Perhaps most important, this series of events illustrates how aggressive acts are often embedded in relationships (see Cook 1992, 1993). It is no accident that the misbehavior of an adolescent girl and her young partner precipitated aggression on the part of her mother and father. Nor was it inappropriate for them to be assisted by the mother's sister and the speaker, who is a clan sister of the adolescent's father. These events also illustrate that, at times, aggression at Mangrove can be understood as a socialization technique. Aggression that might be so characterized accounts for about 11 percent of 656 acts that occurred while I was at Mangrove. Women were the attackers in at least 50 percent of these; both young men and young women were their targets. I discuss this topic further in chapter 3 (see also Burbank 1988, in press). The first event, recorded on April 18, 1988, provides additional examples of "family" involvement in aggressive interactions.

April 18, 1988
[Woman A]: There was a fight last night. We couldn't sleep. Those girls. "Jealous" for [a young man]. [A young unmarried woman was at speaker's house.] [A second young unmarried woman] came up to her there and said, "I'm not calling you *gagu* [mother's mother], I'm calling you troublemaker." When she was coming back [from a visit] [the second young woman] was at the area of the shop and they had a fight there—wrestling. [The man they were fighting over] kicked [the second woman] right in the forehead for making trouble and [her brother] got after [the second woman] with a stick. He beat her with it for "making trouble." She went and hid in [speaker's] house. Then [the brother] went to [their mother] and pushed her and was dragging her by the hair, but everybody called out and told him not to do that to his mother.

About 5:00 P.M. I observed [the first woman's mother] marching along the bottom road from the single women's house toward [the mother of the second woman's] house. [Another woman] followed a few minutes later, went in same direction. [Woman S] said she had just gotten back from [another settlement]. Came because [her daughter] had been in a fight. She had been "argument" with [second woman's mother]. Girls were fighting over [the man]. [First woman] is "bruised." She didn't go to work today. [She went out and saw the second woman.] "What for you been come on?" "I'm just going for a walk with this little boy," replied [the second woman]. Then later when [the first woman] was going back, [the second woman] was up by the shop, hiding. Then she started swearing at her and they had a fight. They were swinging each other. [The second woman's mother's sister] was fighting with [the second woman's mother]. VKB: What for? A: Stopping her, she wanted to fight.

[Woman A]: [The first woman's mother] was "talking," "growling" on the road yesterday. She went into that house where [the second woman] and "those girls" were. She was growling at them. When I am here don't fight with my daughter. She has a weak chest. . . . I could make that video (that you are watching) *gurdu gurdu* [sacred and thus unusable]. They were all just quiet, they didn't answer back. If she had wanted to [hit that girl] she would have taken a stick. Maybe she felt sorry that [the second woman] got a hiding from two men [the man they fought over and her brother].

This case also illustrates how aggression may be used to counter or stop aggression, a topic that is discussed in chapters 3 and 4.

April 18, 1988
[Woman A]: Shop was cursed today early by [other settlement] mob. Q: What for? A: "When they drunk they can cursem easy." Burned by about 10:30–11:00 A.M.

The perceived connections between aggression and alcohol are discussed in chapter 3. It should be noted that the "mob" who cursed Mangrove's shop may not have been present at the time. Today with shortwave radio and radio telephone, people elsewhere can curse things at Mangrove and then notify the settlement of their actions.

April 20, 1988
Early break for schoolchildren this A.M. Not clear why. Lots of children playing under [elevated] school [building]. Noise [of children's play and conversation] turns to one that indicates something is happening. Suddenly young boy [teenager] appears, hurls rock at children under school. Fortunately hits pillar as thrown with full force and could really hurt (even kill) a child. Children scream and scatter. A few minutes later [Woman R] says some of the young boys might get spear or rifle. Meeting about petrol [sniffing] going on. [Police aid] talks as does [another man] who says, according to [Woman M], that petrol is bad for the mind. [Woman M, and Woman C]: Boy who threw rock at children also threw rock at his father [name]; he is [name]. He was one of the main sniffers before, he was unconscious from sniffing once. And in the hospital. He stole a container full of petrol and is sharing it with all his friends. One of the sniffers is [one of the speaker's brother's sons].

[Woman S]: One of the sniffers was [one of her brother's sons]. [Her brother] was chasing him and [his mother] gave him a hiding with *nulla nulla* [woman's fighting stick]. Then they took all his long pants, jeans and locked them in a room. He has only short pants and singlet and because he is not used to it he is staying inside.

Inhalation of petrol is an activity largely pursued by adolescent boys and girls. Two adolescent girls once told me that it "makes you mad; screaming and laughing" (Burbank 1988:130). Many adults decry the acts of theft and vandalism that often accompany sniffing. They also express concern about the damage that petrol can do to their children's health. (For recent discussions of petrol sniffing in Aboriginal communities, see Brady 1985, 1991). The connections that Aboriginal people perceive between sniffing and aggression are discussed in chapter 3.

April 20, 1988
[Woman M]: Last night she was lying down [at her sister's] because she had a sore rib cage when [her brother's daughter, a young married woman with children] came in to see her aunties. Told [speaker] she was going to fight two girls from [another settlement]. She was very, very angry, because those girls came to her house, knocking on the door, when she was asleep, wanting to fight with her. She didn't know those girls. It was for her husband. So [speaker] got up and went with her. She was only one and they were two, but she knocked over both of them. Then [speaker] slapped her on the behind and told her to stop and "forgive" them.

[Woman S]: Because [married woman] knocked down those two girls from [another settlement] they cursed the shop. . . . They put it to their father [woman's father] who just died. [A man] burned the shop early. That man is his full uncle. They wanted to leave it for one week, but [the man who cleared it] said there are old people and children here [who need to get food from the shop]. When [a woman] gets back she will give those girls a hiding for putting her uncle [using her deceased uncle's name in a curse].

As this case illustrates, people's reactions to fights can vary. I do not know if this young woman "forgave" her two challengers as her father's sister suggested. Her opponents certainly did not appear to forgive when they cursed the shop. I discuss the emotional aftermath of fighting in chapter 4.

April 22, 1988
[Woman W]: [A man] was throwing stones at [a woman's] house. VKB: What for? A: You know, when they playing card and someone win and take ten dollars [out of the pot]. [Another man] was stopping because "uncle" [is responsible for nephew's behavior]. [Speaker] was also talking to him, telling him not to throw rocks.

April 25, 1988
[Woman M]: Today [a woman] was growling at [teenage girl] mob. While

Slade [high school] mob was in Darwin they went to halfway house kind of place where [woman's teenage son] was. He was to have been released this week, father had even gone to Darwin to get. He was [teenage girl]'s boyfriend and went with her to sleep with her at Bagot [Aboriginal reserve in Darwin]. [His mother] was "really angry" because now he will not be released.

April 26, 1988
[Woman A]: [A man] went after his wife with a rifle. She was at [a neighbor's] eating when she saw him coming. Maybe they had been fighting, [speaker] didn't know. [A married couple] told her to run, so she did. He was after her and he shot the rifle. Good thing she was hiding behind a tree. [Speaker] thinks police will come for this. Didn't know why he did this except: "He is a murderer, he always killing [striking] wife, he can't keep wife," and "He is really jealous." Not like his brothers [enumerates four men's names], they treat wives proper way. [Man] was married before to [woman] but he was always killing her and she left him. Then he went to [another settlement] and got this one.

[Woman W]: She saw [man who shot at wife] going to get some bullets and she saw all the sisters, i.e., [the attacker's sisters] walking [watching what their brother was doing]. She wondered what was going on. The other day he was going to throw a shovel spear [spear with a metal blade] at his wife, but [speaker] told him not to throw it and he didn't.

[Woman M]: Talking about [man's] attack on wife with rifle. "He is a really bad one." VKB: Why do you think he is like that? A: [No response]. He used to always do like that with his first wife [name]. So she left him and when I saw him with his new wife, I felt really sorry for that girl.

These statements underline an important contextual aspect of Mangrove—the number of people willing and able to protect women and men from the worst consequences of aggressive action, a point I shall return to in chapters 4 and 6. Nevertheless, the effects of aggression are not the same for all people at Mangrove. Overall, women are injured significantly more often than men ($z = -4.68$, $p < .0001$). Men die almost four times more often then do women, but this is a nonsignificant difference. Women are injured slightly more than twice as often as men in aggressive interactions between men and women ($z = 4.94$, $p < .0001$). Injury inflicted in same-sex altercations is not, however, negligible. Statistical associations of gender and injury suggest that about 43 percent of the injury received by women is inflicted by other women; they suggest that of the total injuries inflicted on men, approximately 55 percent are inflicted by other men (Burbank 1992a).

April 28, 1998
[Woman A and daughter-in-law]. They are going to have a meeting about [the

man who died yesterday].... That man was young and well. He was talking and drinking tea with his sons and then he just died. [Woman A] was thinking about how somebody young like that could die all of a sudden.... Maybe somebody was sneaking around and shot him.... Or maybe he went outside at night and somebody got him then.... [Both speakers] predict that there will be a fight at the meeting. [Senior man] been talk "We gonna find out who murdered him." They get shovel spear and rifle.... Maybe at the meeting they are going to say to one man, "You been murdering him," and his son and brother are going to get spear and take partner.

[Woman W and husband]: [Speakers] were talking at the meeting, telling everybody not to throw spear, not to fight. But now [male speaker] said no meeting because too much fighting. But they are thinking about who killed him, because he wasn't sick and old. [A man] threw a spear. It almost hit [a teenage boy], by accident. [A young man] shot a rifle. Everybody was coming to the meeting with shovel spear.

In chapters 4 and 6, I discuss links between physical and supernatural aggression.

Counting only the people who normally reside at Mangrove, these events involved as attackers, victims, or those who assist or intervene in aggressive interactions at least forty different individuals, ranging in age from 15 to 66. The average age of these participants was about 36. (I do not know and therefore do not include in this calculation the age of the young woman whose husband shot at her.)

A similar picture of widespread participation in aggressive interactions is presented by an analysis of the total number of cases that I collected. One hundred fifty-six of the women and 164 of the men had participated at least once in an aggressive event, whether as aggressor, victim, or in some attendant role. It must be observed that according to my residence survey of 1988, Mangrove was home to 178 women and 156 men.[10] The fact that the number of men in these cases is greater than the number that resided on the settlement in that year reflects the changing nature of the settlement's population. People die and come to maturity, of course. They also sometimes move from one settlement to another.

Although almost every adult at Mangrove appears to have participated in an aggressive interaction in some guise, there are, not surprisingly, individual differences in frequency and kind of participation. For example, an examination of fights occurring in 1977 and 1978 gives the distribution shown in table 1. Aboriginal statements addressing the sources of this variation are presented in chapter 3.

Similarly, an analysis of men's and women's roles in aggressive

Table 1 *Distribution of Number of Fights for 1977–1978 per Individual*

	Number of Times Individual Fought							
	1	*2*	*3*	*4*	*5*	*6*	*7*	*8*
Men	31	8	7	3	2	—	1	1
Women	33	11	2	1	—	2	1	1

events suggests some variation along gender lines. A most notable difference between men and women is found in the roles of those who "initiate" aggression and those who are its "targets." Men perform 57 percent of all "initiates" roles; women perform 43 percent ($z = 3.39$, $p < .0007$). Men take the role of target in only 39 percent of the total; women, in 61 percent ($z = -4.19$, $p < .0001$). The implications of this gender difference are addressed in chapter 6.

3

The Cultural Construction of Anger and Aggression

That experiences of the physical and social world are apprehended—and thus created or re-created—through cultural symbols (e.g., Geertz 1973; Lakoff and Johnson 1980; Murphy 1971; Sahlins 1976; Shweder 1990) is a premise I have long accepted. Though I believe I would learn something about Aboriginal women's experience of aggression by being hit by one of them, I anticipate learning more by discovering how culture mediates this experience for them. To do so, I explore the ways in which anger and aggression are conceptualized by women at Mangrove, primarily by looking at what they say about it. I also examine some apparent structural correlates of the way anger and aggression are culturally constructed. These structures I assume to be both the creation of these constructs and a preponderant source of the circumstances that reinforce them (e.g., Merlan 1988; Ortner 1984, 1989; cf. Abu-Lughod and Lutz 1990; Knauft 1985).

My exploration of Aboriginal culture has, of course, been guided by my understanding of what "culture" is, and this has been greatly influenced by the work of Ward Goodenough (e.g., 1956, 1970, 1971) and his formulation of culture—derived from his understanding of learning—as a phenomenon to be identified with the individual. My approach here should not be confused with the introjection of Western individualism into an Aboriginal ethnopsychology (for discussions of this issue, see Gergen 1990; Ito 1987; Myers 1986; Shweder and Bourne 1984). Instead, to use the words of Liz Stanley and Sue Wise (1990:43), I assume that " 'individuals' do not exist except as socially located beings," a premise that is central to this work.

Focusing on the individual as the primary unit of cultural analysis has, from the beginning of my work at Mangrove in 1977, provided me with a field heuristic that resonates with my intellectual, emotional, and philosophical goals as an anthropologist. Most critically, this theoretical formulation of culture elevates subject understanding to the ideal, if unobtainable, goal of ethnographic description. It invites anthropologists to base their abstractions of "culture" on what people outside academia have to say and to verify their abstractions, at least to some extent, with these same people (Goodenough 1971).

Goodenough's formulation of culture is also a useful heuristic for understanding variation and change (cf. Reid 1983). If, as Goodenough (1971:20) asserts, the "ultimate locus" of culture "must be in individuals rather than in groups," then "sharing," the definitive characteristic of culture for so many in the anthropological community (e.g., Geertz 1973; Keesing 1974; Peacock 1986), becomes something to be discovered rather than something to be assumed. Along with Goodenough, I assume that it is advantageous for people who live and work together to operate according to similar standards. What might be called "sharing" is achieved when individuals adjust their versions of standards to those attributed to others—attributed on the basis of what others do and say. It is in terms of these attributed standards that individuals guide their own behavior to communicate with others and to predict and interpret their behavior in turn. When communication or prediction fails, individuals can revise their version of the standards to better accord with other people's expectations. Culture, then, is a matter of approximate understanding rather than shared meaning.

Though today I prefer words like "ideas," "knowledge," and "cultural models" to "standards," it is Goodenough's insight that the individual is the locus of culture that underlies the manner in which I proceeded as a fieldworker and in which I describe aggressive behavior as I learned to perceive it from Aboriginal women at Mangrove. I came to see my task in the field as one of revising my standards to accord better with those held by people around me by attending to what others said and did. At Mangrove, of course, those others were Aboriginal women. But clearly this is a process much like learning to understand and function in any new setting, whether as a freshman in the U.S. Congress, a first-year graduate student, a hospital patient, or any number of other situations encountered by Westerners, at least, during the course of their lives. I assume here, of course, that the things people do and say indicate, not replicate, mental constructs, that abstraction we call "culture" (Quinn and Holland 1987; cf. Gergen 1990).

Because I believe that the extent to which ideas are shared cannot be assumed, I wish that I had been able to supplement informal methods of learning with systematic interviews of a selected sample of men and women. I did not conduct such a survey, however, judging it too intrusive. Thus, the process by which I learned about aggression at Mangrove is more like the kind of social learning I have mentioned above; it took place, often in informal conversation, among a limited number of people who were usually women. But as an anthropologist at Mangrove I was more limited in my ability to interact with diverse others than I would be in my own society. I learned about aggression at Mangrove, in the sense that it was described and explained to me, from about forty-six women and older adolescent girls. However, the description of aggressive behavior presented here does not necessarily represent the ideas of all these women. Some spoke to me at much greater length than others. Three women whom I shall call Rosalind, Lily, and Tina guide, instruct, and befriend me whenever I come to Mangrove. There are, perhaps, five or six others with whom I also spend many hours. It is not surprising that I have learned more from these women than from those with whom I talk only occasionally, and this bias in perspective is no doubt represented here.

Assuming, however, that people occupying similar social niches are likely to have similar experiences and talk about them in similar ways, it is reasonable to believe that what I learned about aggression from these forty-six women is similar to what I would have learned from any other forty-six women at Mangrove. These women may speak English with greater facility than some others and undoubtedly are more willing to interact with a non-Aborigine, but I believe they are a representative sample of the women of Mangrove. Among these are mothers and childless women, Christians and women with important roles in Aboriginal religious practice, married and unmarried women, teenagers and "old women," women who work at Western occupations and women who fish for their sustenance, women who had once been nomadic wanderers and women who have known only settlement life.

Newly arrived in the midst of a people whose etiquette, rules, and expectations are largely unknown, the anthropologist must at first rely on her own knowledge as a guide for behavior. Our own culture may help us in early contacts and interactions with others. It certainly lets us perform such necessary activities as finding a place to sleep and food to eat, and, to the extent that there is a congruence between certain domains of the two cultures, it may aid interpersonal communication.

But congruent yet not isomorphic elements can also get in the way of learning. I see learning a new culture as not unlike completing a fill-in-the-blanks puzzle. At the best of times, the blanks get progressively shorter. But in the day-to-day life of the field-worker, they are always filled, if not by elements of the host culture, then by components of the anthropologist's culture.

A description such as I desire to present here—emphasizing the experience of other people—must always be, to some extent, a distortion, for at least two reasons. First, the "continuous unfolding, elaboration, and readjustment" that no doubt characterizes the process of social understanding cannot truly be captured in an ethnography (Gergen 1990; cf. Abu-Lughod 1991). Second, there is inevitably a confounding of the author's understanding with the subjects' understanding (e.g., Lutz 1985, 1988; Middleton 1989; Rosenberg 1990). To what extent do I present the men and women of Mangrove as creations of a Western imagination? This is a question that the reader must always keep in mind.

In her work on emotions in Ifaluk, Lutz provides an extended discussion of the problem of understanding, or "translation" as it is sometimes referred to in the anthropological literature (e.g., Kirkpatrick and White 1985). An emotion word, she says, is "an index of a world of cultural premises and of scenarios for social interaction" (1988:210; see also Kirkpatrick and White 1985; Rosaldo 1984; Schieffelin 1985). Cultural translation goes awry when a word that is accessible stands for a whole that is not. At Mangrove, I worked in a pastiche of Aboriginal English, Kriol (an amalgam of English and Aboriginal languages), and the Australian language spoken on the settlement. When, for example, I learned that the word *riyaldha* means "angry," I thought that I knew what the speaker meant. And in a way I did, as will be seen below. But as will also be seen, in other ways I did not; the scenario that the word "angry" evokes for me is not that which is evoked for an Aboriginal woman. To understand "angry" at Mangrove, I had to learn to envision new scenarios based on new scripts and new theories.

This description, then, is my approximate understanding of some Aboriginal women's ideas about aggressive behavior. In order that readers may better understand my interpretation, I try to re-create something of my experience at Mangrove. I do this, for the most part, by presenting examples of the kinds of things that women say about aggression. Even here, however, it is not possible to entirely separate "them" from "me," and the reader should observe that these texts are only approximations of what was actually said. When interviewing women, I took notes and attempted to take down their words verbatim—but not, of course, always with success. As I mentioned in chapter 1, I also attempted to remember the actual words that people spoke in conversation and write them down as soon as possible afterward. But I know that I did not always remember with precision. I have also edited some of these statements, translated Australian and Kriol words, and rendered many into standard English (following Colby's [1966] suggestions).

Cultural translation also requires that the concepts of both societies be rendered explicit (Lutz 1985, 1988). As I have indicated, the array of Western theories on aggression, both folk and formal, is vast and unwieldy, and I cannot even pretend to present its outlines in this work. I will, however, in conformity with my attempt to separate Aboriginal conceptualization from my own, try to make explicit my own thoughts about aggression. Though these now have been informed by Aboriginal ideas for more than ten years, I attempt to tease apart the strands of experience from Western and Aboriginal sources.

Edward Schieffelin (1985) has observed that cultural anthropologists routinely assume that words provide an entrée into the conceptualization of other people. This description begins with just such an analytic tactic: an investigation of the words "trouble" and "angry." But the meaning of words cannot be derived from the words themselves (Kirkpatrick and White 1985; Quinn and Strauss 1989; Rosenberg 1990; Shapiro 1990; Schieffelin 1985). I "look beyond" (Rosaldo 1980b:24) the words "trouble" and "anger" by analyzing associations and metaphors found in the texts of women's talk about anger and aggression. This kind of analysis, common in cultural and psychological anthropology today (e.g., Kirkpatrick and White 1985), rests on several assumptions I shall briefly discuss below.

My methodological interest in associations derives from a belief in the psychoanalytic principle that nothing people say or do is accidental and without meaning (Brenner 1957), a principle bearing a certain resemblance to current theories of connectionism that assert that "whatever is apprehended together in the individual's experience comes to have strengths of association in the mind" (Quinn and Strauss 1989:5). Unlike Freud (1920a) and his followers, however, who use "free association" as a technique for exploring the "unconscious," I, like other psychocultural anthropologists (e.g., Howard 1985; Rosaldo 1980b, 1984; White and Kirkpatrick 1985), explore the more or less conscious and deliberate connections that Aboriginal women make between anger, aggression, and other realms of their social universe.

My analysis of metaphor is based on a similar set of assumptions. These arise from George Lakoff and Mark Johnson's (1980) observation that metaphor is more than a literary device. Metaphor enables and thus permeates language and thought; it allows us to replace the intangible with the tangible, the abstract with the concrete. "War" may be used to conceptualize "argument" because we experience "war" in terms of physical space and occurrence, that is, more easily than we apprehend the ephemeral, sometimes ineffable quality of those interactions we call "arguments" (Holland and Quinn 1987; Lakoff and Johnson 1980). But I do not limit my dissection to the metaphors of Aboriginal women alone. Metaphors assist but also limit thought. To continue with Lakoff and Johnson's example of "argument" as "war," this metaphor, they say, may blind us to the possibility that arguing is not only a form of attack but also a form of cooperation, an attempt at understanding. We can learn to see the world differently by viewing it through new lenses (Ortner 1984). This process not only involves the discovery of new metaphors but also leads to new experiences of the world in terms of these metaphors. This requires that our normal way of perceiving be set aside; to do this, we must identify our ways of perceiving (Lutz 1985, 1988). In later chapters I examine some of the metaphors that Westerners, particularly social scientists, use to structure their experiences of anger and aggression.

My analysis is, of course, selective. It cannot be otherwise, and I leave most of our metaphors untouched. These, I hope, will be scrutinized by others. I also hope that the new and different perspectives that diverse authors can bring to the study of women, anger, and aggression will someday create a more vivid and many-sided picture of human aggression than I am able to paint here.

Anger and Aggression

What I understand as aggression is signaled by Aboriginal women when they use the words "trouble," *wungari,* or "fight." "What does the word 'trouble' mean?" I ask. Rosalind answers first, Tina second.

Means any sort of trouble. Might be if you've got trouble for somebody else, for one of the girls and I hear you growling and I go talk to that girl, "Hey, you got trouble." "From whom?" "From Vicky. She's been talking about you." Might be you and that girl have one husband. "Oh . . . she covet my husband. He's not for her, he's mine." Well, I go tell her that she's got trouble. "What for?" "Oh, you've been stealing her husband, she said." Well, that girl is gonna get up and talk to you. And you say, "Oh, you've been stealing my husband." And you are gonna get up and get a stick and that girl is gonna get a stick too and you are gonna fight with that stick. Sometimes trouble when you go on a date; someone sees you and tells other people. Oh trouble, that means trouble for a man or any sort [of thing] that we don't like to talk about, ceremony way [supernatural aggression]. Sometimes trouble means they can talk behind your back and you don't listen. And afterwards, someone is going to tell you, "That someone was talking behind your back when you couldn't hear." But you are gonna talk, "Why can't he come and talk to me in front of everybody." That kind, they call it "trouble."

Somebody comes up telling you, "You sit down, you've got trouble." Like if you steal, you've been stealing something, you've got big trouble. You can't come outside; by and by they'll kill you. . . . Like you've been stealing tobacco or food for a ceremony. They can kill you with a spear, tomahawk. You go to get wood; might be there they kill you. A cheeky man kills you with a spear. Then they fix you up, just like a doctor. Then you lay down, you sleep. They tell you, "Three days you stay, you feel sick, in one week you die." You get up now. You don't see them. They've got a song [to ensure that]. You've got a mark, that's where he struck you with the spear and then shut [the wound] up. You go and sit in camp, see a girl, you get wild, grab a stick. You get wild because of that mark. You get up now. "You've been talking at me. You've been swearing. Come on, you and I will fight." . . . Right, well she might strike you now, she's got a stick or just with her hand. Well you die now. Like next morning you die. Or you feel sick [and you die].

As Rosalind's reply indicates, "trouble," "wungari," or "fight" can be used to mean aggressive behavior, verbal or physical. In American English, the word "fight" is used in a similar manner; it can be used to signal a physical battle, but it can also be used to mean any kind of "hostile encounter" (*Merriam-Webster's Collegiate Dictionary*, 10th ed.). In both cases, however, conceptual and linguistic distinctions are made between verbal and physical aggression. At Mangrove, both "fight" and "wunguari" are used to distinguish physical aggression from "growling," "rowing," and "arguing," that is, aggression limited to verbal attack.

Argument is the same, like "growling." Sometimes if you don't want to use [the words] "teasing" or "growling," just "finding fault." "Fight" is like "wungari." You are going to fight now, get a broom or a stick and go and hit her. "Fight," that means you are going to wrestle now.

Only word, that'll do. That's nothing. He *gula* [a verbal or minor physical altercation], but he can't fight. He gula, but he stops. That fight, that's [something else], when he's wild properly. Well two fellows fight, two fellows are wild, two fellows run and grab spears straight away. That's a proper fight when he's wild.

A fight is when maybe a girl gets involved in trouble, just like when a single girl goes out with a married girl's husband and when [the married woman] finds out, she goes looking for that young girl to fight. . . . [Or] when they argue or when they grab each other's hair, they call that a fight. When they argue they still call that a wungari, but in the other way, they don't call it a fight.

But verbal aggression and physical aggression are also conceptually linked in the sense that the former is said to have the potential for provoking the latter.

When a person you love growls at you, you don't get temper, but when you don't love that person you get angry and fight.

Swearing, in particular, can make a fight inevitable.

"Big penis," this is a bad word. If you say it that man might strike you. "Big vagina," this is really bad. If you say it there will be fighting.

Women talk about "trouble" and they talk about people who "make trouble." People who make trouble do not necessarily behave aggressively, though they may, but their behavior is such that an aggressive act will likely follow.

Maybe somebody makes trouble and he runs away and hides himself in the house . . . and some man wants to spear him.

I have come to understand "trouble" as a word signifying a complex of potentiality that begins with "make trouble"—action that is expected to provoke an attack, whether verbal, physical, or supernatural. From the moment that people make trouble, there is an anticipation of danger, physical attack, even death. This eventuality is indicated, perhaps, by the polysemy of the Kriol word "kill"; it can mean either "strike" or "kill." Danger, physical attack, and death are not seen as inevitable, however. In chapter 4, I describe how this anticipation affects the ways in which people respond to aggressive behavior at Mangrove.

When women at Mangrove talk about aggression, they often talk about anger. That is, their descriptions of aggressive events often include words in Aboriginal English, Kriol, or the Australian language that I understand to mean "anger"—"an intense emotional state induced by displeasure" (*Merriam-Webster's Collegiate Dictionary*, 10th ed.). The chest or abdomen is said to be the seat of anger as well as other emotions. Anger is associated with heat, as is illness. Both sick and angry people are "hot." According to Lily, when a man kills or injures another human, it makes him "hot inside, sick and old and gray." Underarm sweat is used to cool the body and brow of a feverish person. It is also used to remove the sweat of a dead man from his widows' bodies and bring to an end periods of food restriction. It is not, however, to my knowledge, used to calm an angry person. But an angry person is allowed to "cold," that is, cool off, suggesting that anger, like illness, is seen as a deviation from health or normalcy. Rosalind once spoke about anger as a pumping of the heart.

Cheeky is when they growl at them and something pumps that heart for them and makes them cheeky, . . . hot. Cheeky is like angry.

Over the years that I have been visiting Mangrove I have asked many of the women I know what makes people "angry." I have also collected women's conversational comments about anger. These statements illustrate the kind of things Aboriginal women say they get angry about and the kinds of things they think makes other people in their community angry. Myers understands anger among Pintupi people of the Western Desert as an experience in which "a subject evaluates some entity in the world as unjustifiably harming or threatening him or her and desires punishment for the causer of harm" (1988:597). I understand anger at Mangrove in a similar way—primarily as a negative evaluation of an actor's current circumstance—but wish to emphasize the communicative role that anger plays. We do not, I think, need "anthropological tradition" to tell us "that strong emotion is a sign of social import" (Rosaldo 1980*b*:35). If indeed we did not already intuit this to be the case, recent constructions of emotions as judgments (e.g., Myers 1988) or as "discourse on problems" (Lutz 1990:88) would suggest this to be so. Along similar lines, John Kirkpatrick and Geoffrey White have observed that behavioral departures from the "normal or desirable," like fights, invite folk definitions and interpretations that "may demarcate the margins of the social order as a whole" (1985:24). Anger and aggression, at least as I see them at Mangrove, signal that something is important to the person expressing them. These expressions often include information about what that something might be. Thus, to understand what makes people at Mangrove angry—usually the same things they say can lead to aggression—is to understand a great deal about the things that matter in their lives.

Women say that when some people will not do as they are told, it makes other people angry. Being told what to do or what not to do can also make people angry.

> I wanted to sleep late but that old man woke me up so I would make a fire and boil tea. I was really angry with him yesterday. He kept telling me, "Do this, do that."

The nonperformance of expected roles and duties can make people angry. A number of women mentioned that men and women would get angry if their spouse did not perform expected economic tasks. For example, one woman said a man would get angry if there was no food or tea at home. Rosalind said a woman would be angry if her husband refused to go hunting or fishing.

Violation of expectations in the sphere of ritual is also cause for anger. An "old woman" once told me how angry she was because funeral rituals were completed before all the relatives of the deceased arrived at the settlement. "Wait until we get back [from the outstation we planned to visit], then I'm going to put more rain clouds than they have ever seen [bringing rain in retaliation for the slight]." Lily once told two other women that her husband was angry because several men trespassed on sacred ritual ground in his country. Conversely, sometimes ritual deployment is cause for anger. For example, people were said to be angry when others "cursed" an area, placing it in the domain of the sacred and thus off-limits for fishing (discussed in detail in chap. 6).

Death is associated with anger, especially when sorcery is the suspected cause. This is Rosalind's response to my questions about emotions associated with death.

> Nearly all of the people are going to be sorry and worried and cry for that person. Unless, if that person died all of a sudden . . . they are gonna be worried for that and ask who did it and have a big argument for the body. . . . They are gonna get wild, properly, and get a spear and walk along the road and shout and growl and ask who did it. "He can't die for nothing, maybe you mob did it night time."

Relatives also get angry and accuse others of neglecting the deceased. For example, when Tina was talking with a neighbor about the recent death of an old man and the imminent return of his sons from another settlement, she predicted the following:

When those men get back, hey lookout, spears are gonna be everywhere. They are gonna be wild for that old man, his sons. [They are going to be wild] at [two classificatory sons] because they weren't minding him.

Aggression of any sort is said to be a cause for anger. Take, for example, verbal aggression, or "growling" as it is often called.

If they are gonna growl at each other and if they go more and more growling and one person doesn't like to growl but the other keeps going, then the person is going to get angry, and the other persons will get angry too.

According to one young woman, even the memory of aggression can provoke anger.

When you see a person's face after they growled at you, I feel angry inside and a bit . . . frightened.

Aggression directed against a relative or friend can also make people angry. It was said that men and women may get angry if someone growls at their family or fights with their brothers or sisters. One adolescent said that hearing gossip about a friend makes young girls angry. Many women talked about anger in association with the perceived mistreatment of a child.

New mission time teachers belted the children with a belt. . . . Parents would get angry and chase the teachers with a stick or spear.

Conversely, a relative's bad behavior—a brother stealing from the shop, for example, or a sister sniffing petrol—can make people angry.

According to statements from many of these women, the realms of sexuality and marriage hold great potential for anger. For the adolescents, stealing a boyfriend or girlfriend makes young people angry. The teenage boys were said to get "mad" when the girls would not come to sit with them; teenage girls get angry when boys refuse their requests for dates. Similarly, "stealing" a husband or wife, that is, elopement or adultery with a married man or woman, makes both men and women angry.

[My husband] would get angry and wild if I went with other men.

Material goods and their distribution provide recognized cause for anger. Returning from a day of fishing, Lily's husband was asked by a "sister's son" for one of his catch. She told me he gave the fish but was angry that the man had asked for it. In some situations, as Marcel Mauss (1967:11) pointed out, "one gives because one is forced to do so." It is possible that however reluctant he was to give, Lily's husband was aware that not being given something may also make people angry, for example, being denied money, food, or the use of a truck. "Stealing" has the same effect. One day in 1978, Lily and I were interrupted in our conversation by a loud banging on my trailer door. Tina burst in looking for the culprit who had stolen tea and damper from her camp. "Next time I'm going to make tea and put glue in it. I'm going to make damper [bread] and put fly spray in it and leave it laying about." "That was one mad old woman," remarked Lily. "You'd better store her food in here to keep it safe."

As a white middle-class woman in American society, I have been taught to think about aggression and anger as separate entities. One feels anger but may then act aggressively or not. Aggression is a potential but not a necessary outcome of anger. This Western construction of anger and aggression is illustrated by the words of another anthropologist working in a lowland New Guinea community.

The association of anger with violence is still quite strong for Gebusi. Indeed, one personally annoying aspect of fieldwork was trying to convey that I was angry without taking the extremely improper step of standing up and gesturing to hit someone. To *say* that I was angry had no effect unless the verbal expression had a clear behavior accompaniment; the potential for violence was crucial. (Knauft 1985:325)

The work of W. Douglas Frost and James Averill (1982) suggests that this conceptual separation may be widely shared in America, at least in the middle class. One may, according to this formulation, learn, and choose, to express anger in a nonaggressive fashion (e.g., Lerner 1985). For example, books on child care suggest that a parent respond to a child who has hit another with something like, "I understand why that made you angry, but it is not O.K. to hit your brother."

The way that Aboriginal women speak suggests that while they do not see concepts of anger and aggression as unitary, like the Gebusi (Knauft 1985), they do not separate the two in the same manner or to the same degree that many of us do. For example, on my first trip to Mangrove, I asked Lily's mother what made people feel "anger." She prefaced her reply by translating the English word "anger" into the Australian language and then back into English. Here is her modification of "angry": "She's angry, and she's going to fight." On another occasion, I asked Lily's mother if you could tell by looking at people if they were angry. Yes, she said, "Somebody is coming up, you see him angry, walking to get a spear."

In 1988, I asked another half-dozen women to tell me what makes men and women angry and how an angry person would act. After describing various causes of anger, four women said that men would act in an aggressive manner, mentioning such acts as picking up boomerangs and nulla nulla and chasing people with spears. All six women said that angry women would act in an aggressive manner, mentioning such acts as picking up sticks and trying to hit another person. Here, for example, I did not have a chance to ask the second part of the question.

VKB: What makes women angry?

AW: When another person swears at her or talks about her to other people, talking yarn. Like me, like yarn, they were saying I was sleeping with [a man] when [my husband] was at [another settlement]. It made me angry. I was swearing at [a person].

The linkage of anger and aggression in Aboriginal women's thought is perhaps most clearly suggested in the linkage of the words "angry" (riyaldha) and "fight" (wungari) (Heath 1982; Hughes 1971).[1] Sometimes the word "wungari" is compounded with "riyaldha," as in *ni riyaldha-wungari,* "He is angry." Sometimes "wungari" is used as a synonym for anger. "He is wungari, he is going to talk to those men," said Lily of her husband after several men had violated the sanctity of his ceremonial ground. "That old lady is wungari. She is growling at me," said Lily's daughter, quarreling with an elderly relative. Describing a fight, Rosalind explained how, before attacking, a protagonist hid her feelings.

There was a fight last night. We couldn't sleep. Those girls were jealous for [a man]. Last night [one young woman went outside to perform a task. While she was outdoors another young woman walked up to her]. "What are you doing here?" [the first young woman asked.] "No, I'm just walking around," [the second replied]. She was hiding that fight.

Similarly, the Kriol word "cheeky" can be used to mean angry and aggressive.

Cheeky is like angry. They get temper quick. Some people don't get temper quick.

Both "cheeky" and "wungari" have the further meaning of dangerous. A death adder is cheeky, a tree snake quiet. Wasps are only cheeky if you hold them in your hand.

It is not surprising that aggression and anger are linked in Aboriginal women's descriptions and predictions of the everyday events of their lives.

When I know my husband is playing up [with another woman], I lose my temper and go and grab that woman and hit her.

Sometimes for the young [adolescent] boy, if mother does not cook his meal, he gets angry and throws tins and firewood.

She is going to be really angry and she will growl at all the sisters [because of a death]: "Why didn't they take care of that old man?"

Nor is it surprising when anger is used to explain aggression:

Around 6:00 P.M., a ten-year-old girl and her similarly aged girl friend ask to visit. I tell them no, my little boy is tired and needs to have a bath and go to bed. Upon this refusal, the ten-year-old stands by the screen door and tells me that I am not kind. "When you came to the women last night, we were kind to you. Now you are not kind to us, you are cruel. I am going to tell [your classificatory sister] that you are cruel. I have only [two of your classificatory sisters] for [grandmothers]. I have no [white grandmother]. I can't come here tomorrow. There is a lot of long grass here and snakes." And then the girl friend speaks with the ten-year-old whispering instructions from around the corner of the house: "[The ten-year-old] does not call you [grandmother]. She calls you enemy. You are cruel because you won't let us in tonight." But after I continue to refuse, the ten-year-old says, "Vicky, I am sorry. I was too angry."

Jealousy and Aggression

Emotions other than anger are also associated with aggression. One resembles what we call "jealousy." Like the word "anger," the word "jealous" is linked to aggression in women's conversation; at times it almost seems to be used as a synonym.

Well, might be that man doesn't like that woman because she is growling and growling and jealousing, well he is gonna just leave that woman.

Jealousy is associated with anger.

> She might be jealous. He might have been looking at another woman, that's why she's angry. She might be jealous of her sister.

But sometimes jealousy is spoken of as cause in itself for aggression.

> They are fighting because she is jealous, that girl. She was chucking flour everywhere.

The suspicion or certainty that a spouse or lover has another partner is, perhaps, the paradigmatic circumstance associated with feeling "jealous."

> Yesterday when [the speaker, a woman] was coming back from town, she and [another woman] got off the plane at a nearby community. There [a third woman] came up to [the second] and told her that her husband had run off with another woman. [The speaker] tried to calm her down, but she stayed there to go after her husband and the girlfriend. [The speaker] doesn't get jealous when people tell her a story about her boyfriend. If she sees him with her own eyes, that's when she will get jealous.

According to Aboriginal women, there are many ways to recognize sexual desire and sexual affairs. Recognition of these signals can also lead to suspicion and jealousy. Inactivity and neglect of marital duties, for example, are grounds for jealousy.

> A no-good wife is one who just sits, takes no notice when he tells her to do things. This will make him angry and he will belt her. She is being silly way, she is going another way, to another man. When she just sits and thinks, it might be because another man is pulling her heart away from her husband. She is not going to stay with him. A no good husband does the same thing. His wife asks him to go hunting, make a shade, he won't do it. He just sits and thinks about another woman. A man will think when his wife is like this, "Might be, she doesn't love me." He will belt her with a stick on the back, leg, arm, or head just to give her a lesson.

Lily said that a wife's refusal to have coitus with her husband indicates infidelity. Suspicion may also be aroused if a man and a woman are seen smiling at one another or sitting, walking, or laughing together. According to one of Lily's sisters, even two women laughing together may invite jealousy.

> [Another woman] and I were laughing together this afternoon and I said to her, "You better not laugh. Your husband might get jealous." [2]

Spending time alone with a member of the opposite sex or accompanying a man or a woman into the bush or an unoccupied house is suspect behavior. For example, after interviewing a white settlement official for several afternoons in the rare privacy and stillness of his air-conditioned office, he told me that one of his Aboriginal colleagues had asked him if he was thinking of taking me as a second wife. Walking alone may even arouse suspicion, for lovers who wish to tryst signal their intentions to one another or send a messenger naming the spot, then leave camp from different directions, meeting later at the prearranged location. [3] Watching a person of the opposite sex also signals sexual interest.

Because a young man is jealous he will do this and that and give his wife a hard time. A young girl is jealous of her husband just because she sees somebody look at him when he walks around. He says, "I'm not going to those girls, I'm going with those boys." They are going to fight, jealous [of] each other. It's the same with that young man, "Oh, you are going to those men," just because they are sitting watching her as she goes by. He might hit or punch her.

Jealousy and aggression are also associated with pregnancy. In making these connections, woman at Mangrove are not unique. In other parts of Aboriginal Australia, "uncharacteristic and excessive" behavior is attributed to pregnancy (Tonkinson 1978:62). The first of the following quotes is from a woman named Elsie Roughsey of Mornington Island, Queensland; the other is from a woman at Mangrove.

When a woman is pregnant, at first she fights a lot with her husband. Lots of things maker her feel angry, growl, fight. Folks say, "that husband and wife fight too much, going to have baby." (Huffer 1980:48)

Aboriginal way we say it is like that: when a woman is pregnant she growls at her family. We Aborigines know this.

Some women say that pregnancy, or more specifically, the baby inside her, makes a woman angry or aggressive. Others say it makes her jealous.

[Pregnant women] start getting greedy and don't like their family, but I never get like that. . . . They sometimes get jealous, they tell their husband not to walk around [after other women]. The baby inside makes them angry.

One woman said that pregnancy makes husbands angry, but others said the baby causes anger only in its mother. No one I asked offered a theory about how or why the baby does this. One woman said it began to do so early in pregnancy, but Rosalind saw the process as one that could continue even after birth.

Maybe that girl is gonna be pregnant and that baby is gonna tempt her mother, that girl is gonna make fights all the time because she is starting to have that baby. . . . Old people can tell that way when they fight, that means they gonna have a baby. . . . She is gonna be jealous all the time. Maybe [her husband] kills fish or goes hunting, gets bullock meat and comes back. Only he can let mother, sister—close up sister—[have some], but not long way one, [his wife is] gonna be jealous for that girl. Only her family and her husband's family, she is gonna let them ask him for beef or fish. But nobody else. And after when she has three or four kids, that's the time temper is gonna fade away and she is gonna love anybody after that. . . . [Before] she is jealous for girl and for beef.

As Rosalind's words indicate, people are said to be "jealous" not only of relationships but also of things, like "beef." For example, in 1978 when a number of clans obtained new motorboats, a woman told me her husband had been stranded up the coast from Mangrove. Someone, she said, had put water in his boat's gas tank because he was "jealous."

The way people speak about jealousy suggests that it is perceived as a widespread cause of aggression. For example, Rosalind once speculated that Charlie Pride, a favorite country-western singer, was shot in the back because someone was jealous. A group of schoolboys told me Elvis had been killed for the same reason. I shall return to the topic of jealousy in chapter 5.

Intoxication and Anger

He exaggerates, but Collmann's remark that "the analysis of interpersonal violence among Australian Aborigines has developed no more than the analysis of drinking liquor" (1988b:170) nevertheless captures much of Westerners' conventional wisdom on alcohol and aggression. One tenet is that alcohol counters inhibitions (MacAndrew and Edgerton 1969); a second, that aggression is a consequence of relaxed inhibitions (Klama 1988). Although much in the anthropological literature challenges ideas about alcohol's role as a determinant or facilitator of violence (e.g., Bohannan 1960a; Levinson 1989; MacAndrew and Edgerton 1969; Riches 1986), connections between alcohol use and aggression are made by a number of Aboriginalists (e.g., Myers 1986; Reid 1983; Sackett 1977, 1988; Sansom 1980; Wilson 1982).

Women at Mangrove also associate anger and aggression with alcohol.

Alcohol makes a man's [chest area indicated with hand] burn. They get really angry.

These women are not the only Aboriginal people to make this association. In her analysis of domestic violence in the Northern Territory, Bolger states that "most of [the women] regard alcohol as the most important contributor to their distress" (1991:46). And Sackett reports that people at Wiluna in the Western Desert say "drunks" "look for trouble" and "always have to have a fight" (1988:70).

Sackett has suggested that Aboriginal drinking patterns have been modeled on those of the "hard-drinking miners, station hands, and drifters of rural Australia" (1977:93). Australian drinkers seem to have made a similar impression on Gebusi people in Papua New Guinea.

Many Australian patrol officers were justly renowned for drinking binges. This pattern has been continued, in the eyes of Gebusi, by national patrol officers. Stories filter into the village of officials who become heavily intoxicated and provoke severe fights, defying all efforts to restrain them. The drunken individuals were described as "wild men." The context in which government officials were said to drink was almost invariably described as a "party." Significantly, people have begun to use the loan word 'party,' *fati*, as a colloquial referent for their own ritual feasts. Given these associations, it is not surprising that when Gebusi finally were able to consume alcohol at a "party" of their own, their collective behavior paralleled closely the drunken comportment of government staff personnel. (Knauft 1987a:92)

Careful scholarship by Maggie Brady (1991) has disabused us of the notion that intoxication is a new experience for Australian Aboriginal people. Indeed, she mentions that Aborigines brewed a "mild pandanus-cider" in an area near Mangrove (Basedow 1929 in Brady 1991). I do not know if people of the Mangrove area gathered or manufactured intoxicants in the past. Liquor may have been obtained prior to white contact from Macassans who camped nearby (Turner 1974). But as Brady has remarked, it is unlikely that experience with these intoxicants prepared Aboriginal people for the "sheer volume of substances"—alcohol, petrol, and drugs such as marijuana—available today.

Mangrove is a "dry" settlement. This policy, initiated by the missionaries, has been subsequently upheld by the Aboriginal community. A long-term resident missionary said that until 1977 this rule had been violated only once or twice, but during 1977 and 1978, alcohol was brought into the settlement on at least thirteen occasions, which were noted because each was marked by an aggressive event (Burbank 1980*a*). By 1981, the Northern Territory Liquor Commission had undertaken a survey of Aboriginal groups' preferences regarding alcohol in their communities. Mangrove chose to remain dry, and new laws and strict enforcement have meant that little alcohol is brought into the community, though Aboriginal people may still acquire it in nearby areas where its sale and consumption are not restricted.

Many of the Aboriginal women I know do not like or approve of drinking (see also Reid 1983; Williams 1987). Here, Rosalind tells of the meeting with officials of the Northern Territory Liquor Commission.

You know, like long time [ago] we had the biggest meeting here about beer and some—all those people who know how to drink—wanted this place to turn to beer, but the community was very strong. Those [whites] came here and we had a big meeting. And after that we had a meeting at the shop and all the men were sitting outside the office (all the [white men] were listening) and arguing about the beer and that [white] was asking, "I'm gonna ask you mob community, what this place gonna be, this place gonna be wet or dry?" And all the woman shouted "Dry, this place gonna be dry." We talked, this place is gonna be dry and that [white] talked, this place is gonna be dry. That means they won't bring beer in. . . . We made them wild, community made them wild. . . . "You mob wait there," [some men said]. "We'll get spears." . . . They wanted this place wet.

According to Aboriginal women's formulations, when people drink, they get "drunk" and act aggressively.

When they are drunk they go and talk to a man or woman, "Hey you. You wanta fight?" "Oh, we can't fight, because we are not drunk. You are drunk, you."

Lily told me that women from Mangrove advised those in a nearby community not to allow the establishment of a drinking club because "their husbands will drink and fight and kill them." One of her sisters, who stayed with me for a while in 1978, came in unusually early one evening because some of the men had been drinking. She said she was frightened that a man she had refused to marry would put a "curse" on her (see chap. 6) in his drunken state, then added, "When men drink they come back and bash their wives." Children also apparently associate "drunk" with aggression. For example, one day I observed a mixed-sex group of young children play *bunguru* (the Kriol word for drunk). They all pretended to drink from an empty bottle of Tab, which they called "beer." "Give me some, too." They then proceeded to "break the shop," by striking a tree. Another example is provided by a story written by one of Lily's daughters when she was a schoolgirl.

On Friday afternoon [my brother] and his friends went to the hill to play hide-and-seek and after they went to the pictures and it rained a little bit and we didn't see the picture because drunken men were silly and so we went home and two men were fighting for beer and the men stopped and went home and slept till morning. They didn't fight, they were friends again.

Intoxication from petrol sniffing (Burbank 1988) should be mentioned in this discussion as it is occasionally associated with aggression and with being "mad." It does not, however, seem to be associated with aggression to the extent that alcohol is. Only rarely is interpersonal aggression attributed to the intoxication caused by petrol sniffing. Indeed, petrol sniffing is regarded as antithetical to aggression in one way: it is said that intoxicated individuals should not be struck while they are high on petrol fumes because doing so could cause severe injury. I have never heard this said of alcohol intoxication. Nevertheless, a number of cases of disciplinary aggression (discussed below) have been precipitated by the acts of youthful petrol sniffers.

Intoxication from drug use is not in evidence at Mangrove and thus is even less pertinent. I was told that one woman who had spent some time in Darwin was cranky from smoking marijuana; I have heard no other mention of drug use in the Aboriginal population of Mangrove or of its association with aggressive behavior.

Why People Are Aggressive

Sansom identifies a distinction, used by the Aborigines of Wallaby Cross, between "[that fellow] always gonna go wild—silly" and the man who goes "wild for reason" (1980:100). The things Mangrove women say about aggression, the words they use, and the associations they make paint a picture that is, for the most part, remarkably familiar. The ways in which they talk about aggression suggest that aggressive behavior is seen as the outcome of both what we might call the "character," "personality," or "temperament" of actors and the circumstances in which they find themselves. There are events that are expected to lead to anger and fighting, but there are also perceived differences in the people who might be affected by them. There are "cheeky" indivduals and "quiet" individuals: "Some women here are quiet. Some women think themselves good fighters."

What is the source of this similarity? Is it a result of the way that I have "recontextualized" Aboriginal words in this analysis (e.g., Gergen 1990; Rosenberg 1990)? Or are "anger" and "aggression" experienced by Westerners and Aborigines in such a way that we have developed similar theories about them (e.g., Brown 1991; cf. Valentine 1963)? I begin this analysis with "cranky" and "mad," as these terms most clearly illustrate the relevance of both situational factors and personal characteristics in talk about aggression.

On the one hand, "cranky" is used as a simple synonym for "angry" and "aggressive."

If their husband wants another woman, [women] are going to get cranky and fight that man and woman. The women get sticks and fight for that man.

On the other hand, "cranky" can also be used to indicate what I would understand as an irascible character or a mental illness.

AW: The other old lady, she used to feel cranky, and she used to chase us round and round the house.
VKB: Why did she chase you? Why was she so cranky?
AW: I don't know. [She] had a heart attack and the head . . . she used to feel no good, that head, and she used to get up and chase us and she used to cry.

The multiple but related meanings of cranky are demonstrated in this answer to my question, "What does *yinagaladi* (no-good-head) mean?"

When someone is a bit cranky in his head or when he gets mad or when somebody has no sense or when they are growling at each other.

Anger is associated with the abdomen, but aggression can be associated with the head or the mind. For example:

[A man] went up to the school and growled at [two teachers for their treatment of his sons]. . . . He goes off his head if someone growls at his kids.

Aggression, not just as a behavioral response but also as a more enduring trait, is attributed to head injuries.

[There are two little boys] . . . might be [one] wants to tease[4] [the other] for no reason, because his brain is working a different way. You know when little baby, girl or boy, falls off from mother's arm to the ground. Well, he might fall head down and after, when he grows big, his head is gonna work a different way now. That means he can't behave himself when he grows big. He's gonna be teasing all the time.

Lily once described another woman as "cranky fella." When I asked why she labeled her in such a manner, she replied that once when the woman and her husband were fighting, he hit her with a hammer and broke her eardrum. "Now she can't hear on one side." When people fight and refuse to stop even when others intervene, it is sometimes said that they "can't hear," that "they have no ears." Conversely, what we might call a "mature" or "sensible" person is one who can hear from "long way." Others seemed to accept the designation of this woman as a "cranky fella." In 1988, it was reported that she was in a hair-pulling, rock-throwing, stick-swinging fight with another woman over some missing teabags (though one woman hypothesized that the fight was really over injury done to the woman's husband and son). In discussions of this fight, it was said that "she has something in her brain that makes her cranky, so she thinks someone is growling at her." The fight occurred during a Bible camp, and it was decided to hold a "healing service." I was told that all the visiting ministers gathered round the woman and placed their hands on her head "to heal that thing in her brain."

Aggressive behavior is an accepted part of life at Mangrove. Women's comments, however, indicate that some aggressive acts are seen as more violent or injurious than they should be.

[My eldest son] is not much wungari, but [my other son], because something is wrong with his head will get a [metal-tipped spear] if someone swears at him over cards.

Acts explained with reference to "something wrong with his head" point to another theme in women's discourse on aggression, what I would label "the irrational," in the sense of "lacking usual or normal mental clarity or coherence" *(Merriam-Webster's Collegiate Dictionary,* 10th ed.). Aggression attributed to alcohol intoxication, for example, is assessed as irrational.

[A week or so previously a group of men were drinking near one of the "wet" settlements] [my son] and [another man] got into a fight. [The other man] punched [my son] on the neck and arm and then hit him on the body with a stick. . . . [Just a few days ago, my son] took a spear to go after [the other man]. But I told him, just forget it. He didn't know what he was doing because he was drinking. Just leave it now. So [my son] didn't throw the spear.

But so is simple anger and aggression.

When two women are gonna fight, fight each other; one has a stick and the other has one. They can fight from morning to teatime and still they fight. They try to stop them, they won't take any notice. "No, I won't stop. I'm still gonna go after [her]." Maybe old people gonna feel tired of stopping them and they are gonna say, "She won't stop, she's still gonna go forward. We tried to stop her, she won't take any notice of us."

The assessment of aggression as irrational is also indicated when a person who has not been drinking or sniffing petrol but is angry and fighting is described as "drunk."

Being cranky does not always require an immediate cause. Some people just are.

[My daughter] is cranky, she is mad and swears at her father. She has always been like this.

Women say that some people are more aggressive than others.

If a man makes his wife bleed . . . her mother will growl at him if she is a gentle one, but if she is a cheeky one, she is going to hit him for her daughter.

Others are less aggressive.

Some kind men, if they don't see anything cooked, tucker or tea, or maybe he comes back from hunting, he won't growl at his mother, just asks for fat and just cooks his own [fish].

People, both men and women, who display behavior judged as aggressive more often than others are described as *andhawungari* (literally, greedy for fight; Heath 1982) or "troublemaker."

Some people, all the time trouble. Some girls are rough fellows, andhawungari. . . . They make trouble all the time.

As do people elsewhere in Aboriginal Australia (Merlan 1986), women of Mangrove talk about family resemblance. Some say, for example, that children "get" their faces and feet from their fathers. But it is not only physical qualities that may be shared. Lily, for example, remarked of a little boy whose father had died, "He looks just like his father. . . . He was a really good singer. . . . He looks just like his father, he will be a good singer like him." There is also a perception that some family members may share degrees of aggressiveness. Once, for example, when discussing the aggressive behavior of a man whose father had killed one of his wives, Tina said, "He was a little bit old when he went mad; might be son is gonna follow father." "Why is a kid a bully?" I asked one of Lily's sisters. "Maybe because he followed his father when he was young, or a little girl followed her mother; they were like that when they were kids."

When women talk about aggression for "no reason," they may be talking about people who are regarded as more cheeky than others.

Ngunij [translated by Heath 1982:146 as "jealous (over a woman)"] means jealous for just no reason. . . . Like when [a man] doesn't get that little girl, [his wife] says dirty words and hits him for no reason. "[Husband], you never get [the baby]. You always hide girls at the village."

But they may also be talking about the difference between what I would call a "distal" and "proximate" cause. Rosalind, for example, here distinguishes "the real cause" of a man's anger from anger for "no reason."

When that promise man [betrothed] gets another girl sometimes his promise girl gets another man. Then the man gets jealous. [A man] made friend [love] with [a woman] when she was here. Then when she went back to [her community] this week he went back to [his promise]. . . . The other night [his promise] was at school watching TV. [He] wanted to talk to her and was calling to her, but she didn't take any notice of him. So he went in and hit her. He smacked her for nothing. I was asking him, "What for you been smack [your promise]." He answered me, "For nothing. She wouldn't come when I called her." "Well," I told him, "It's your own fault. You took that [other girl]."

Words that we use to describe personality or character may be used differently, suggesting that "the person" is not viewed with the same sense of fixity as in the West. For example, in the following statement, "bully" is a temporary act rather than a kind of child.

I used to get bully to [Wendy]. My grandfather used to get pandanus tree nuts. I used to get them from [Wendy]. Grandmother used to cut them for her and I used to go bully and take one or two. And grandfather used to chase me.

The aggressive behavior of left-handed (*balajagu*) people is a fixed characteristic but for physical reasons.

When a balajagu throws [a spear], some can't jump. They are struck on the body, struck straight away. Maybe an old man can dodge that balajagu spear. He's alright. He looks properly. Not that young fella, he might be struck straight away. . . . [The left-handed person], he's just like that from the time he is little. He picks up a stick and plays just like that. Well, that's all together now [the way it will be from now on].

Left-handed people are more dangerous because those who are right-handed have difficulty seeing what they are doing.

If a man stands up for spear and if one man throws with his left hand he is gonna strike that man. Right hand is little bit little bit; left hand is one go. Even if they are boxing, they will win, except if they fight left hand to left hand. But not if one fights with the right hand. Right hand can't manage, can't see which way that left hand. That means he is gonna get hit every minute.

What Is Aggression?

David Riches (1986:11) has observed that violent acts are easy for us to perform and easy for us to understand as hurt. They are thus "highly appropriate *both* for practical (instrumental) *and* for symbolic (expressive) purposes." I agree that aggression is most productively viewed as many things, for example, as a means of dominating, resisting domination, expressing frustration and anger, self-assertion, competing, or fulfilling sadistic fantasies or motives (e.g., Attili and Hinde 1986; Whiting 1969). Aboriginal women's talk suggests that they too recognize a multiplicity of motives and purposes in the aggressive behavior manifest in their community.

Women at Mangrove talk about the potential effects of aggression on its targets.

VKB: How did you feel after that fight you had with [your sister-in-law when she was growling at your brother]?

AW: Not good, upset. But then we said sorry and we don't fight anymore. When they come here and have an argument, they never, she never, lets her voice go loud, they talk softly so I won't hear them.

And they talk about the sanctioning effect of aggression.

VKB: I hear [a man] punched [a man] in the nose.

AW: He did it for his own good [to stop him from smashing the school stereo].

Women talk about aggression as a means of punishment, especially the punishment of adolescents.

Today when you were off fishing, [two adolescent girls] came and sat here with me. I saw [one of the girl's classificatory fathers] come out of his house and come this way. I thought he was coming to talk to me. But he came right up to her and said, "I know you've been fucking your [classificatory] brother in that house. If you can't go live with your mommy, go live with your auntie." Then he swore at her and kicked her two or three times on her jaw. Blood came out of her nose. [The other girl] ran away. I didn't get up because I have this sore backbone, but I told him, "That'll do." I told [the girl] she should go to her auntie, too. She went over to [my sister's house] and slept all day.

It should be understood that according to the norms of her community, this adolescent had committed incest. When I told Lily that the girl had been kicked, her only comment was, "That's because he saw them walking together. They are brother and sister. That's not right." Sometimes women explicitly describe such aggressive acts as a means to an end. For example, a stated intention of wounding a young girl in the foot or leg is to keep her from "running around" with boys (Burbank 1988). I do not agree with Myers, however, when he says that "results . . . confirm the meaning of . . . actions" (1986:162). Who can say with certainty that the results one sees are those intended by the actor or even those experienced by the victim (Liddle 1989)?

Women talk about aggression as a means of self-defense. I asked seven women what they would do if another person started to hit them or fight with them. They all answered that they would fight back. The most restrained response was given by a woman who said she would have to be hit three times before she would hit back.

The statements of some women indicate that aggression is seen as a means of resisting the dominance attempts of others. Here, for example, is Rosalind's reply to my question, "If someone started an argument with you, what would you do?"

You are gonna answer back. You are not going to let her argue with you all the time. You are gonna turn back and growl at her, too. You're not going to let her [be] boss over you.

And here a young woman explains her actions when she was attacked by another woman.

You know what I am like. I don't like anybody to push me around. Even when they argue with me, I just hit them.

Even justified reprimands may be resisted with aggression. I asked three women what they would do if someone like their mother growled at them because they had done some "silly thing." Two said they would "take it" if they were in the wrong, but all three talked about answering back. "Sometimes I start talking back. . . . I feel angry and start arguing and saying silly words [swearing]." I return to women's discussion of aggression as a means of dominating others and as a means of resisting that domination in chapter 6. Aggression is also seen as a means of "payback" or revenge.

[A man and his son were in the midst of a fight, the other son] didn't do anything, didn't say a word. He went to have his morning tea. . . . And they shouted to him to look out, but not soon enough and he got speared here in the thigh. He just took out that spear and said, "We two are gonna have a pain." And threw and hit [his brother] here [indicates just above hip bone]. Both had a pain.

A discussion of the perceived motives and purposes of aggressive behavior at Mangrove cannot conclude without a return to the theme of aggression as an expression of anger. "What can you do if someone is angry?" I once asked Lily. "You can't do anything," she replied, "only stop them from fighting, throwing a spear."

[A man] wanted a permit to bring alcohol to Mangrove. At the meeting everyone raised their hand against it. [The man] went and got a spear. He almost hit his wife when he threw it. His uncle stopped him. He didn't mean to hit his wife, that was an accident. He just threw it.

Wishing to better understand their perceptions of aggressive purpose, I asked seven women why women hit at each other with sticks. I also asked six of them why men chase people with spears. Their answers emphasize aggression as an end in itself, the expected, if not inevitable, outcome of anger. There is little attention to "instrumentality" in these answers. The women answering my questions did not say things like, "She is hitting her to teach her a lesson," or "She is hitting her because she is wrong." Three women mentioned external circumstances giving rise to aggression—intoxication, previous aggression, and jealousy— but, as I have said earlier, these states themselves are often used as synonyms for anger. Intended effects of the aggressive acts were mentioned, but with the exception of one woman who talked about men's and women's reputations as fighters, the effects sought were the immediate injury of the opponent. "She likes to hit her so she can break her leg or knee, so she can send her to the hospital." The vast majority of women answering these questions explained the aggressive acts largely in terms of anger or aggression. For example:

Maybe she hits back because already she gets angry.

Because they start arguing, that's why they hit each other with sticks.

They want to strike somebody, that's why they've got that spear.

I argue in the following chapters that Aboriginal women's emphasis on the expressive purposes of aggressive behavior provides a key for understanding their experiences as aggressors and victims.

4

The Control of Aggression

In spite of their seeming readiness to fight or otherwise expose themselves to the aggressive behavior of others, women at Mangrove do not talk about themselves as particularly aggressive people. Their perceived ability to fight for themselves and others is perhaps best characterized as "taken for granted." They recognize that aggressive behavior is learned and may be taught but seem neither to encourage nor vaunt this ability. Similarly, their role as peacemakers is an aspect of daily life that is taken for granted (see Bell and Ditton 1980; Kaberry 1939). From the Aboriginal perspective, women's involvement in overt expressions of aggression is "natural." From my perspective, however, this involvement is largely a product of the ways in which anger and aggression are culturally constructed, and these constructs include precepts for action and reaction.

That women at Mangrove recognize aggression's potential for serious harm is seen in Tina's discussion of the weapons people use.

In olden times women here didn't have nulla nulla, only spears and tomahawk. That tomahawk can open up the head, brains spill out; look, some women have scars. That spear can make the heart and liver come out. Nulla nulla is better, only blood from skin, that's all.

But if aggression is an inevitable outcome of anger, how can people be protected from its deadlier effects? Overt aggression at Mangrove is not regarded as extraordinary, deviant, or even antisocial. Nevertheless, women express considerable concern that no one be seriously injured.

Steps are occasionally taken to ensure that others do not become angry, and fighting is sometimes discouraged. But, by and large, the expression of aggression is expected. Most efforts to control its destructive potential are thus focused on the structuring and containment of aggressive acts.

Lily's Fight

I illustrate these points with an extended analysis of one fight. Lily is the protagonist, Marguerite is her teenage daughter, and Bret, a young man in his mid-twenties, is her son. This fight took place in a community about forty miles from Mangrove where Bret and many other people from Mangrove were living at the time.

June 4, 1981
Marguerite: "I am going to [a nearby community]. Lily is going to [the same place]. Some women, our full cousins, broke Bret's arm. . . . We are going to give the same [broken arm] back to them."

June 6, 1981
Lily: "Yesterday I went to [a place] and had a big fight with the women who broke Bret's arm. There has never been a fight like that here at Mangrove." They fought from the time they got there on the plane until they came back. Lily was fighting those three women, her [classificatory brother's daughters]. "They are really dangerous. They can really fight. They fight with nulla nulla, really big ones." Yesterday Lily was feeling really "horrible" and "upset" and "weak." She was thinking, "How can I fight those women? They are really big fat ones and I am only a skinny one." Lily went to [the place] and fought them "straight away." They kept trying to hit her head, but she blocked them with her nulla nulla. They hit her in the chest, but [Lily's sister] put a bandage on it and it's O.K. [Lily's sister] was fighting, but she doesn't know how to use a nulla nulla, and they hit her finger. She had to fly to [a nearby town with a hospital], and maybe they will have to cut it off. . . . "Those women can cheat. They come and hit you from behind." But [Lily's two sisters-in-law] were there "helping," . . . only talking, "We are watching you. You can't cheat." . . . "Only those women didn't really break Bret's arm. They only hit it here and here [each forearm] a little bit. [Lily said to them], " 'I'm sorry. I was fighting you because I thought you broke Bret's arm and sent him to the hospital.' I told them sorry and that fight is finished now. I told them to come to Mangrove, they are our family."

When asked if women attack each other at their place of work, in the aisles of a supermarket, or at town meetings, most white middle-class

Americans would probably say that women do not fight. In the unlikely event that they did see women fighting, they might say that they were "lower class," "drunk," or "crazy" and certainly that their aggression represented chaos—a breakdown of all rules and civilized behavior. Aboriginal women from Mangrove might say that Lily was "mad" or "cranky" when she attacked her son's attackers; however, her fight represents a culturally patterned event from start to finish.[1]

First, the manner in which Lily and her opponents fought was, for the most part, expected and rule-governed behavior. Women have their own weapons for such fights—*mabargu,* or *nulla nulla,* three- or four-foot-long sticks of eucalyptus wood, used both to strike at an opponent and to block an opponent's blows. Body extremities such as legs, arms, and fingers are fair targets. To judge from health clinic records, the injured finger sustained by Lily's sister is similar to injuries sustained by many women on the settlement. Soft body parts and the head are not to be hit. However, in attempting to hit Lily on the head, her opponents were not acting in a completely lawless manner; it is recognized that someone who is very angry may well attempt such a blow.

You shouldn't hit someone on the head, but you do if you get wild for something like food or about your children.

Indeed, a part of learning how to fight with a stick is learning how to protect the forehead.

You have to be careful of the other woman when you fight. Watch her eyes [to see where she is going to strike].

Because fighters cannot be counted on to follow the rules, people at Mangrove depend on noncombatants to ensure that no one is seriously hurt. The extent to which this expectation may structure aggressive behavior is illustrated by the following account of a fight observed not at Mangrove but among the "Murngin" of northeastern Arnhem Land.

The writer observed one nirimaoi yolno [camp fight] when, for some unaccountable reason, the contestants' friends did not attempt to hold them. They had counted on being restrained when they rushed at each other while hurling threats of death and covering each other with obscenity and profanity. When they reached each other no clubs were wielded or spears thrown; the men stood breast to breast and obviously felt a bit ridiculous. (Warner 1937:157)

That Lily's account does not mention *wajar*—the Kriol word for people who take part in a fight to ensure that serious injury does not occur—

probably reflects only the fact that the fighters stopped of their own accord after Lily's sister's finger was struck. It would be very surprising if there were not several people standing by, ready to intervene had the fight taken a more serious turn.

To intervene in a fight, people must have certain information. First, they must know that a fight is taking place, who the aggressors are, and the reasons for the aggression. The public nature of day-to-day life makes these facts almost immediately available. Over the years that I have been visiting Mangrove, new Western-style houses with larger rooms and facilities like kitchens and bathrooms have been provided for the settlement's inhabitants, and I have seen more and more activities move inside. For example, in 1981, Lily and Rosalind both cooked on outdoor fires; in 1988, they both used stoves in the kitchens of their new houses. Nevertheless, much of life at Mangrove is spent outside, and many activities continue to be performed in public, within view and earshot of other people. Fighting is an event that usually takes place out of doors and is thus easily monitored by neighbors and kin. Residential arrangements are such that those who should intervene for one another usually live in close proximity (see Biernoff 1974, 1979). If interested parties are at some distance when an altercation breaks out, the cries of antagonists and observers soon bring the event to their attention. People at Mangrove watch and talk about their neighbors and kin; they are generally aware of ongoing issues, problems, and conflicts. It can be presumed that when a fight breaks out, the people most concerned have a good idea of its etiology even if proclamations and accusations of participants do not inform them of its immediate cause.

I turn now to the cause of Lily's fight, the reputed injury of Lily's son, Bret. At Mangrove, women and men are expected to protect their children, even when they are adults. It is also expected that such protection may sometimes take the form of aggression. For example, on another occasion in 1981 Marguerite made the following remark:

Those [other teenage] girls won't fight with me, only growl. They won't fight with me because they know my mother. My mother's mother . . . knows how to fight with nulla nulla, my mother's mother and my mother. They know my mother will take partner with me. They don't fight with me when she is here. Only growl.

Lily is not the only person to fight over harm to her children. In the same year, a man hurled a spear at another whom he accused of hitting his little boy. The spear didn't hit him, I was told, but stuck about six inches into the tractor on which he had been riding. In chapters 5 and 6, it will be seen that many other people at Mangrove have fought for similar cause.

Lily's protection of her son illustrates not only a reason to fight but also an Aboriginal expectation that, I believe, underlies and explains much of the action of people drawn into fights started by others: the parent or caretaker/child relationship entails ongoing, often reciprocal, protection and control (cf. Myers 1986).[2] Indeed, Lily's fight and others like it may be seen as examples of caretaking: "Some people here at Mangrove, they take partner for their kids, they start a big fight now." "Family" take part in each other's fights. When fights do not involve a "close relation,"[3] an onlooker should not take part. In this case intervention would be inappropriate and might even, said Tina, result in an attack on the newcomer.

According to women's accounts of aggressive events, mothers—both actual and classificatory—play a significant role in the control of aggressive behavior; their participation is an expected extension of their nurturant role. Lily's mother, for example, described her intervention as "minding," a word that is used like "looking after" (see Myers 1980) to indicate caring for children: "Your brother [age 47 at the time] was going to throw a spear, but I stopped him. I'm minding all those kids."

Women are held responsible for the aggressive behavior of their children, young or old. Here, for example, are a young woman's remarks after one of her clan brothers fired a shotgun, slightly wounding a second clan brother and his father. To my knowledge, this was the first time that a gun had been used at Mangrove to wound another person. The young man who used the gun had been sniffing petrol, and the incident was perceived as one of great potential danger. The women the speaker refers to were visiting another settlement when the shooting occurred.

[Those mothers of the boys and their sister] should be here looking after their husbands and sons. Their sons almost killed each other. And those three are off acting like young girls. When they come back I am going to ask [a woman] for six eggs. I'll tell her I'm hungry, but that's only gammon [a lie]. I'll throw two at [the mother's sister], two for [one mother], and two for [the other mother]. If that old man had died, I would cut off all three of their heads with a galiwanga [a large knife]. I have a long one there at the house. I don't want any wajar [intervention], nobody be wajar for me. Poor [youth who shot the gun]. They took him off to jail.

Thus, a mother, or mother substitute, who intervenes in a fight on her child's behalf is simply fulfilling a requirement of her maternal role.

Mothers do not only protect their children by using aggression, however. Aggression can also be used against the "child." The severe punishment of young children is neither expected nor tolerated at Mangrove. This is not to say that adults never physically discipline children, for they do. I have observed men and women hitting, yelling, or threatening children on a number of occasions, though it is my impression that aggression against children has increased over the years that I have been visiting Mangrove. Some women say that hitting children is something that people learned since coming to the settlement. However, children are usually safeguarded from severe physical chastisement. An adult who severely harms a child can expect to be harmed in turn (see Berndt 1978). This changes as children approach physical maturity. When judged to be the same size as adults, children may be legitimate targets of aggression. For example, Lily once told me that when she discovered that her sister's son (who was 21 years old at the time) had taken her fourteen-year-old son along to break into the settlement's shop one night, she hit him on the back with a broom. Seeing this, Lily's sister, the young man's mother, came running at Lily but took no further action when Lily told her what her son had done.

The importance that relationships may have for aggressive interactions is indicated by work that H. B. Kimberley Cook (1992, 1993) has done on women's aggression in another part of the world. In the Venezuelan community of Margariteño, women *parar el macho* (stop macho behavior) with acts of physical aggression. Asking how this could be so, as Margariteño women are smaller and weaker than men, Cook observes that in all cases where women use physical aggression against men, the women "were either mothers or sisters or female relatives of the men involved" (1993:71). She suggests that it is the emotional bond between mother and son that enables women to use force without fear of retaliation. In Aboriginal Australia, it has long been apparent that perceptions of relationship constitute a pivotal component of the context in which aggression takes place (e.g., Berndt 1965; Hiatt 1965). This is clearly the case at Mangrove.

When it comes to intervening in aggressive events, women do not stand alone. The mother's brother and the child's father are held to be responsible for the child as well. Thus, men are expected to join with their wives and sisters or stand in their place when intervention requires

male participation. Reciprocally, adult "children" are expected to intervene when their mothers, fathers, or mother's brothers are involved in
aggressive affairs. The following remark illustrates this point: "[Two
men, sons of one man] were going to fight that [other man], because
[the first man] is their daddy, he has been minding them."

The righteousness of Lily's cause is reflected in the fact that she was
assisted by her sister and two of her sisters-in-law. Same-sexed siblings
are seen as potential allies, that is, as those who "take partner" in fights.

[Men] get angry when somebody fights with their brother and strikes them.
Then they fight with that person. Women get cheeky if someone fights with
their sister. Then they will get up and fight, too.

Opposite-sex siblings are enjoined from fighting with each other, an
injunction that is in line with other aspects of the brother/sister relationship, which can be characterized as one of caution and avoidance
(see chap. 6). It was said, however, that women can assist and restrain
their brothers when they fight, though Lily told me that restraint
should be limited to verbal rebuke; a woman should never touch a
brother. There was less agreement about a man's role in his sisters'
fights. Several women insisted that men should not be involved in their
sisters' altercations. Women also suggested that a brother's presence
would prevent women from fighting.

Two sisters can fight or girls together might be swearing, but they don't like
brother listening. He might spear that girl [his sister]. Before they were like
that, bush [time]. They were like that. . . . "We can't fight, our brothers could
hear."

What brothers might hear when sisters fight is swearing, a common
element of fighting. A man is expected to attack all sisters that might
be present if he hears swearing in their presence. Saying that men could
participate in their sisters' fights, Rosalind also points out the difficulties of doing so.

It might be two or three against one, [a man] can stand for his sister. But if
those girls are gonna swear at that sister, he can't fight for his sister.

Lily said men would avoid their sisters' fights so as not to hear someone
swear at them.

A brother wouldn't stop his sister [from fighting], he would go away if he saw
her fight with her husband or anybody because they might use a bad word.

Nevertheless, some women apparently expect their brothers to assist them when they are attacked. For example, I was told that after being attacked by a man who wanted one of her daughters in marriage, a woman argued with one of her brothers: "You are my brother, you should be taking side with me." I shall discuss this apparent lack of consensus in a moment.

Lily's sisters-in-law were also acting according to expectations when they helped her in her fight. In-laws are not, however, supposed to take sides against one another or fight with one another. This is made clear when they do.

> We were shame because two [in-laws] were fighting. . . . [People] said, "You should shame, you can't fight with your mother-in-law. No one ever does. [One of the women] is the first one."

Mothers-in-law have a special role to play in aggressive events, for not only is one not supposed to fight with a mother-in-law, one is not supposed to fight in her presence.

> When a son-in-law sees his mother-in-law, he can't fight. If [my son-in-law] wants to throw a spear at [a woman] and I am standing with her, if he sees me standing there, he won't throw it, that's the Law.

Interference in fights is not limited to the occupants of the kin categories I have discussed here. As the following answer to my question about who might stop a husband and wife from fighting underlines, there is someone who can be expected to intervene in any altercation.

> When husband and wife are fighting their children can stop them. Or the mother of the girl can grab her or the mother of the boy can grab him. Or their uncle can stop them. If their mother won't take notice, then their father's sister or mother's mother or father's mother or anyone of their real family can stop them. Somebody would always stop them.

For example, as I mentioned in chapter 1, Lily's mother once told me that she had assisted a classificatory sister because the young woman's mother and father had gone fishing. In other words, she stepped in because she was there and they were not.

Onlookers must not only decide whether or not to take part in a fight; they must also decide what action to take. The perceived ferocity of an attack and the perceived reason for it appear to affect this series of decisions that I have modeled as follows:

If a member of my family is attacked I should intervene.
But not . . .
If my family member deserves a hiding (for starting a fight for no reason, drunkenness, infidelity, neglect of duties, and so on . . .
However . . .
If my family member is about to be seriously injured I should take partner with him or her no matter what the fight is about.
Or . . .
If my family member is about to seriously injure another I should stop him or her, no matter what the fight is about.

The appearance of serious injury causes other rules to change. For example, people who might not normally assist one another or fight with another may now do so.

If you make your husband bleed then his sister is going to fight you because seeing her brother's blood gives her a shock. People might call out, "You two sisters-in-law fight. You have no right. You should shame." But that girl will say, "I'm fighting with my sister-in-law because she hit my brother and made him bleed."

It is in circumstances such as these that a man can be expected to side with his sister against his brother-in-law or a woman attack her son-in-law. The threat of severe injury also requires that an aggressor be stopped, even though his or her action might be viewed as a just one.

[When one woman was having an affair with another's husband, the two women had a fight.] "He's mine!" "He's mine!" First they fought with their hands, then they pulled each other's hair, then they fought with nulla nulla. . . . [One] knocked [the other down]. [Another woman] rushed in and beat [the felled woman] with a nulla nulla. The men, everybody, pulled her off because she might hit that backbone.

Interference can be verbal or physical. Women often reported that words had been used to stop an aggressor.

I talked to him, I told him that if he kills his wife he is going to be all alone; he won't have anybody to cook for him or do everything for him. He has a small baby and if his wife dies there will be nobody to mind that baby.

Words can also be used to help an aggressor. Recall, for example, Lily's account; her sisters-in-law said to her opponents, "We are watching you. You can't cheat." Marguerite added that one of Lily's father's sisters also helped, saying, "You hit them my girl."

People who interfere in a fight may act aggressively. Words may be used in an aggressive manner. Once, for example, a man fighting with another was assisted by his mother and his mother's sister who yelled at his opponent, accusing him of marrying a close family member and inappropriate marriage partner. Physical acts may also be used by those interfering in a fight. Women might, for example, strike an aggressor to stop the aggression.

Once when [a woman's betrothed] was drunk he stood outside her house and swore at her. [The woman] got up and beat him from head to toe, gashed his mouth, dragged him to the wash house and beat him with a hose. She would have done more but her mother pulled her off, and when that didn't stop her, hit her on the head.

There are other factors that women appear to consider once they have determined that an aggressor should be stopped. What I have called the "temperament" of the aggressor is one of these. Is he a "cheeky" or a "quiet" man? Tina suggested that the former is more effectively stopped with words than blows.

Everybody talked to him, but they didn't strike him because he's a cheeky fella man and if they struck him he would just go more.

The restraint employed should also be appropriate to the circumstances. For example, words should be used when a woman wishes to stop a brother. Women who might intervene in an aggressive incident also appear to consider the degree of anger displayed by the aggressor.

If a man is mad then we leave him alone. We can't stop him. We let his uncle stop him.

She's drunk, she can't hear when people call out to her to stop. . . . [Her father's sister decided] she couldn't stop her.

Women, said Lily, leave interference to men in situations they see as "dangerous." These appear to be those in which the aggressor is male, the display of anger is intense, and weapons such as spears and rifles are employed. This is not to say that women never stop men armed with weapons, for they do. "I'm not frightened. I can go through spears," said Lily's mother, after stopping one of her grandsons from attacking another man. But women say they leave intervention to men when they see their own efforts as potentially dangerous or ineffectual. Men are seen as the second line of defense: "If a woman tries to stop a man and he won't notice her, then a man will stop him."

The Aftermath of Aggression

In the end, Lily discovered that Bret's arm had not, in fact, been broken by the women she had attacked. According to her account, she said, "I'm sorry," reminded her opponents that they were "family," and invited them to visit her at Mangrove.

What did Lily mean when she said, "I'm sorry"? I associate feelings that I call "regret," "guilt," or "shame" with this linguistic formula. Yet afterward, to my eyes, Lily displayed none of the psychological aftereffects that Westerners (perhaps especially white middle-class women) might expect should we behave in like manner. I would characterize her mood in our conversation about the fight as "proud." Recall, for example, her words, "There has never been a fight like that at Mangrove."

The Kaluli people of Papua New Guinea say, "How is one to know how another man feels?" (Schieffelin 1985:174; see also Gerber 1985). And I agree. I include my thoughts on Lily's feelings not to convince anyone that she really felt this way but to illustrate the process by which I learned to understand aggression as an Aboriginal rather than Western construct. Lily's story of her fight, particularly the account of her "apology" and my reaction to it, is a relatively concrete instance of such learning and thus an important example of the kinds of experiences that directed my exploration of aggression at Mangrove. In short, Lily said she was "sorry," but I did not think she seemed at all sorry. What did that suggest about the way in which aggressive behavior might be experienced by the women of Mangrove?

There is currently in anthropological thinking an emphasis on emotions as social constructions that can be observed in human interaction, particularly in people's talk about emotions (Lutz and Abu-Lughod 1990; Lutz and White 1986). Myers's early work on Pintupi emotions illustrates this perspective.

Consequently, Pintupi concepts of the emotions should be seen as an ideology, as models of and models for how one *should* feel and behave. They constitute a moral and cultural system that articulates and informs a particular view of social life and the self for the Pintupi, an official representation of what is going on. (1979:345)

Robert Levy (1973:271) has said that "emotions seem to be feelings which convey and represent information about one's *mode of relationship as a total individual* to the social and nonsocial environment." Myers (1979:375) has suggested that we see emotion concepts "as a way of representing action and selves in light of a moral order." Citing Lutz and White (1986), Geoffrey White and Karen Watson-Gegeo (1990:11) observe that emotions "are the subject of socially organized discourse—a cultural resource that is interactively produced to formulate particular kinds of identity, experience, and moral assertion." Following the general orientation of these perspectives, I explore emotion concepts associated with the aftermath of aggressive interactions at Mangrove as an additional means of understanding women's experiences of them.

As Lily's story indicates, fights and other aggressive events do not usually make an obvious difference in the everyday appearance and functioning of the community at Mangrove. They may, however, be associated with negative or devalued emotions or states. For example, several days after she wrestled, scratched, and threw sand at another woman who attacked her in like manner, it was said that a woman was feeling too "sick" to take a short trip. Another woman told me that after fighting with her husband she felt "frightened." Lily explained the departure of a health worker from her job at the local clinic after arguing with the white nurse in charge: "We Aborigines, we are different. If somebody growls at us and hurts our feelings, we don't like to stay." A man who was pushed by another during a fight subsequently refused to drive his attacker's truck. Following an argument with two of his sisters, another man reportedly told them he would no longer help them.

As a means of exploring further the aftermath of fighting, I asked seven women how they or others would feel (or had felt) after real or hypothetical fights and quarrels. Five women answered questions about both actual and hypothetical events, two about only one or the other. Three women said they would be or would say "sorry." But again the question arises, what does "sorry" mean in Aboriginal English? Only one woman explicitly associated "sorry" with negative feelings, saying, "They feel sorry and sad and unhappy." Jeffrey Heath (1982:168) gives *nugiwang* as the Australian word for "Excuse me!" and says it may be used when avoidance etiquette is unintentionally violated. But the two women who translated their "sorry" into the Australian language did not use this word. One used a word that Heath translates as the "exclamation of pity," "poor fellow" (ibid.:212), but another used a word that means "tired." It is difficult to conclude that "sorry" is unequivocally meant and understood as an apology, that is, as an admission of transgression and regret. It can as easily be understood as a signal that a fight is over as does Tina's formula for aggression and its cessation: "They should fight, shake hands, and finish." However, at least one woman reportedly expressed a concern about the manner in which her aggressive behavior might affect others.

Yesterday [a woman] was growling at us. I was sitting there with my sister. But we just sat there and didn't say anything. She was growling about how we always growl at her. And she saw me today and asked me if I was angry with her and I said no, I wasn't angry.

Two other women talked about physical sensations as a part of the aftermath of fighting; they spoke of being tired, weak, short of breath, and feeling a little pain. In addition to the woman who associated "sorry" with "sad" and "unhappy," three others spoke of negative emotional states, using words like "worried," "frightened," "bad," and "not good." Two of the respondents also talked about shame, that is, they talked about feeling "shy"—a word that is used interchangeably with "shame" in Aboriginal English.

Shame

"Shame," *mbuliyn* in the Australian language of Mangrove, is a word that is associated with aggressive behavior. One of my first experiences with behavior said to be a manifestation of "shame" occurred in the early months of my first visit to Mangrove; I noticed that groups of women studiously avoided looking at me as I approached them. I found this very disconcerting and assumed, perhaps rightly so, that they wanted to avoid me. But as time went by, I found that women who were expecting me to visit and expressed what seemed like genuine welcome when I arrived beside them also avoided looking at me as I walked toward them. "Why," I asked Lily, "do people look away when someone walks up from a long way?" "Old women," she replied, "don't like us to stare at them, they are too shy. It makes them shame. They might think something is wrong with the woman who is staring at her, she might be jealous or wungari." "Staring" indicates hostility.

If a woman is looking at me all the time when I go past, watching my eye, that means we have one man. She doesn't like that.

I fought with that woman because she was looking at me. She wanted to fight.

"Shame," in contrast, is indicated by averting the eyes.

Shame is, nevertheless, described as a feeling that may motivate aggression. For example:

[A man strikes the office with an ax] because he is shame of what he did to his wife [in a fight]. He is shame because [her parents] growl at him and he is not going to have their girl again, and he was very angry and got an ax and cut the shop.

Shame may be a response to aggression.

When everybody is there and someone growls at a man or a woman, they have feelings and they are going to shame for that.

It may inhibit aggression.

A man was after a woman for his second wife. When she was running around with two other young girls, he once beat her but stopped because he was shame when the other girls saw what he was doing.

Or it may occur in the aftermath of aggression.

When someone in the family does something wrong, the family shames. Like if your father kills someone you would feel shame.

Shame thus is both a motive for aggression and antithetical to aggression.

Shame is an emotion associated with wrongdoing, the violation of expectations and norms (cf. Hiatt 1978; Myers 1979).

When somebody, two [in-laws], have a fight and one stares at the other and says, "I don't call you [in-law]." And makes other people feel shame. "Why does she have to say that," people say. . . . They stay at home and maybe two or three days stay inside and come out when they don't feel shame any more.

Shame follows an accusation.

Boyfriends looking at [young girls], makes them shame. . . .The young girl says to the young boy, "You can't stare at me." [He replies] "I can stare at you any time because you were meeting [another young boy]."

And it follows public knowledge of wrongdoing.

When they do wrong and all the people know, everybody, because we know, that's why they feel shame, boys and girls.

Shame is an emotion said to be felt by a transgressor, by those who witness the transgression, or by those whose "family" have violated social norms.

If [my daughters] are single girls and they have a baby. Ooooh. That makes me shame.

It is associated with refusal and rejection.

A young girl and a young boy, maybe the man got married to another girl and that young girl really loved him, that makes her shame. She won't ever cut across his pathway, she will never want to see him. She will be shy.

Shame, *nga-mbuliyn*, "Don't look at me, I'm shy." Men looking at women make them feel shame, feel shy. That girl doesn't want that man, she doesn't want him to see her. . . . Or if somebody goes to take something, like a tin and someone calls out, "That's mine, you can't take it," she's going to leave it, she's shy now. If someone won't give her food, ngi-mbuliyn.

The association of the word "shame" with wrongdoing, public censure, and rejection suggests that women who say that they or others feel "shy" after a fight perceive some aggressive behavior to be wrong. This is a possibility; certainly, some acts of aggression—particularly those that result in serious injury or death—are regarded as wrong. But it is also possible that this shame is associated less with the aggressive behavior, the verbal or physical attack, than with the circumstances in which it is enacted. Lily, for example, seems to be saying that she had been misinformed about her son's arm and was sorry to have fought when it was only bruised rather than broken (though I think that many women would say her aggression would have been justified for any physical attack on her son). But this is not the same as being sorry for fighting or the same as being ashamed of fighting.

Revenge

The end of a fight does not necessarily mean the end of anger. As one young woman put it, "Some people forget, some people never forget." Six years after Lily's fight, I asked the sister who had fought by her side how she had felt afterward. Here is her reply.

I still felt bad, still angry. I wanted to go back and fight with [the woman who hit my finger]. I wanted to do the same thing to her. But they told me I had beat her cripple, she couldn't walk properly, she was bruised for months.

An act of aggression can bring an act of retaliation or revenge. When, for example, two sisters were attacked by a woman who hit one in the ribs and the other over the head, causing her to bleed, Lily predicted that they would fight again, "because of that blood." Eight days later, they did. Although Tina said that the fight would "finish" if the woman with the head wound did the same to her attacker, the sisters were apparently satisfied with an unarmed match. Afterward it was reported that they said, "We are finished now. We don't want to fight anymore. We are going away to the bush now." The healing service for the "cranky" woman (chap. 3) did not keep her opponent from confronting her several days later: "You always talk rough to me. . . . I'm going to throw a stone and cut your face just the same way as you cut mine."

Revenge is particularly to be feared, not just by an aggressor but by the aggressor's whole family, if an act of aggression has been especially injurious.

When a man [injures or kills] somebody, wungari will come to his family—everybody, father, mother, mother's sister, mother's brother, mother's father, everybody, the family. At [a nearby place] a man killed a woman. His fathers, sisters, uncles, his two old mothers were taken away to keep them from the trouble.

And revenge is not limited to direct human agency; it may take the form of supernatural aggression. Various equations between supernatural and overt acts of aggression have long been reported in the anthropological literature. Years ago, for example, A. Irving Hallowell said,

It can now be understood that, while there are no *official* records of murder among the Saulteaux, this does not correspond with the psychological realities of this society. Within their behavioral world, murder has occurred again and again but always as the result of sorcery, not of overt physical aggression. (1955:282)

Other writers have emphasized sorcery's role as a means of controlling acts of physical aggression (e.g., LeVine 1961; Whiting 1950).

Links between overt and supernatural aggression in Aboriginal Australia have been noted by some ethnographers. McKnight writes, for example,

There is an intricate connection between fighting and sorcery, as is indicated by the general term for sorcery, i.e., "spearing in the bush." Many of the Mornington Islanders were constantly on guard against sorcery, and many accidents, deaths, and general misfortunes were attributed to it. People were locked in a vicious circle, for fear of sorcery and sorcery accusations brought about anxiety, conflict and fighting, which in turn resulted in fear of sorcery. (1986:147ff.)

W. Lloyd Warner (1937:148) reported that out of fifty "Murngin" revenge killings, "five supposedly guilty magicians were killed by the clan members of victims of black magic." The imputation of sorcery as the cause of death can lead to revenge expeditions and physical attacks (e.g., Myers 1986; Tonkinson 1978; see also Knauft 1987b).

The conceptual salience of this linkage at Mangrove is suggested in the remarks of a man discussing the importance of good behavior for those who are initiated into the men's secret religious life.

Some boys can never go in [to the ceremony]. . . . Because if you go to the sacred side and after play up, then trouble to innocent people, father's mother, mother's mother, mother, uncle. Before if that boy made any trouble he would get twenty spears—killed straight out. Before, no secret trouble, no behind back trouble.

Maria Lepowsky (1990:184) reports that men and women on the South Pacific island of Vanatinai say much the same thing: "Before we killed with spears. Now we kill with sorcery." And the substitution of sorcery for spears has reportedly been made for much the same reason, the imposition of Western laws forbidding physical violence. Here Nancy Williams's conversations with Yolngu people on the relationship between killing and sorcery are illustrative.

Yolngu often referred to the suppression of revenge killing . . . that followed the imposition of Australian law in terms that implied they were grateful. Considerable ambivalence was apparent, however; for example, when they spoke of the bringing of peace by the Christian mission. Ambivalence was also expressed in terms of uncertainty over appropriate punishment and deterrence, since the death penalty (or the threat of it) was no longer available to them. As one clan leader put it, Yolngu had two ways to deal with people who committed serious offences: to talk to them, and to kill them. The old men had been talking and talking, the leader said, but they had to face up to the problem of how to punish people who committed offences for which they should have been killed. It was better not to kill, he said but what punishment would take its place? He implied that one result was increased reliance on sorcery. (1987:151)

Aboriginal women at Mangrove also link the physical and the supernatural in their talk about aggression. In the following account, two women relate a dream that followed the sudden and disturbing death of a clansman. As McKnight (1986) observed above, the act of sorcery is visualized as an act of spearing.

AW1: We didn't know this [that the man was murdered] before, but [my son] had a dream. [The dead man] came to [my son] in the dream and told him, "They took me in a truck to the bush and then I was walking. There were two billabongs. I was walking there. You can see my footprints there. And when I was walking between the two billabongs, somebody there killed me."

AW2: With a [metal-tipped spear].

AW1: After he died he had a cut here [shoulder shown] and here [back of neck shown].

Referring to the same death, two other speakers link sorcery and physical aggression together in a "cause and effect" sequence.

[At a meeting for the dead man, a man] talked, "We are going to find out who murdered him." They get [metal] spears and rifles. . . . Maybe at the meeting they are going to say to one man, "You murdered him." And his son and brother are going to get spears now and take partner.

As Tina has said (chap. 3), after a murderer secretly spears someone, he heals the victim's wound, leaving an invisible "mark." The victim lives for two or three days after the spearing, then dies suddenly of apparent sickness, an accident such as a shark attack, or in a fight.

"Trouble" incurred for whatever reason may be general or specific in its aim. The individual who provokes supernatural aggression may or may not become its victim. Trouble can travel from one member of a "family" to another. A man, for example, who murders another may provoke sorcery, but it may ultimately strike his sister or mother in his place.

AW: New mission time, the first one to pass away was [a man's] little brother. It didn't matter that [another boy] was in the middle of the water and [the little brother] was near the shore, the [poisonous] jellyfish got him. Somebody was doing something to him before.

VKB: You mean he had a mark?

AW: Yes.

VKB: Why would they do that to a little boy?

AW: They do like that when they can't get his father.

The perception that any member of a "family" may suffer for the misdeeds of another undoubtedly affects ideas about the role of "family" when it comes to aggressive behavior (cf. Whiting 1950). People whose actions protect others from harm may also see (or only see) these actions as a means of protecting themselves and other members of their family.

Belief in supernatural aggression may also limit and contain physical aggression in another way: by deflecting culpability from a known individual, seen as an unwitting agent, to an unknown assailant, one who has employed supernatural means of aggression (see LeVine 1961). In these circumstances, the necessity and appropriateness of revenge, at least against the known perpetrator, thus become questionable. I illustrate this point with a case of murder and ritual revenge.

Shortly before I returned to Mangrove in 1981, a man from the community was killed by another during a visit to a nearby settlement. As the accounts go, before his attacker was taken away to jail by the Australian authorities, people from Mangrove went to the settlement for *magaranganyji,* a highly structured form of aggressive retribution.

In olden days there was a big wungari called *mana magaranganyji* that happened after one man killed another man. . . . Only men would fight. Women would stop the spears with a long stick. They would knock them out of the air. . . . The man would stand up alone and people would throw spears, or the man would stand up with his brother or uncle and the other line would throw spears one at a time. After they throw the spears they are satisfied; no more wungari.

In olden times when a man killed another man he would have to stand up for the dead man's relations. At that time, old women could stand there with poles and knock the spears out of the air. But if people said, "No, you can't stop the spears, he has to get a mark," they wouldn't. A man might jump spears from early morning until dinnertime. If he jumped them all, finally a relation of the murdered man would walk up to him and stab him with a spear in the leg or the shoulder. Then the trouble would be finished, that man would be free. . . . If a man doesn't stand up for the spears, the trouble will go to him, his mother, brother, sister, and his children.

In the case of the magaraganyji held in 1981, the attacker jumped all the spears. Afterward, a senior man in the victim's clan walked up to the attacker and struck him on the shoulder with a spear thrower. As these are generally made from short, lightweight pieces of wood, it is unlikely that the blow was intended to do any real harm.[4] Lily explained that people did not think he was really responsible for the death. As another woman put it,

[The dead man] was in Darwin and then he went to [the settlement] and maybe he had trouble in Darwin from somebody because when he got to [the settlement] he was growling and [the attacker] didn't hit him very hard. You know how Aborigines do things sometimes.

Reunification

Shame, unhappiness, regret, and a desire for revenge are not the only possible affective outcomes of fighting. Speaking of another fight she had been in, Lily said that afterward she and her combatants were all together, hugging one another. Three of the women whom I asked about feelings after a fight used words indicating neutral, if not positive, emotions: "happy," "calm," and "alright."

AW: Did you hear that [a woman] and [her husband] had a fight last week? That old man had a spear.
VKB: Did he throw it?
AW: No, he was just [hand motion of threatening with].
VKB: What for?
AW: For [their ten-year-old son's] sake. He threw a rock and hit [his mother]. She was very angry and gave him a hiding. [Her husband] said, "You shouldn't give him a hiding, he's too skinny." She said, "He's skinny and spoiled."

This fight account illustrates one of the most significant aspects of aggressive interactions at Mangrove: the likelihood that they will occur between familiars, if not intimates. This is expressed in one of the replies to my questions about how people feel after they have been fighting and arguing.

You are going to think about what you did [to your opponent] and maybe, late afternoon, you feel sorry for him and so you go and say, "Sorry we've been fighting." But the other man says, "It's alright we've been fighting because we are two relations, close family."

The people who attack you one day are the people who may protect you the next. They are also people who see you from day to day and remember what you do. It thus makes sense for the aggressors and the victims of Mangrove to ask for and receive forgiveness as soon as possible, anticipating the next aggressive round when players and their roles may be slightly rearranged. Insofar as the people of Mangrove who fight with each other know each other, the context of aggressive interactions replicates special conditions of the prisoner's dilemma when the "best" strategy is to "cooperate" initially, immediately "punish" deviation from cooperation, and "forgive" willingly (Axelrod and Hamilton 1981; Klama 1988). The patterns of aggression, intervention, and forgiveness manifest at Mangrove may display a kind of universal logic (see Myers 1988) but one that makes good sense only when it is expressed in a community like Mangrove.

The social arrangements of Mangrove appear to facilitate the ease with which relationships strained by aggressive behavior are repaired and restored. Wondering how people who had fought and injured each other were getting along after the fact, I asked several women about dyads who had once been antagonists in fights. I asked, for example, about the woman (mentioned above) whose head had been struck and the woman who had struck it. I was told that they were "good friends now" because one had married the other's brother; they were now sisters-in-law. Another woman told me about a fight she had with her husband's lover. Afterward she was "still angry" and did not "forgive them." She wanted to leave for another community, but her father-in-law did not want her to go. "He wanted me to stay, so I stayed and I'm still here."

Observing that Aboriginal people "engage in elaborate work to preserve harmonious relations," Kenneth Liberman has wondered "how such extremes of congeniality and personal violence can coexist" (1985:49). (Knauft [1985] poses a similar question about Gebusi society.) Liberman proposes that the focus Aboriginal people place on interpersonal relations "make both congenial fellowship and violent argument more likely" (ibid.). Myers has reached a similar conclusion about violence and "relatedness" in Pintupi life.

When the capacity to complete oneself through relationship with others is threatened or prevented, the resort to violence establishes one's own will. At the same time, the ever-present possibility of conflict lends enormous value to sustaining shared identity as a precondition for social action. (1986:179)

The statements from women at Mangrove similarly suggest that the multiplicity of long-term relationships and the affective and behavioral expectations associated with them draw people together even as aggressive interactions push them apart (see Gilmore 1987; Gluckman 1956, 1965). I would, however, propose a slightly different formulation of the relationship between fellowship and violence at Mangrove. People there can fight with each other, risking estrangement, because there is so much keeping them together (see Macdonald 1988; Shokeid 1982; Simmel 1955).

When aggressors expect to see each other again (and, most important, can remember their opponents' previous behavior), restraint may be an unbeatable strategy (Klama 1988). In the gemeinschaft of a place such as Mangrove, it pays to follow the rules. Patricia Draper (1978:40) has described how the homicides of very aggressive !Kung San "were in fact political assassinations" (see also Lee 1979). In Aboriginal Australia, "an assembly of men might reach a decision to execute an individual whose violence had become a matter of deep public concern" (Hiatt 1986:14). Even in societies where aggression is the prerogative of the individual rather than the state, there can be severe penalties for displaying aggression beyond the norm. As Martin Daly and Margo Wilson (1988:226) conclude after a survey of sixty cases in the HRAF probability sample, "Lethal retribution is an ancient and cross-culturally universal recourse of those subjected to abuse" (see also Otterbein 1986).

When fighting with strangers, however, aggressors may perceive no reason for pulling their punches. Robin Fox (1968) has observed how the dramatic but highly structured and relatively harmless aggression of Irish villagers becomes no-holds-barred brawling in the anonymity of an urban pub. He predicts that, generally, violence between strangers will be violence without rules. At Mangrove, there may well be a difference in the aggressive behavior displayed among "close relations" and people who are essentially strangers.

When [a woman] was a young girl, three or four men [who speak a language other than that spoken in area around Mangrove] came here and grabbed her. She called out and was heard by her husband's brother who was near camp cutting wild honey. He jumped down from the tree, grabbed some spears, and went after her. He grabbed her back from the men and then fought them. One ran around behind him and threw a spear into his hip bone. He threw a spear and broke one man's ankle. At this point three of his brothers heard the fighting and came from the area where they had been hunting feral cattle. By the time they arrived, the foreigners had run out of spears. The three brothers grabbed the wounded foreigner and held him up telling their wounded brother, "Kill him or he will kill you and steal your woman." One of the brothers said, "Kill him or I will kill you." The wounded brother thrust a spear into the man's stomach. "You didn't kill him hard enough," said his brother and stabbed the man in the stomach again. He then proceeded to break the man's bones with a nulla nulla: arms, legs, and skull. His brains came out. He was dead. The other foreign men left. The men from Mangrove put the dead man up on a platform, picked up their spears, and left.

This text is notable in two respects. First, the violence of the encounter is unlike any of the instances of aggression that currently occur at Mangrove. It clearly upset the speaker, even as she told the story. Second, it is not insignificant that this level of violence took place between men from two language groups. It is true that these groups are connected by intermarriage, myth, and ceremony (Turner 1976). People from both speak each other's language, and even these opponents might have stressed their kin ties on another occasion. But they are also people who "speak another language," a people who are not one's own.

This difference between the aggressive treatment of "family" and strangers underlines the effects that cultural expectations have on the aggressive behavior that the people of Mangrove display toward each other. It is not normally acceptable for people to seriously harm or kill each other; their actions and the actions of the people responsible for them must conform to this standard. In this small community, people live their lives in the public gaze. Most people have always known each other, and everyone has a reputation, though it can change from day to day. Even in the last few years when more substantial houses have reduced alfresco living, residential arrangements ensure that few acts go unwitnessed. The sociocultural milieu of Mangrove is characterized by precepts of aggression as behavior that will remain within specified limits, and there are social and physical arrangements that ensure these expectations will usually be met.

Accompanying the Western assumption that overt aggression represents chaos is the corollary that overt aggression rends the social fabric, destroys relationships, and weakens group solidarity (Gilmore 1987). Particularly interesting in this context is our metaphorical usage of material goods to stand for relationships. Observing that American marriage is often seen as "manufactured product," Naomi Quinn (1987:174–175) lists things that Americans say about their marriages.

These include the words "strong," "building," and "foundation"—all words that we also routinely use, as laymen and as anthropologists, to talk about "society." Referring to social structure, for example, Max Gluckman (1965:108) talks about the "interweaving of ties," Mary Douglas (1973:89) of a "network of links." Speaking of exogamy, Roger Keesing (1975:19) says, "It serves the same general functions of making groups interdependent and of weaving them together with strands of kinship." White and Watson-Gegeo, like so many of us today, talk about the "cultural construction and maintenance of social relationships" (1990:13). Gilmore (1987:171) provides a further example when he writes at the conclusion of his work on aggression in an Andalusian village, "The most salient themes in their village society are those of desire and restraint, struggle and tradition, aggression and gregariousness: seemingly contradictory threads, but woven together by the genius of their culture into the iron fabric of a good life." But if relationships are things, they can be torn and broken; we speak, as above, of aggression "tearing" at the "fabric" of society, of "broken" marriages, and "ruined" friendships (Quinn 1987). And, I suggest, we often think of such "damage" as "beyond repair" (e.g., Lakoff and Johnson 1980; Lakoff and Kovecses 1987).

Aboriginal people at Mangrove emphasize different metaphors for relationships and, I would argue, consequently understand the effects of aggression on them differently. Relationships are not perceived as things, nor are they as easily broken. There are, for example, words not just for single kin positions but for relationships as well: *nigamanyij* refers to two brothers; *amurij*, to a grandchild and his or her father's father/father's sister (Heath 1982:121, 199). As is the case in other parts of the world (Shweder and Bourne 1984), the body is used as a metaphor for relationships, though this may be more prevalent in other parts of Australia (Heath 1982). In sign language, for example, the breast signifies child, and the calf, sibling (see also Schebeck 1978; Shapiro 1979, 1981). Short of death, an injured body gradually, or rapidly, transforms into a well body. Healing is routinely observed as cuts and bruises inflicted in the quotidian accidents and conflicts of life mend. The willingness with which bodies have long been cut, pierced, and scarified for ceremonial and cosmetic ends[5] suggests an expectation that wounds will heal. Nancy Scheper-Hughes and Margaret Lock (1987:21) have said, "The confident uses of the body in speaking about the external world conveys a sense that humans are in control." The use of the human body to speak about relationships at Mangrove implies that the integrity of relationship is seen as an organic process and one that can overcome many perturbations.

In these sociocultural circumstances, aggression need not be seen as unvaryingly dangerous, evil, or bad; in these circumstances, its potential for drama, discourse, and catharsis can be appreciated, if not actively encouraged. In these circumstances, aggression can even be enjoyed.

One night as I was sitting with Tina in her camp, she began to laugh and told me she was thinking about her [grandfather] when she was a little girl. She was with the women who were gathering corms in the mud. The wife of her [grandfather], who wore a pubic apron of possum skin in those days, went a little way from the others, pretending to gather as she slowly moved away from the group. She put down her *cooliman* [carrying vessel] and ran off with her husband's younger brother. The women noticed she was gone and went to look for her. They found her cooliman and sang out, "Gagagagaga, your wife has eloped." Her husband got up with a boomerang, nulla nulla, and spears. He stood up there with his legs apart, yelling at the women, "You fucking bastards, you didn't watch her." He hit them with his boomerang. "Waaah, he's striking us for nothing," they said. Then he went to look for his wife. He found her tracks, took his sister's sons to find her, but he couldn't. He came back and hit his head with a boomerang, crying, "My wife has eloped." "I never saw another man do that," said Tina. "Maybe they did that in olden times." He went off again to look for her. His sister's son found her, then passed her back to her husband. He left her alone but went to find his brother. They fought with boomerang and nulla nulla. They wrestled. People just let them fight to see who would win. Well, he didn't strike that girl and she slept in camp for two nights, then eloped again. Again she went with the women to gather, then crept away to join her lover. Again the women discovered her absence, called out that she was gone. The lovers were found. [Grandfather] stood there with his legs apart shaking his nulla nulla, calling out, "Let's fight." His brother did the same. They fought from dinnertime to sunset. Good fun that eloping.

5

Women and Aggression

Years ago, Collier (1974) observed that serious attention to women's conflicts can reveal critical social issues that might be missed if they are dismissed as mere "domestic squabbles" or "cat fights." Here I explore Aboriginal women's intragender aggression with the intention of demonstrating what this analysis can tell us about these women and their relationships with others. I also illustrate the multidetermined characteristic of these aggressive interactions and the consequent importance of employing multiple frameworks or concepts for their explication.

Women are among the initial actors in 495 of the 793 cases of aggressive behavior that I collected. In 285 of these cases, women are clearly the instigators of aggressive behavior; in 147, women are the victims of other women. A discussion of these cases, with a particular focus on fighting as the most common and most dramatic expression of aggression, is the substance of this chapter.

Table 2 lists the categories of aggressive acts associated with women as initiators of aggression. With the exception of murder, women initiate the full range of aggressive interactions manifest at Mangrove. I begin my exploration of these interactions by asking about motive. Motive can, of course, be addressed at many levels—from examining the behavioral repertoire of the human species and the female sex to looking at factors precipitating fights in specific settings (Konner 1982). Here I am particularly interested in what Aboriginal women say about their own actions. According to the accounts of people at Mangrove,

Table 2 *Women's Aggression*

Type of Aggression[a]	Women vs. Men[b]	Women vs. Women	Solitary Woman
Fight	29	61	1[c]
Fight?	1	14	—
Discipline	15	24	—
Display	—	—	9
Display in fight	—	1	7
Murder	—	—	—
Verbal aggression	13	35	33
Curse	—	1	11
Threat	2	3	2
Suicide attempt	—	—	3
Mirriri	—	—	—
Miscellaneous/ Not clear	4	8	8
Total	64	147	74

[a]See chap. 2, n. 6, for details of these categories.
[b]Only includes cases where women initiated aggression against men.
[c]The categorization of this case reflects the complexity of human interactions and the difficulties we sometimes have pigeonholing them.

women attack others for a variety of reasons. These are summarized in table 3.

I identify three broad themes that make sense both in terms of Western concepts of aggression and in terms of the sociocultural context in which they are manifest at Mangrove. These are, first, aggression as defense or self-defense; second, what has been labeled "prosocial" aggression, that is, aggression that appears to stem from a concern with conformity to social norms; and, finally, aggression that is a form of competition. I focus here on the third category of motive, that of aggression as competition. I also restrict my discussion to cases of aggression between women. Aggression between men and women is the topic of chapter 6.

Table 3 *Reasons Associated with Women's Aggression*

Reason[a]	Women vs. Men[b]	Women vs. Women	Solitary Woman
Child	5	7	9
Marriage	—	3	—
Spouse	2	1	1
Jealousy (U)	1	12	2
Premarital sex	4	23	3
Jealousy (M)	7	17	4
Subsistence	8	5	5
Other goods	4	6	3
Delinquency	7	2	1
Intoxication	6	2	—
Aggression	2	12	10
Misbehavior	5	14	5
Ritual breach	—	5	5
Swearing	4	3	—
Emotions	—	1	1

[a]I have summarized the reasons offered by Aboriginal people as follows:

1. Child: Perceived mistreatment or neglect of a child, or disposition of a child not liked, e.g., residence. Should be biological child or ward of aggressor, e.g., wife's child. Child may be adult. If child is a classificatory relation, see no. 11.
2. Marriage: Conflict over or disruption of marriage arrangements.
3. Spouse: Attempts to acquire a spouse. Includes getting rid of a spouse that is not included in no. 4, 5, or 6.
4. Jealousy (Unmarried): Jealousy over boyfriends or girlfriends where all are unmarried. Does include "stealing" of a betrothed partner of an unmarried person.
5. Premarital sexual behavior: Includes illicit dating, "running around," elopement of unmarried partners.
6. Jealousy (Married): Includes jealousy of married partner, suspected or real adultery of partner. Because of polygyny, this may include a married woman getting a new husband but not a married man getting a new wife (see no. 3).
7. Subsistence goods: Critical goods such as money, food, and tools, or concerns over these.
8. Other goods: Includes items like cards, clothing, and cassette tapes.
9. Delinquency: Acts such as breaking into the shop, graffiti, and stealing.
10. Intoxication: Intoxication from petrol or alcohol. Includes people fighting because they are drunk or fighting with someone because the other person is drunk.
11. Aggression: The perceived previous aggression to self or relative, e.g., gossip or suspected sorcery.
12. Misbehavior: Includes misbehavior or mistreatment of another, e.g., not working, not helping.
13. Ritual breach: Breaches of ceremony or ritual etiquette, e.g., misuse of supernatural, nonparticipation in ceremonial activity. Does not include incidents related to Christianity.
14. Swearing: Use of swear words.
15. Emotions: Emotions or states other than sexual jealousy, e.g., mad, jealous (if not sexual), *mirriri*.

Cases were also coded into a miscellaneous category (e.g., concerns about the weather, sending a relative to the hospital) and an unclear/unknown category.

[b]Only includes cases in which women initiated aggression against men.

Competition

I have chosen to center this discussion around a consideration of women's aggression as competition for two reasons. First, because this framework, which encapsulates both biological and sociocultural arguments about gender relations, is one of the few that has been employed in the rare looks at women's aggressive behavior around the world; and second, because Western ideas about competition between women share a similar ideological space with ideas about women and aggression (e.g., Flax 1987*b*, 1990; Miner and Longino 1987).

It is not always clear what people mean when they talk about competition. Competition may be "striving" or "rivalry." "Rivalry" is most pertinent to this discussion. When two individuals both pursue resources perceived as insufficient, they can be said to be in competition. As I want to use the word here, a race in which there is no reward for winning is not a competition. It is a situation in which individuals are only "striving" to do their best. In contrast, "rivalry" exists between two people who are pursuing the same resource, like a job or a spouse. Whether or not they ever confront each other, or even know the other is in the running, they are in competition (see Daly and Wilson 1983).

Should competition and aggression always be equated? Considering only the motives of competitors or aggressors, the answer is no. People may act aggressively without competing. Here, for example, is a case of aggression at Mangrove that I would not, at least initially, categorize as competition.

Yesterday, shop time, [a woman] was in the office and [another woman] saw her and went into the office and they were growling—because [the first woman's sister's daughter] was teasing [the second woman's daughter]. Then just after supper, just before sun go down time, the whole lot [the second woman, two of her sisters-in-law, her mother-in-law, and another woman] came marching down to [the first woman's mother's] house. [The second woman and her mother-in-law] had sticks and [the second woman] hit a trash barrel. But they only growled at [the first woman's sister and her husband—the parents of the girl who had been "teasing"—and mother]. [The first woman] wasn't there. [The second woman] said, "You don't let your children be cruel to my children when I go away." [The first woman's sister's husband] was growling too, and so was [her sister]. Her "family," her mother [and two of her mother's half-sisters] were trying to stop her, but she just kept growling. I don't know how she didn't get that temper and [start fighting physically]. She used to be like that. [One of the sisters-in-law] said, "Don't growl at me, I have a pretty leg." And then she just walked away. That means she knows someone is sleeping with her brother [real or classificatory]. I don't know if anyone is. [The first woman's mother] picked up a rock, but she didn't throw it. [Another of the second woman's daughters] had a baby for that man; they don't like [the first woman's sister's daughter] to go after him. [A young woman] was angry at [the first woman's sister's daughter] for that and that's why she was teasing [the second woman's daughter]. [The first woman's sister's daughter] was trying to get that boy.

The "second woman" would probably say that she attacked the mother of the adolescent who had attacked her daughter only to protect her own child. Similarly, people may compete without aggressive intent, that is, with no intent of harming the other. For example, a woman may take a married man as a lover because she "loves" him, not because she wants to "hurt" his wife.

Competition and aggression, however, are experiences not only of initial actors but also of those who are affected by the acts—the rivals and victims. Effects of behavior as well as motives for behavior should therefore be considered in an examination of the relationships between aggression and competition. If, for example, the first woman's sister was less able to care for her daughter after being attacked by the second woman and her kinswomen, the battle between these two groups of women could be interpreted as an example of competition between women; while "the other woman," insofar as she uses resources that a man would otherwise contribute to his wife and children, may be doing harm.

Anthropological Perspectives on Aggression and Competition

Overt competition between women, like aggression between women, is both a taboo for many Western middle-class women (e.g., Miner and Longino 1987) and only rarely a topic of academic interest. Nevertheless, sporadic discussions of women's competition are found scattered throughout the anthropological literature.

Jane Collier (1974) and Louise Lamphere (1974) are, perhaps, the first anthropologists to address the topic. They treat competition as a variable phenomenon, dependent on specific sociocultural configurations. According to them, a woman's place in the developmental cycle of the domestic group and the way in which power and authority are distributed within the family are critical determinants of its manifestation. For example, in patrilocal, patrilineal extended families in which power and authority reside in the male hierarchy, women seeking power and resources are set less against men than against one another. Mothers-in-law and daughters-in-law, co-wives, and sisters-in-law are women who are expected to compete in these circumstances. The classic example of the friction so often displayed between mother-in-law and daughter-in-law is a case in point. These women, say both Collier and Lamphere, are competing over their respective son and husband and the power they may gain through him (see also Gallin 1992; Miller 1992; Wolf 1968, 1972).

In Sarah Hrdy's *The Woman that Never Evolved* (1981), a reconstruction of evolving female primates and an endeavor to bring women into the evolutionary picture, female competition has a central place. "Competition among females is one of the major determinants of primate social organization, and it has contributed to the organisms women are today" (189). According to Hrdy's argument, female competition and female aggression as a form of competition are major components of female reproductive strategies. They are evolved traits, endemic to the female of the species and as such, says Hrdy, must be considered in analyses of human social life and in blueprints for social change.

Looking at women from a perspective derived from evolutionary biology, Ilsa Schuster (1983, 1985; see also Brown and Schuster 1986; Schuster and Hartz-Karp 1986) has suggested that female aggression should be seen as a form of female competition. "Aggression is related to competition for scarce resources," she says and predicts that women will display aggressive behavior "when confrontation becomes a viable means of attaining scarce resources" (Schuster 1983:320, 1985:2). Schuster proposes that the "incidence of aggression among women is related to the intensity of competition for the scarce resource" and suggests that "aggression will become manifest when it becomes worthwhile" (1985:25), that is, when "environmental" factors such as population density, the availability of economic resources, and the extent of social stratification are such that aggression becomes necessary in the competition.

Schuster acknowledges sociobiological theory as the source of her framework but does not provide a step-by-step outline of the route she has taken from her considerations of "reproductive success" to the aggressive behavior of Zambian, Chinese, and other women. I need such an outline for my purposes, however, so here I reconstruct it. The focus to date in evolutionary biology has been, almost exclusively, on male competition. According to this theory, in which the measure of evolutionary success is the differential reproductive success of individuals, females, because of their greater investment in offspring, are the limiting resource for which males must compete (Trivers 1972). Access to resources that can be converted into offspring (e.g., food) limits female reproduction, so females are expected to compete for scarce resources. Males, however, whose reproductive success is limited by access to females, will compete for such access—either directly or indirectly—for resources that are "attractive" to females (Daly, Wilson, and Weghorst 1982; Hrdy 1981; Hrdy and Williams 1983). On the basis of such reasoning, Martin Daly, Margo Wilson, and Suzanne Weghorst (1982; see also Daly and Wilson 1988) predict that men and women will be "jealous" for different reasons: a man, of his partner's sexuality; a woman, of her mate's time, energy, and wealth.

Schuster (1983, 1985) has interpreted many examples of women's aggression as competition over the scarce resource of "socially desirable men." But women's competition over men could also be predicted with reference to the importance of fathering in human society. Human families are characterized by a long-term "collaboration" between men and women who rear their offspring until adulthood (Lancaster and Lancaster 1987). Thus, by the logic of Trivers's hypothesis, women could be expected to compete for men when the male contribution to offspring gives their mother a reproductive advantage (Ayres 1976).

Aggression and Competition at Mangrove

Can an evolutionary perspective help us understand the unique, historically particular moment in which women at Mangrove attack each other? Rarely do women at Mangrove appear to compete for things that might be regarded as resources. Only five cases of aggression between women were attributed to conflict over subsistence goods; only six cases were attributed to conflict over less essential

Table 4 *Reasons for Women's Fights*

Reason	Number of Fights
Child	4
Marriage	2
Spouse	1
Jealousy (U)	8
Premarital sex	7
Jealousy (M)	12
Subsistence	2
Other goods	4
Delinquency	—
Intoxication	—
Aggression	4
Misbehavior	3
Ritual breach	—
Swearing	2
Emotions	—

goods like tape recorders and tobacco. "Subsistence goods" was a reason significantly associated with aggression between men and women but not with women's attacks on each other.[1] When it comes to "men" as a reason for aggression, however, women's attacks on each other are much more frequent. Thirty cases of aggression between women were attributed to jealousy or conflict between unmarried women over a man, a husband's real or suspected adultery, or a husband's attempt to bring another wife into the household—all situations in which women are pitted against one another in competition for a man's favors, if not resources.

According to Schuster (1983, 1985), women's competition for men is like competition for any resource; the intensity of the aggression varies with the importance of the prize. The favors of high-status men make life more comfortable for educated Zambian women, but reliable male partners may be a matter of "sheer physical survival" for poor urban women. Thus, educated rivals threaten each other over the telephone, while their slum counterparts attack with broken bottles.

Table 4 lists the reasons for Aboriginal women's fights. Among these, what we would call "sexual jealousy" and the knowledge or suspicion that a husband is having an adulterous affair are the most com-

Table 5 *Injuries Inflicted in Aggression Between Women*

Reason	Injury		
	With Weapon	Without Weapon	Not Clear if Weapon Used
Child	2	1	—
Marriage	—	—	1
Spouse	—	—	—
Jealousy (U)	4	4	—
Premarital sex	4	5	14
Jealousy (M)	5	11	3
Subsistence	2	2	—
Other goods	1	1	1
Delinquency	1	1	—
Intoxication	1	—	—
Aggression	1	4	—
Misbehavior	1	—	1
Ritual breach	—	—	—
Swearing	2	2	—
Emotions	—	—	—

mon. It should also be noted that twenty-one of the thirty cases of aggression between women for these reasons involve fights. Fighting at Mangrove entails physical aggression and is thus potentially more injurious than verbal aggression. But "intensity" is a relative concept. Any physical aggression might seem "intense" to a Western middle-class woman. Do the women of Mangrove think that their fights over men are "intense," or at least more "intense" than their fights over other issues?

Table 5 lists injuries inflicted by women on other women in association with the reason for the interaction. "Jealousy" of both married and unmarried women is clearly the cause associated with the most injury. Note that in table 5, I have listed all physical injury inflicted by women on women, not just that inflicted in events that I have labeled "fights."

Models of women's evolved biology and behavior emphasize "the overarching need of female mammals in general and women in particular to acquire resources necessary to bear and rear offspring" (Lancaster 1989:96). Predictions derived from sociobiological theory would lead us to expect aggression from women competing over men's resources. Women, according to this framework, would not be expected to compete over male sexuality (e.g., Daly and Wilson 1988; Daly, Wilson, and Weghorst 1982). Assuming that the rewards of liaisons at Mangrove are primarily sexual in nature, whereas marriage entails a commitment of resources to a man's partner and offspring, differences between the actions of "girl friends" and wives might be expected. The focus on "reproductive success" in the formulations of sociobiology also suggests that differences between women with and without children might be found.

Women's aggression at Mangrove does not provide overwhelming support for either possibility, however. It might be predicted that because women convert resources into offspring and defend these resources from intruders, married women with children would be more likely to initiate a battle with their husbands' lovers, who should have little to gain from such confrontations. In nine of the thirteen cases in which a wife and a "girl friend" fought, it was possible to ascertain which woman initiated the encounter. In five cases, wives (four with children and one without) initiated aggression. In one instance, a woman "taking partner" for a wife initiated aggression. In three cases, however, girl friends reportedly started the fight.

Of course, it may be that girl friends at Mangrove are competing with wives not for a man's sexual favors but for his resources. The likelihood of this possibility is discussed below. It is also possible that wives are competing with girl friends for a man's sexuality, but this is not predicted by evolutionary theory.

I also looked at the total number of participants in the twenty-one cases in which women fought over men, reasoning that greater numbers might reflect a societal perception that some kinds of contests between women are more important than others. It might be, for example, that more attention is paid to fights in which at least one combatant is married and has children. Here I found even less support for the predictions of evolutionary theory. Of the eleven cases of aggression in which the relationship at issue was a marriage with children, an average of 3.9 people participated. In the two cases in which one of the aggressors was a married but childless woman, 6.5 people participated. And in the eight cases in which unmarried girls fought over "boyfriends," 4.1 people took part. In two of these cases of fights over "boyfriends," combatants were pregnant or had a child; one woman fought over the man who reportedly impregnated her, and the other fought over the brother of her child's reputed genitor. In these two cases, 3.5 people reportedly participated in the fight.

I also categorized these cases on the basis of whether or not one of the combatants had a child rather than on the basis of marital status. In the thirteen fights in which women had children, an average of 3.8 people took part; in the eight fights in which women did not have children, an average of 4.9 people took part. Only the greater number of fights involving married women with children suggests that fighters themselves might think that competition over a married man with children is more important than competition over men who have not fathered children.

It is possible that fights associated with other reasons should be considered in this discussion. For example, recall the conflict between the families of two adolescents because one "teased" the other. Even though the stated cause was the defense of a child, it is possible that the aggressors were really motivated by the adolescent's interest in the youth who had fathered a child with her opponent's sister. I do not want to second guess the men and women who have told me about aggression at Mangrove, however, and so limit my analysis only to fights that reportedly are over men.

Sociobiological predictions about behavior do not require that actors be conscious of their motives (Daly and Wilson 1983). What is critical is that actions increase individual reproductive success, not that individuals intend them to do so. But clearly, as the above analyses indicate, we can understand very little about women's aggressive behavior at Mangrove without reference to their perceptions and interpretations (see Klama 1988).

Competition: Adaptation or Reflex?

Calling women's competition the "dark underside of the feminist dream," Hrdy (1981:190) sees women's "universal commitment to compete" as a trait that evolved in an environment in which place in the female hierarchy was so central to reproductive success that "female status has become very nearly an end in itself" (128). Today's women may be "highly competitive, manipulative, and even murderous" though they may be competing only for "points" (129). To compete and aggress against one another, women do not need to perceive that they are rivals for a scarce and valuable resource but simply that they are rivals.

A number of anthropologists today are attempting to bridge the nature/nurture dichotomization of our discipline rather than deny its continuing influence on the way we construe questions about gender, kinship, and hierarchy (e.g., Brown 1991; Chisholm 1992; Smuts 1992; Shore 1988; Worthman 1992). Harold Scheffler's discussion of gender and kinship captures the spirit and intention of this discussion of gender, aggression, and competition.

What is wrong with [the standard theory of kinship] is not its attempt to explain the ubiquity of kinship concepts and practices by positing certain, as Clyde Kluckhohn once put it, "invariant points of reference supplied by the biological [and] psychological . . . givens of human life." . . . It is, after all, one of those "givens" that humans *do* reproduce bisexually and *do* produce helpless offspring who *do* require physical and psychological nurturance for many years. The real defect in the standard theory is that it constructs some of those "givens" in a blatantly sexist fashion and then uses them to constitute the ethnographic facts to be explained. (1991:374)

Evolutionary biology points us in the direction of human potentials, of behaviors, or learning biases, that probably were adaptive in our evolutionary past (Tiger and Fox 1971; Tooby and Cosmides 1989). But it is a mistake to assume that these same behaviors or propensities to learn some things more easily than others are necessarily adaptive in the particular circumstances of a given historical moment (Burgess and Draper 1989). It is also a mistake to assume that by identifying them as "adaptive" we understand very much about them. Western middle-class women are as much creatures of evolution as are Aboriginal women. They are also rivals for men. Why, then, do they not fight over men, at least in the ways that Aboriginal women do (e.g., Remoff 1984)? Viewing women's battles over men—even if these battles are a form of competition—as adaptive strategies for survival does not necessarily advance our understanding of women's aggressive behavior. Nor does viewing them as contests in which a woman's reproductive success is at stake. We can accept that it is easy for women to learn rivalry in some circumstances. But clearly it is by delineating the circumstances in which this rivalry is learned that we can best address our questions about the actual forms that women's competition and aggression take (cf. Schuster 1985; Smuts 1992). And so this analysis of women's aggression returns to the framework originating in the work of Collier (1974) and Lamphere (1974) and directs attention to the sociocultural context in which the women of Mangrove compete and attack.

Aggression and Hierarchy

Recent anthropological discussions of "gender hierarchy" have required a rethinking of the "egalitarian" nature of "simple societies" (Flanagan 1989; Yanagisako and Collier 1987). I am uncomfortable with attempts to assess any kind of overall "status" of Aboriginal women, a point I return to in chapter 6. Nevertheless, too many links between "gender," "aggression," and "dominance" have been identified in the anthropological literature for me to ignore the potential of a framework based on the premise that aggression and hierarchy are mutually relevant concepts. Assuming, at least momentarily, that aggression is a "resource" (Riches 1986) and observing that access to this resource is not distributed equally throughout the community of Mangrove, my approach bears some resemblance to that advocated by Sylvia Yanagisako and Jane Collier, who say that when we begin our analyses of social relations with "the premise that all societies are systems of inequality" (1987:39), it forces us to ask "what social processes organize the distribution of prestige, power, and privilege" (ibid.:40). It also bears resemblance to examinations of women's aggression that acknowledge power relations. The precedent here is set by Schuster when she writes of women's interactions in Zambia, "Interfemale aggression is . . . understandable only within the context of the relations of the genders to the social stratification system" (Schuster 1983:320; see also Glazer 1992; Glazer and Abu Ras, in press; Schuster 1985; Schuster and Hartz-Karp 1986).

Influenced by the work of those who approach emotions as social constructions (e.g., Abu-Lughod and Lutz 1990; Lutz and White 1986; Myers 1979), I also assume in this analysis that aggressive acts are social practices that both construct and are constructed by a given social "reality" (cf. Ortner 1984, 1989). Abu-Lughod and Lutz (1990:14) ask how "emotion discourses establish, assert, challenge, or reinforce power or status differences." David Gilmore (1987) and Ilsa Schuster and Janette Hartz-Karp (1986; see also Glazer and Abu Ras, in press) have suggested that overt aggression can maintain the status quo. I ask how acts of aggression—a form of discourse, if you like—can reproduce or transform facets of the social hierarchy.

Many anthropologists before me have conceptualized links between aggression and hierarchy. For example, Lionel Tiger and Robin Fox write,

> The impulse is to accept the established hierarchy—which enhances stability and makes matters easy for the dominants, who can maintain their dominance largely by ritual means. Ultimately, of course, there is the threat of force—the primeval canine tooth—but most of the time subordinates will defer to badges of rank and thus to those who wear them. (1971:39)

Myers (1988:600) has said that the prevalence of anger—the emotion we most commonly associate with aggression—varies with the degree to which a social structure is characterized as "egalitarian" or "highly ranked."

Theoretically conceived, the causal arrow between hierarchy and aggression points in several directions. Taking a cue from the primate literature, Michael Bond and Wang Sung-Hsing (1983:61) hypothesize that "there will be less overall aggression in societies where hierarchial relationships are widely found and generally accepted." Similarly, Robert LeVine (1965:193–194) has observed that "hierarchial status relations (either through the appointment of one chief wife who dominates or through a rank ordering of all)" lessen co-wife conflict. Showing the reverse face of this relationship, "status ambiguity . . . in potentially competitive situations, allows competition to become so intense that conflict results" (LeVine 1961:8). Hierarchy, however, may not suppress all aggression but only that of subordinates. Writing of Ifaluk, Lutz says,

> It is much more often the case that persons of higher rank or status are justifiably angry toward those of lower station than the reverse. The chiefs are justifiably angry at community members, adults are justifiably angry at children, older women are justifiably angry at younger women, and brothers are justifiably angry at their younger sisters. The direction in which justifiable anger flows is predominately *down* the social scale. (1988:169)

Or hierarchy may facilitate aggression. This is a basic premise of feminist perspectives on family violence (e.g., Breines and Gordon 1983; Edwards 1987) that I discuss in chapter 6. Sometimes, hierarchy affects not the occurrence but the form of aggression. Marc Swartz (1990), for example, tells us that both the relatively powerful and the relatively powerless in Mombasa's Swahili society use "aggressive speech." There are differences, however, in the forms of speech used by people occupying different statuses which reflect the shared understandings that constitute status members and their actions. Aggression may also work against hierarchy. Riches (1986:11–12) suggests why the use of violence for "advancing one's social position" may be regarded as "a 'natural social experience.'" It is something that almost anybody can do. Similarly, Gilbert Herdt (1986:161) states that "hostile attacks become a means of restoring a balance of power between two persons."

Women, Polygyny, and Competition

In a cross-cultural study of family violence, David Levinson observed that "fighting between women occurs almost exclusively in societies with polygynous marriage" (1989:49). In his brief discussion of this intriguing correlation, he links co-wife conflict to physical aggression between "women in general," often because of sexual jealousy (ibid.:32). This and a theoretical tradition connecting polygyny with gender inequality (e.g., Murdock 1949) suggest that Mangrove's recent history of plural marriage provides an important backdrop for this discussion of women's constructions of their aggressive and competitive behavior.

Just a few decades ago, when the mission was first started, polygynous marriage was the norm; the majority of today's grandmothers once lived "one fire," that is, in a polygynous household. But polygyny violated Western mores and was discouraged by the missionaries. Today, though Australian federal law now recognizes plural marriage as a legitimate Aboriginal social arrangement, few of Mangrove's women share their husband with a co-wife (Burbank 1988). In 1988, for example, only one man had two wives who lived together in the same camp.

Around the world, conflict, jealousy, and rivalry are associated with the co-wife relationship (Burbank 1987b; Murdock 1949; Stephens 1963). In East Africa, for example, where "the relationship between co-wives is considered to be more fraught with jealousy than any other social bond," the Gusii word *engareka* "means hatred between co-wives" (LeVine, 1962:39); Luo women call their co-wives *nyieka*, "my partner in jealousy" (ibid.:40). Across the Atlantic in Surinam, the Saramaka word for "fight" is "to make [act like a] co-wife" (Price

1984:53). On the Melanesian island of Alor, "it is considered good form" for the first wife of a man to attack the second when the latter is first brought into the marriage (DuBois 1944:110).

Hostility between co-wives often appears to stem from competitive motives. D. W. Ames, for example, says of West African Wolof women, "Quarreling or open fighting between the wives may result when a covetous wife openly wheedles extra gifts from the husband" (1953:108). For the Mam of Santiago Chimaltenango, Charles Wagley observes, "Co-wives are supposedly always enemies. . . . They are jealous of each other's sexual relations with the husband and, when both have sons, each fears that her sons will inherit less at the division of the father's land" (1949:46). While of the Siriono of eastern Bolivia, Allan Holmberg writes,

In non-sororal plural marriages sexual jealousy between co-wives is sometimes intense. Since food and sex go hand in hand in Siriono society—and there is a scarcity of the former—the wives with whom the husband most frequently has sex relations are also the ones who generally get the most to eat. Consequently, co-wives frequently vie with one another for the sexual favors of their husband. This sometimes leads to bitter fights and quarrels. (1969:126)

Similar observations have been made of co-wife relations in Aboriginal Australia. L. F. Warner, for example, reports the words of a "Murngin" polygynist.

My wives growl at each other all the time. The two old ones are good friends, but they are jealous of Opossum. They say to her, "Why don't you get another man? This man is our husband. He made our children come. He belongs to us. He doesn't belong to you."(1937:79)

Writing of the Aranda, Geza Roheim describes this incident.

Ilpaltalaka was on her way to Njala with other women when her husband and Tjuwa-tukuta came with two new girls, *mbanja*. She saw him coming with one of the girls, and said: 'What girl is this?' He said: 'My wife.' She beat the girl with her yam stick. (1933:253)

Mervin Meggitt (1962:109) describes quarrels between co-wives as "very bitter." After surveying much of the ethnography on Aboriginal Australia, Gillian Cowlishaw (1979:201) concludes that conflict between women is "endemic" in polygynous unions. In the case of Aboriginal Australians, however, it is not clear what provokes co-wives' jealousy and conflict.

What are the implications of polygyny for gender hierarchy in Aboriginal Australia? Does its presence signal a concentration of power and authority in male hands, with women set more against one another than against men? Some who have looked at polygyny in Aboriginal Australia assign a positive impetus to women in its formation. Others present it as an institution imposed on women against their will. "The initiative to form such a marriage union," says the Marxist, Frederick Rose, "came mainly from the women." In need of "mutual assistance" when their child care responsibilities were greatest, the women of Groote Eylandt tended to "aggregate" around an older hunter at the "peak of his productivity" for it was successful hunters who could provide for the "collectives of co-wives" (Rose 1960:241, 1968:206). A. P. Elkin (1964) and Nicholas Peterson (1974) see polygyny as a means of ensuring that a man and his wife will be taken care of in old age. For William Irons (1983), Australian polygyny represents a compromise of male and female reproductive strategies. Men's reproductive success is, on the one hand, maximized by access to many fecund women. Women's reproductive success, on the other hand, may be compromised by polygyny when it limits their opportunities to bear and raise children (Ayres 1983; Irons 1983). But for the Tiwi, according to Irons, the economic importance of women's coalitions is such that they "are willing to share a husband . . . as a means of holding their female networks together" (1983:191). Hiatt, in contrast, sees polygyny as a "favoured male reproductive strategy" that co-wives, as competitors for a husband's "sexual and nurturing" services, "accepted . . . under duress" (1985:35).

Irons (1983; see also Ayres 1976, 1983) argues that women tolerate polygynous marriage to different degrees. Where polygyny confers some benefits on women either because of male wealth differentials or because it permits women to maintain important female coalitions, women's tolerance may be greater than where polygyny represents only male coercion. Nevertheless, Irons continues, at least some jealousy will characterize all co-wife relationships because competition for a husband's favors is inevitable in any polygynous marriage.

Do memories of polygyny at Mangrove suggest that women once preferred this form of marriage or perceived an advantage in such unions? What was their tolerance for co-wives? Does a history of competition between women feed the fights of today? I explore these possibilities in a discussion of food, children, and work in polygynous households.

Food, Children, and Work
in Polygynous Households

None of the women and men who talked to me about polygyny were currently living "one fire," though a few had, at one time, been married polygynously. Others were, at best, the children or grandchildren of polygynists. Polygyny, however, has left a legacy of opinion at Mangrove; lack of firsthand experience does not keep people from expressing their views on this social arrangement.

One day in passing, Lily remarked that one of her now-deceased classificatory husbands "was always saying, 'You can all be my wife because I am a good hunter and because I am a good singer and dancer.' " I asked five women, including Lily and Rosalind, if men who were *walajgari*, that is, poor hunters, would be denied wives by their bestowers. The replies suggest women think that hunting prowess has little to do with a man's success as a polygynist. Rosalind first answered that such a man might not be given his betrothed; instead, one of his more successful brothers would receive her. But some people, she added, would not "break their promise" to give him a wife. Here I might note that such a promise might be made when a boy was as young as four or five, an age when little would indicate the kind of hunter he might become. Another woman said that such a man would be given only one wife. Her companion disagreed, however, saying he would be given several wives, for other men would share their catch with him. Another woman made a similar statement. "Brothers" and "mother's brothers" were those who would share with a poor hunter. Rosalind said a father-in-law might share, if only for his daughter's sake. Lily added that nearly all men hunted successfully in the past. In interpreting these remarks, it should be kept in mind that hunting prowess might be regarded as a transitory condition rather than a fixed ability. Poor hunting might be regarded as a passing occurrence, reflecting, perhaps, mood, interest, or luck rather than lack of skill.

One older man shared his grandfather's words on polygyny; men had many wives to provide an abundance of food for the ceremonies. This man pointed out that wives could also get food if the husband was not a good hunter. These remarks in conjunction with the responses described above suggest that men are perceived as the primary recipients of polygyny's economic benefits. They also suggest that at least some men and women at Mangrove do not think of polygyny as an arrangement that provides women with any particular economic advantage. Women recall, or imagine, that in the past they could depend on a number of people besides a husband to provide them with food, if they could not get it themselves.

People at Mangrove have explained that men desire multiple wives because they desire many children (Burbank 1988). An earlier analysis of fights precipitated by men's attempts to obtain additional wives suggests that this is indeed an important motive. Of the seven men involved in these cases, four had wives who had borne no living children, though all had been married for at least four years. Another man's wife had one child but had borne no other in four years. The remaining two men's wives had a number of children apiece, one four, the other eight, but at the time that their husbands were attempting to take another wife, one was past childbearing age and the other was using a birth control device (Burbank 1980a).

As I point out elsewhere (Burbank 1988), a desire for children is not necessarily the same thing as a concern with reproductive success. People at Mangrove say that they want children to help them and look after them as they grow old.

They might like a girl because a girl can help her mother carry the baby and things, help mother when mother is sick. [They might like] a boy to help father in [ritual] business, or fighting, or for hunting. . . . Girls stay and look after mother and father when they are old. Boys go after food for them. That's why they want them.

Men and women also say that they want children simply because they make them "happy" and keep them "company."

Some women at Mangrove today see a cooperative advantage in polygyny.

Your husband will go to work in the morning and you will get everything ready for *smoko* [morning tea]—tea and maybe some beef. Then he goes back to work and you have to get everything ready again. This is very hard. When you have a child that gives you even more work. But if you have a little sister she can make it easy. She can mind the baby and you can do the washing. Like olden times when two sisters were one fire. The young one could go hunting with the man and the other one could stay, make a shade, make a fire, make damper. The other two would bring back fish. This makes its easy for that biggest girl.

Sometimes they are good friends together, talking together, fishing together, hunting for sugar bag [wild honey] together, all good friends together. They help each other. Maybe one has three or four children, well one young wife will help her. If they want they can work together, some cleaning, some carrying wood, some making fire and cooking.

Even today the presence of a second wife in the marriage may reduce a woman's household tasks. After a successful hunt, when two sea turtles had to be cleaned and cooked, a polygynist said to his first wife, "You are going to work." "No," she replied, "you've got a young wife." Conflict is also seen, however, as a characteristic of polygynous households. Lily, at least, expects co-wives to fight.

[Two women] should be one fire. If they were, bam, bam, bam, bleeding here [body part shown] and here [body part shown]. If you and I were one fire, we would fight and fight.

Why do co-wives fight? Are they competing? Insofar as women fight over a husband's time and attention, their action may be said to stem from competitive motives. Comments about co-wife aggression implicate a variety of motives as the source of these acts. It is interesting to speculate on the meaning of the following statement in this regard.

A girl gets wild because her husband takes her sister hunting. She sits down sulky. When they come back he says, "What's wrong with you?" She doesn't fight with him, she fights with her sister—wrestling.

This might be a fight about a husband's subsistence contribution. People on a hunting trip often cook and eat part, if not all, of their catch before returning to camp. But the privacy of the bush also provides a setting for sexual intimacy. Hence this woman might have been fighting with her sister over their husband's sexuality. She might also have missed the pleasures of a hunting excursion. Meat was mentioned as a reason for co-wives to fight, but so were feelings: "Oh, you don't love me, you don't want me anymore." And so was what appears to be sexual jealousy. Observing another woman to be "sulky," Tina concluded it was because she had been fighting with her husband's other wife. "Maybe that husband is sleeping too much on her side [of the fire] or maybe [they are hanging] a blanket on the door [for privacy] too often."

One day a woman remarked that (as I had been incorporated into the kinship system) I should call her husband (classificatory) "husband." She added that if her husband and I should run off into the bush, she would come after me with a stick. It is not clear if this woman would chase me because of an imagined tryst with her husband or because she might see this sexual foray as the first step in a campaign to bring an additional wife into the marriage. As a classificatory "wife" to her husband, I would be an ideal candidate for the real position. I suggest that the ambiguity of this scenario signals a perceived continuity in the competitive potential of a co-wife and "the other woman." As the following case from the Aranda illustrates, the possibility of polygyny may also symbolize the potential disadvantage faced by women who desire monogamy or the sexual fidelity of a male partner.

> Kaliraka had also several wives. He was always after a girl called Lultjaa. He used to follow her when she went to dig for witchetties. Once Ilpaltalaka's mother caught them *flagrante delicto,* and immediately started a fight with the girl. Kaliraka simply said: "You fight in vain, for I can keep you both if I want to." (Roheim 1933:253)

As polygyny is no longer against the law and men may once again take more than one wife, the preponderance of monogamous marriage today may be due largely to women's refusals to tolerate a second wife in the marriage: "I don't want that second wife, [I want to be the] only wife for him. . . . I can leave you now. I'll go to another man." The facility with which a woman can leave a man, remain single, or remarry likely represents an important change in women's current experience. Factors that allow women to leave their husbands with relative ease are discussed below.

Aggression as Competition at Mangrove

VKB: Where did you get your nulla nulla?
AW: [An old man] made it for me, and one for [my girl friend], when we were [single]. He made it in case we had to fight any married woman. I still have mine, but [my friend] doesn't.

Just as it is recognized that co-wives may fight, it is recognized that other women may come to blows or otherwise attack each other because of a man. But what women intend in these battles is an open question. Is their aggression used as a means of winning a lover or keeping a husband? Do women at Mangrove see themselves as competitors in these aggressive encounters? Or are they simply expressing their anger?

Some statements suggest that women may actually try to avoid seeing themselves as competitors. Said one young woman of her fight with a married woman, "She was fighting with me because her husband did a wrong thing. He took me away." Lily's mother explained a fight between a man's wife and the woman he had run off with as "that boy causing trouble," an interesting reversal of the kind of blame men often assign to women as the cause of their conflicts (e.g., Collier and Rosaldo 1981; Hiatt 1965). The unwillingness of some women to see themselves as competitors is not confined to this Aboriginal community in Arnhem Land. Here a contemporary American woman speaks of her male lover and his wife: "I'd feel guilty if I had wanted to steal him, but I didn't. I didn't want him. I worked to keep them together. If he had left her, I would have just turned tail and run" (quoted in Richardson 1985:100).

However, the "other woman's" ability to break up a marriage is recognized in this woman's plaint at the end of a fight over her former husband: "You know why I left [my former husband] before. Because you young girls kept taking him away. I knew. That's why I went with those [other men]." And here, in an account of the breakup of her daughter's marriage, are the words that a woman puts into the mouth of the former husband as he addresses his new wife: " 'You just came and put yourself in and I would have still been with my wife, but you, wrong woman, came and came between us and took me to be your husband.' " The ability of a wife to defeat a rival with aggression is given credit in this apparent capitulation by a woman whose boyfriend's wife confronted her on three different occasions, according to her report (at least once with a "ninja" sword): "I don't want to go to [another settlement where the boyfriend lives]. I just hate it when women growl at me and tease me. I want them to just leave me alone."

Men and Resources

Some women, it appears, see other women, if not themselves, as rivals whose aggressive behavior helps them compete for boyfriends and husbands. But do they see the men of Mangrove as scarce and valuable resources? Are they worth fighting for?

Various social innovations associated with settlement dwelling suggest that husbands are not essential for the well-being of women. Some easily identified factors that appear to make it possible for a woman to live comfortably without a husband are an ethic of cooperation and sharing within the extended family or kindred, welfare, jobs for women, and little or no emphasis on wealth differentials or status through possessions.

The presence of such institutional factors does not, of course, guarantee that the women of Mangrove see things this way. But there are indications that they do. A rapid rise in single motherhood, for example, suggests a willingness on the part of women to forswear or defer marriage (Burbank 1988; Burbank and Chisholm 1990). A look at cases of aggression precipitated by conflict over subsistence suggests a source of this willingness. Aggression is precipitated by subsistence concerns much less often between women than between men and women. The cases include twenty-three conflicts over subsistence goods between men and women but only five between women.

Conflicts over resources between women and men are not confined to married partners. Nevertheless, a woman without a husband (or boyfriend) may be a woman with one less male rival for resources she wants to use for herself and her children. Men, some women say, do not help their wives or feed their families; they just play cards, then take their winnings to drink up in town. "This is a big problem for wives and children. The men go and take all the money and come back broke. The wife waits until he is sober and then she has an argument with him." In 1988, this problem seemed to receive official recognition when Mangrove's Aboriginal community worker arranged for several married women to collect their welfare allowance separately from that distributed to their unemployed husbands.

I asked fifteen women if they would prefer to marry a young man, an old man, or a middle-aged man. The majority said that they would prefer to marry a young man.[2] I then asked which man they thought would make the best father of their children. Seven women stated that young men make poor fathers. These are the words of just one of the women, but her response is almost identical to the responses of three others.

Young boy, he's good enough to give a baby to a woman and then leave her behind nursing that kid. He just goes, makes her get pregnant and then when she delivers, is nursing it in her arms, he doesn't pay any attention to her now. He starts fooling around with another girl.

Yet six of these seven women said they would prefer to marry a young man. This preference, in spite of the perception that young men are not especially reliable partners, suggests that some women might not look to their husbands for economic support or child care assistance. In contrast, two women said old men were less desirable fathers because they were less potent and thus unlikely to father a child in the first place. It may be that some women at Mangrove think of men primarily as a way of getting pregnant but not as a means of support. This perspective on men is, perhaps, indicated when women remark, as they have on more than one occasion, that when women fight over men they are "fighting for nothing."[3]

However, adult status for women, as well as for men, rests on marriage. A woman willing to conform to an arranged marriage need compete with no other to obtain this status, though as a co-wife, she might later have cause to fight. But few, if any, women obtain husbands in this fashion today. Increasingly, adolescent girls "fall in love" and choose their own marital partners (Burbank 1987a, 1988). Though I cannot demonstrate here what the women of Mangrove "really feel" about the men they pursue and fight over, consider the possibility that for someone "in love" the beloved, in his or her unique character, becomes both valuable and scarce, though there may be, in fact, any number of "socially desirable" and willing substitutes.

Women, Men, and Displaced Aggression

There is little about women's aggression over matters of "love" and marriage that requires it to be intrasexual. Why a woman attacks another woman and not a man must be determined, not assumed. I now reexamine these cases of women's competitive aggression in light of this point, the idea of hierarchy, and the concept of "displaced" or "redirected" aggression. Although they are not referring to situations in which displacement is necessarily operating, Alice Eagly and Valerie Steffen provide an apt introduction to this discussion. "To the extent that women's subordinate social status and lesser physical strength vis-à-vis men inhibit their aggression toward men, we could argue that women would aggress more toward other women than toward men" (1986:313).

When aggression is "displaced," it is discharged not on the person who arouses anger or invites aggression in the first place but on a substitute person or object (Buss 1961). According to some perspectives, displaced aggression can be an unconscious, preprogrammed response (Lorenz 1966). But there is no reason that this concept cannot be used along with the assumptions that potential aggressors consciously intend something by their aggression and perceive that this achievement depends on whether or not the attack of a specified target will be fruitful. I want to consider the possibility that although their anger is largely provoked by men, women attack other women because, in their view, attacks on men would not yield the intended results.

The possibility that women at Mangrove displace aggression away from men and toward women on at least some occasions is suggested by the following example.

I have driven a woman, her husband, and her two daughters to an outstation for the weekend. On Sunday, around noon, the husband asks me what time we are going back. The woman also asks me. I say, "Monday morning right after breakfast," as she and I have arranged earlier. She is very much in favor of this to judge from hints and a smile when I suggest it. The husband indicates that he wants to go back this afternoon. Apparently the two daughters also want to go back today. A family quarrel ensues. The woman addresses her daughters. "I don't like to go back because you two never work for me. You never get wood or water or cook tucker [food]. Only me, I do all the work. When you get up early don't look to me for your tucker." The younger daughter, a teenager says, "You two blame me. It's not me to blame." The elder daughter replies, "Well, you live there!" Their mother speaks again, "Everything was fine when Vicky and I made the plan. Alright, we are going back and you two are going to work for me and when I say fillem up wood you are gonna fillem up my wood, and . . ." The two daughters obviously cease to pay attention to her as she talks. Then the elder says, "I'm going to tell my husband that [my brother] has been hitting [my son]." Her mother replies, "You tell [your son's father] and we are just gonna sit here and wait for him to strike us and then we are gonna tell him that you came out to the bush to have arguments. You just put yourself in [Vicky's] truck." Then the woman addresses her husband. "This little girl [the eldest daughter's daughter] has sticks in her ear." The eldest daughter says, "She put them in, she put stones in her ear. I was trying to get them out." Her mother replies, "Yes, that's what you were belting her for today." After this the argument seems to be over. We return to the settlement that afternoon.

Neither this woman nor her daughters attacked the man in this case, though clearly the woman's quarrel was with her husband. Conceivably, this woman hesitated to attack the man because of a concern for his health or compassion for his feelings. As likely, she anticipated that negative consequences would follow this act. Her prediction might arise from her experience with married life; she might expect, for example, that her verbal assault would be followed by her husband's more hurtful physical assault. Or it might arise from culturally constructed beliefs about gender relations and appropriate forms of interaction between men and women. Whatever her motives, her hesitancy to attack a man and willingness to attack a woman in his place clearly have implications for understanding inter- and intragender relations, power differentials between men and women, and the resulting gender hierarchy (Collier 1974; Lamphere 1974).

That women recognize redirection as an aggressive strategy is indicated in the discussion of sorcery in chapter 4. Here is a further example.

[Three adolescent girls] were sniffing petrol. Then [one of them] started throwing rocks at the shop. [A second] said to her, "Don't throw rocks at the shop. The shop didn't growl at you. I growled at you."

Looking at these cases of aggression associated with competitive motives, I suggest that women at Mangrove perceive that aggression cannot compel another's desire, love, or fidelity. I think that Rosalind, at least, believes this to be so.

VKB: Why did [your daughter] leave her husband [after she fought with the woman he wanted as a wife]?
  R: Because he didn't like to [stay married] to [my daughter]. He wanted [the other woman] to be his wife. That's why [my daughter] left.

As will be seen in chapter 6, it is not at all clear that even male aggression is seen as an effective means of domination. Aggression, as women of Mangrove know, creates bad feelings (see chaps. 3 and 4). Furthermore, although women at Mangrove are prepared to fight with men, they perceive that they are not as strong or as fierce as their male opponents. There are recognized physical penalties for fighting with men.

When her husband was getting his second wife, [a woman] would fight with him over that. Once he threw a spear and hit her in the foot.

[A man] cut off [his wife's] hair. She is jealous of him all the time for other women, so he got jealous of her and cut off her hair.

[A man] is very rough with his wife. It made me sorry to see her last time with blood running from her head and her eye all puffed up. He goes out at night and she goes spying on him. She thinks he is meeting girls, but he is not. That's why he has been giving her a beating.

Whatever the physical penalties of fighting, why risk further alienating a straying husband or boyfriend? It might be assumed that women would not attack men whose good feelings they want to encourage. But if a woman cannot compel a man to love her, could she not harass a rival into leaving? At the very least, she could vent her anger on a person less able to retaliate with severity. It might be predicted that in these circumstances, women caught in a triangle of jealousy or infidelity would choose to fight with the other women rather than with their husbands or boyfriends.

A total of eighteen married women were aggressors in the cases precipitated by the real or suspected adultery of a husband (including a husband's efforts to acquire a new wife). Eleven of these women fought (or engaged in some form of aggression) only with their female rivals (though it cannot always be said that the wife initiated the aggression). But five women attacked their husbands, and two women engaged in aggressive interactions with their rivals and their husbands.

The acts of these last two women are mirrored in other Aboriginal communities. For example, Robert Tonkinson has noted of Jigalong in Western Australia,

Polygyny has declined markedly in the last two decades, largely as a result of the assertiveness of women in opposing the addition of a junior wife with all the passion and aggression they could muster. Their strategies have in most cases been a two-pronged attack: at first verbally, on their husbands for attempting to take a young wife; and then physically, on the new arrival and frequently on the husband as well. (1990:135–136)

The majority of women in these cases attack other women, suggesting that at least some might indeed see other women as "safer" targets. Again, the acts of women at Mangrove resemble those in other communities. There may have long been a tradition of women's fights in Aboriginal Australia.

Brawls in which only women are engaged are fairly frequent. The fights usually take place between two women, almost always because a young woman has seduced another's husband. Occasionally more than two women are involved, sisters taking sides with their kin; or several wives of one man may attack his sweetheart, in which case the latter usually calls upon her own relatives for help. The women's ironwood digging sticks are the usual weapons, although if a man's club is within reach the women often use it. They strike each other on the head. The fights are of such intensity that bloodshed always results. (Warner 1937:165)

That aggressive displacement may be an important dynamic in gender relations is most trenchantly illustrated by a case in which a woman attacked her husband, however. An older woman struck the husband she suspected of infidelity but did not attack her putative rival, a white schoolteacher. This fight took place in 1978, when whites were still regarded as powerful figures on the settlement. I suggest that this woman attacked her husband rather than the white woman because in this instance it seemed safer to attack a man. And the attacker, perhaps, felt she had little to lose. As she put it, "I've got [grown] kids to mind me."

At the same time, a not insignificant proportion of these women do attack men. In a few instances, this may be because their "jealousy" is free-floating, unattached to a specific name. But, more often than not, women attacking their husbands for real or suspected infidelity have a specific rival in mind. This willingness on the part of women to attack men indicates that women do not fear male aggression to the point of complete inaction, an important theme in gender relations and one I shall return to in the chapter 6. It also suggests that aggression at Mangrove may not be purposeful beyond the expression of feeling. In these cases it seems likely that women at Mangrove attack their husbands because they have made them angry. Women's willingness to attack their husbands in spite of perceived negative outcomes also reinforces the picture of a society in which enduring sexual/romantic or marital relationships are not highly valued, at least by some women.

I now turn to look at unmarried women's fights over men. It is striking that of these cases, there is only one in which a woman attacks a man. (And this case is indeed an exception that proves the rule, as I demonstrate.) It involved a woman who fought over the man who had once been but no longer was her husband. One might predict that women would be more likely to attack boyfriends than husbands; an unmarried woman betrayed might perceive she had little to lose in alienating the faithless object of her affections. But this is not the situation.

In physical contests with men, women are at a disadvantage and are more likely to be harmed. In chapter 4, I described how fights at Mangrove are public events in which onlookers are willing and able to assist disadvantaged women. Help, however, is not offered at random; it is particular individuals who can be relied on to come to one's aid. In the case of a married woman fighting with her husband, these would be her "family," people like her mother and her father, and her husband's "family," people like her mother-in-law and father-in-law.

In contrast, an unmarried woman publicly fighting with a man would likely be announcing an illegitimate affair, for often such couples are not regarded as appropriate marriage partners (see Burbank 1988). In these circumstances it is probable that her family would not help; they might well chastise her. Similarly, the boyfriend's family would probably be less interested in protecting her than in driving her away. Observe that the second leading category of reasons for aggression between women is that of "premarital sexuality," a category also associated with a high amount of injury. This, I suggest, is why single women do not attack their "boyfriends" when they know or suspect they have been "tricking" them with another "girl." Men are dangerous opponents in these circumstances not because of their intrinsic size, strength, or aggressiveness but because they symbolize a form of deviance often responded to with disapproval and aggression from other family members.

Women, Aggression, and Cooperation

Given past questions about women's capacity to form and maintain "bonds" for political purposes (Hrdy 1981; Tiger 1970; Tiger and Fox 1971) and more or less concurrent concerns to document and explore manifestations of women's "solidarity" (e.g., Caplan and Bujra 1979), I do not want to leave the topic of women's aggression and competition without at least a brief discussion of women's cooperation. As others have pointed out, competition and cooperation are not mutually exclusive behaviors (Seymour 1981). Indeed, cooperation may be a strategy for competing (Harcourt and de Waal 1992). At Mangrove, women clearly support and otherwise assist each other in their battles; cooperation is clearly a characteristic of women's aggressive interaction.

To illustrate this point, I focus on six fights that centered on the dissolution of two marriages. Both of these were long-standing relationships, and in each the husband and wife had several children together. In two of these fights, the wife attacked the interloper, clearly with the support of others. In four of these fights, women other than the wife attacked the "other woman." For example:

Just like a few days ago, a few of the ladies [three women] were fighting about "talkabout." They fought about the old story about your uncle, you know about [another woman's] husband? . . . About that one. . . . All those ladies were having a meeting about Christianity and jealousing and growling at each other at the service place. They were having a meeting about the problem in service time, about all the growling and being sulky about people who never stand up. . . . Some get up and do item [sharing a religious event or feeling] and some never do. Then that snake came out, right for those women. It wasn't a snake, it was Satan. It came right out for them and they killed it. Then [the woman having the affair] came out of her house and she was talking, "I don't like women talking about me behind my back." They weren't talking about her but she thought they were. Then [two women] were just looking at each other like this [speaker looks at me with what I interpret to be a conspiratorial glint in her eyes] and they got up and grabbed her by the hair.

It is notable that in most of these fights, many of the attackers were relatives of the husband rather than of the wife. For example, at least four of one man's sisters and half-sisters attacked him and his paramour on his wife's behalf.

[His sisters] didn't like [a woman] to marry [a man] because he is a married man and has four kids. They were growling at [the other woman], growling at both of them, because [the man] left his children, and his wife, and because [the other woman] left her husband and children and they ran away. They were telling their brother, "You left your wife and kids, you should stay with them," and they said, "Look after your kids." And when [their brother] came to them they didn't give him any tucker [food] or tobacco. Nearly all his sisters didn't give food to him, they were punishing him. And one day he chased them. He threw a spear at them. He didn't like them to growl at him.

In these fights women also took up the cause of a woman whose husband was their own husbands' real or classificatory brother. Although these women may have been defending a classificatory sister, in the one instance in which the relationship between the two women was detailed, the fact that one was married to the other's "husband's brother" received as much emphasis as the fact that the women were classificatory "sisters."

Why should a man's mothers, sisters, or other female relatives come to the aid of his wife, especially since her rival may occupy an identical structural position vis-à-vis these women, that is, as their daughter-in-law or sister-in-law? This is particularly puzzling given the enmity and competition that may characterize relations between female in-laws in other societies. Also, although sisters and mothers assist women in their battles, I recorded no cases in which the sisters or mothers of a woman initiated aggression against a woman's rivals. It may simply be chance that I have no examples of kin-initiated aggression. In addition, only in the case mentioned above does Aboriginal exegesis include a discussion of affinal motives. Nevertheless, I want to consider the possibility that these fights represent more than random occurrences, that they form a pattern reflecting important aspects of women's relationships.

A number of contrasts may be drawn between women's female consanguineal and affinal kin as they are delineated by Aboriginal people. Mothers and sisters are "close family." A mother nurses her daughter, wipes her bottom, and sleeps with her for years; sisters are, at least according to the system of kin classification, identical. Affines, in contrast are women who are expected to be "shy" of one another, and interactions between them are characterized by varying degrees of avoidance etiquette, though this is never as stringent as that between women and their sons-in-law (Burbank 1980a). In aggressive interactions, sisters are expected to stand up for each other, but no one has ever said that they should not fight, and they often do. Mothers protect their daughters from the aggression of others but may themselves attack them. Affines, in contrast, are women who are not supposed to fight; emphasis is given to the assistance that should be rendered. In sum, a woman's female kin are her intimates: they are her cohorts and defenders but also her competitors and attackers; the more distant relationship between female affines is, at least ideally, a unilateral one of solidarity and support.

Affines are brought together because of a marriage. The aggressive actions in these six cases are clearly motivated by concerns with such marriages. Children may be a central aspect of these concerns. This is suggested by the fight between the adulterous husband, his lover, and his sisters. A comment made by one of the sisters some years later supports this possibility.

I was very upset when my brother and his wife were having all the trouble over [the other woman]. When [his wife] was ready to go away, I was crying and thinking about the children leaving the family and I went to [his wife] and asked her if they could stay here. She agreed and I was very happy.

There are some (e.g., Chagnon and Bugos 1979) who might explain this woman's concern with her brother's marriage in terms of inclusive fitness theory. According to this argument, a selective advantage is con-

ferred on individuals whose behavior benefits not only their own reproductive success but also that of their biological relatives. But why, then,
do we not find a woman's consanguines taking similar action? These
relatives are, after all, just as related to a woman's children as her in-
laws; indeed, they can be more certain that they are related.[4] Rather
than look at the contribution children may make to anyone's inclusive
fitness, I think that the answer to this question lies more immediately
in the realm of meaning, specifically, in the meaning that children have
for people at Mangrove.

Children are highly valued. They are the senior generations' old age
insurance. They sustain the ceremonies of the Dreaming and, thus, the
continuity of society. They also make people "happy" (Burbank and
Chisholm 1990). Threats to children's well-being are, consequently,
matters of concern (Burbank and Chisholm 1989; see also Hamilton
1981b, 1982). The perceived mistreatment of a child provokes the
anger of both men and women.

As is the case in Western divorce, the dissolution of marriage raises
questions about the disposition of children. At Mangrove, there exists
a perception that although a woman has rights in her child, after divorce, a father's rights include his child's presence in his household
(Burbank 1980a). There is also a perception, at least on Rosalind's
part, that stepmothers do not necessarily take the best care of children.

[My granddaughter's] father only found[5] her. Mother is responsible. Mother
had her inside and mother had the pain. I told them, I'm not going to let [my
granddaughter] go to her father. She is my granddaughter and she is going to
stay with me. That stepmother is jealous and she wouldn't feed [my grand-
daughter].

Rosalind's fear that her granddaughter would be neglected by her stepmother is not unique. Many of us are familiar with European fairy tales
in which the actions of cruel stepmothers are central. It was a stepmother who sent Hansel and Gretel into the woods to perish and a
stepmother who victimized Cinderella. Work on child abuse by Wilson
and Daly (1987) suggests these old stories still capture much in the
North American stepparent/stepchild experience. Note, however, that
the woman mentioned above, whose brother left his wife for another
woman, was "happy" that her brother's children would be left in his
household. She remarked one day, some time after the departure of the
first wife from the marriage, that his new wife took good care of them.
What is, perhaps, equally important is that affinally related women may
create and cement bonds through children.

I married the first son for [my husband's mother's clan]. I had all the [father's mothers] first baby. That makes me "boss" of [that clan] because I had the first children for their sons. They remember me and treat me as really family. They give me anything I want. If we go out hunting together they will give me most of the tucker, lily roots, oysters. I had the first baby for the [father's mothers].

Elsewhere I have argued that the high value placed on children at Mangrove has a positive effect on women's self-esteem (Burbank and Chisholm 1990). Here I want to suggest that this high valuation also affects evaluations of women's relationships. According to Lily, the speaker above, her husband's "mothers" value her because they value her children and recognize her role in their reproduction, that is, at a minimum, her "pain" in childbirth. I also want to suggest that the way in which children are valued provides a conceptual bridge that conflates, in this Aboriginal society, what we often tend to conceptualize as the distinctive spheres of domestic and political life.

A number of feminist anthropologists (e.g., Joseph 1983; Lamphere 1987; Rosaldo 1980a; Yanagisako and Collier 1987) have, in the last decade, cast doubt on the usefulness of the "domestic/public" distinction for understanding issues of gender and power. Nor do these constructs necessarily capture the reality of hunting and gathering societies (Keen 1989; Leacock 1978; Levinson 1989). At Mangrove, even with its emerging Western-style institutions such as the council, shop, church, and school, the utility of this conceptual dichotomy is questionable. For example, when parents beat adolescents for their sexual activity, these may be acts with ramifications beyond the family or kindred. A mother's or father's actions may be motivated as much by marriage politics as by parent-child concerns (Burbank 1988). However, public arguments about new council members that may involve dozens of people cannot be understood without charting the family relationships of the participants. When a woman rails against her brother, the council president, because the office has been shut and women cannot cash their welfare checks, is this a domestic or a public matter?

In the social universe of Mangrove, where principles of patrifiliation and matrifiliation create significant categories of people, the importance of one's brother's or son's children may extend beyond personal considerations. It is these children who will perpetuate a woman's and her son's clans and rituals. Insofar as women's aggressive actions are motivated by a concern with the well-being of their brother's and son's children, these may well be examples of women cooperating with "political" as well as "domestic" concerns in mind.

Fighting through the Life Cycle

Aggressive behavior punctuates the lives of the women of Mangrove whether they are themselves aggressors, victims of aggression, or observers of others' aggressive acts. Fights for what we might regard as adult cause begin in adolescence.

Together [two adolescent girls] walk into the home economics classroom. Their entrance is greeted by a sort of "humm" or "aaah" from the girls who are already seated around the classroom tables. To my eyes, their stance is defiant. Neither speaks. One girl comes and sits down next to me. The other walks past the table over to a third adolescent girl and hits her with her fist on her back. Both girls are next in the space between the two tables, sometimes on the floor, sometimes standing, both with their hands in each other's hair. The other girls leap up from their chairs and stand around them. The boys come in from the building next door and also watch. The home economics teacher, who left the room when the fight began, returns in about four minutes with the third girl's mother and a male teacher. Together they stop the girls from fighting. The male teacher grabs one of the girls by the hand. The mother hits at them with a stick, then leaves with her daughter. After the fight I am told that the girls were fighting over a boyfriend.

These fights between schoolgirls should not be dismissed as a form of child's play. The median age of marriage for girls in this community is about sixteen (Burbank 1988). When fourteen- and fifteen-year-olds—like the adolescents mentioned above—fight over boyfriends, they are likely fighting over the men they may soon marry or whose children they may soon bear.

Adolescent girls may also fight with a mother who is forcing them to marry a man they do not like.

When I was nineteen, my mother took me to [another settlement] to give to [my betrothed]. When his brothers came up and grabbed me, my mother just let them, but I fought and got away and stayed with my uncle. I had a big fight with my mother and hit her with stones I threw. She tried to hit me with a nulla nulla. Girls get wild with their mother and father when they don't like the man [they are supposed to marry].

Marriage, as much of this discussion illustrates, does not bring an end to women's fights. Married women of all ages may fight with the women that their husbands take as lovers or want as second wives.

Mothers may fight when others hurt their children, not only when children are young but when they are adults as well. Mothers may also be the targets of female aggression when another family member thinks they are mistreating their own child.

One time I had a fight with my sister over her son. He was about [age four]. We were at the beach and I was pulling her hair and kicking her in the face. It was because of [the boy]. She was hitting him and throwing him down in the sand.

As the children in the extended family or kindred mature and become embroiled in various altercations themselves, the women of the family may also become involved. Recall, for example, the altercation between the mother of a girl who "teased" and the mother of her victim.

Women may also use aggressive means in attempts to ensure that older children marry correct partners, or at least to ensure that they do not become involved in an incorrect match (Burbank 1988). In the following example, a young man's sister and his mother's half-sister beat the adolescent girl whom he was seeing. They were definitely "wrong" marriage partners as they shared the same moiety.

The other day [a woman] saw [an adolescent girl sitting behind the house where her brother slept] and she got a "crowbar" and she and [her mother's half-sister] gave that girl a hiding. They chased her to the [outdoor movie area] and belted her there, made her fall down. Then [the woman] came back and called out to [the girl's classificatory father's sister], "There is your child, lying about by the picture place. Go pick her up."

At any time in the adult life cycle, women may fight over money or other desirable goods.

Yesterday there was a fight. [A woman] was sitting in front of her house and [her daughter] was there nursing the baby and growling at her mother for more money from her check [which her mother had just received]. She hit her mother in the face with a bag and threw dirt at her. Her mother said, "Your husband gets pay, you never share that money with us." [Another of the woman's daughters] was there on the veranda and she said to [her sister], "You got your share." [The first daughter] got a stick and she and [her sister] were fighting for that stick, but somebody, I don't know who, got it and then [the two sisters] wrestled. We were all watching and [one sister] tore her dress. Then [the first daughter] had a stick and was standing right in front of her mother, but they didn't fight. Then [the first daughter] was swearing at her mother and her [mother's two brothers] were there [across the street] but they didn't hear because the children were making so much noise. Then [the first daughter] threw a rock and broke some glass in her mother's house.

Women's fights over men take place within a social context where women's aggression is both familiar and routine. Whether they are sparked by competitive or cooperative motives, these fights underline important and intertwining themes in women's lives: their children's well-being, their husbands' loyalty, and their relationships with other women. But while women fight over matters that are clearly of importance, it is not clear what results they expect from their battles. Their actions often seem more expressive than instrumental; it is through their aggressive acts that women communicate their displeasure with a given state of affairs.

Though many in Western society consider it "wrong," we are accustomed to thinking about aggression in terms of costs and benefits (e.g., Klama 1988; Lorenz 1966). At Mangrove, women's aggression has a price, even though attempts to reduce injury are encoded in cultural rules; feelings, if not bodies, are frequently battered and bruised in the quarrels and fights that occur on a regular basis. But women may also benefit from their aggressive interactions with one another. I argue that these interactions train Aboriginal women to think of themselves as fighters (see also Collmann 1988a), an identity that serves them well when their opponents are not other women but men.

6

Women, Men, and
Interpersonal Aggression

Here I look at aggression between men and women at Mangrove, compare it to wife battering in Western society, and use this comparison to evaluate ideas linking male aggression to female subordination. Central to this discussion are the concepts of "gender relations" and "status."

Because of its very centrality to my life, I have never been comfortable phrasing my work at Mangrove in terms derived from the question of women's status. My concern has been that this could blind me to important issues for Aboriginal women and obscure their interpretations of human existence. Nevertheless, in this analysis of women, men, and aggression at Mangrove, the concept of status must be discussed because so much of our thinking about gender, hierarchy, and aggression revolves around it (see Mukhopadhyay and Higgins 1988).

Male and Female Aggression

In a cross-cultural study of sex differences in aggression, Ronald Rohner (1976:64) writes that "female aggression from society to society tends to vary directly with male aggression. That is, insofar as males are aggressive within a society, females also tend to be aggressive (r = .88, p < .01)." As this significant and intriguing finding is discussed no further, readers are left to wonder, among other things, why it is phrased as it is. It could be said that men's and women's aggression covaries or, for that matter, that men's aggression varies with women's aggression. When Rohner says that female aggression tends to vary with male aggression, does he mean that female aggression is somehow dependent on, or a response to, male aggression?

I have described how women at Mangrove often act aggressively with, and because of, other women. These acts can be seen as aggression manifested by women in contexts largely, if not exclusively, defined by other women. But what about aggressive interactions that take place between men and women? There is considerable evidence that human males are more aggressive than human females.[1] When thinking about intersexual aggression in this context, it is easy to assume that much, if not all, of women's aggression is counteraggression, elicited and necessitated by aggressive men. One can quickly conjure up the image of a woman screaming her defense at a husband who has jealously accused her of infidelity or imagine her waving a kitchen knife to fend off his brutality. Our body of popular culture even includes the picture of a woman desperately setting fire to the bed in which her husband sleeps off the exhaustion of his latest round of wife bashing (McNulty 1980)—an extreme and bizarre image that, I suggest, underlines our belief that women's aggression, particularly when it is expressed physically, is "unnatural" (cf. Jones 1980). Studies of family violence in Western society tend to support this view of women's action in intergender aggression (e.g., Browne 1988; Saunders 1988; Straus 1980; Straus and Gelles 1990b). But is this the case at Mangrove? When women fight and quarrel with men, are their actions primarily responsive and defensive ones, or do they initiate aggression against men? When are women victims, and when are they aggressors, and what do their acts say about gender relations? I address these questions below.

Male and Female Aggression at Mangrove

In 736 of the 793 cases of aggression, I am able to identify the sex of central participants. Men and women were involved together as victims and aggressors in 274 of these cases, approximately 37 percent. In 123 of the cases, it is reported that men initiated attacks on women. In 64 cases, women reportedly attacked men.

In another 87 cases, it is not possible to tell from accounts whether men or women initiated fights, quarrels, and other aggressive acts with members of the opposite sex. I find this ambiguity interesting. The question of who started a fight may not be salient information from the perspective of the women who told me of these events. If so, what does this mean for their interpretations of intergender aggression and gender relations? For the purpose of this discussion, however, I will assume that accounts specifying which sex initiated aggression are representative of those in which this information is missing. I therefore conclude that men initiated attacks on women more often than women initiated attacks on men. But women initiated aggression against men on so many occasions that these cannot be seen as rare or deviant incidents.

Men at Mangrove attack women in several ways: verbal, physical, or supernatural. Most commonly, men take physical action; they may strike a women with their hand or fist, attack her with weapons such as a *woomera* (spear thrower), knife, or hatchet, or chase her with a spear. Here, for example, a man attacks several women.

At 11:05 A.M. I saw [a man], hook spear in one hand poised for a throw and a bundle of spears in his other hand, run toward five or six women at Tina's sister's house. The women stood facing him, yelling at him. He then walked over to [another house], then returned to his own house. Tina thought he was chasing the women for elopement. Tina's sister's daughter, however, said that [a woman] had argued with him and he thought the women had been telling [the woman] a story about him. She didn't know what the story was. She added that he first threw a spear that almost hit a man who was sitting down. Later Lily said the story was that he was spying on [the woman's] daughter and that she, Lily, had stopped him; she grabbed him.

Men also attack women with words; they may "growl," "tell them off," or threaten them verbally. Threats may also be nonverbal. The following is an example of the sort of incident that might be described as growling.

[A man] told [two women] to make a fire and cook food so their husbands would stop coming and taking food from his wife.

In the following case, a man threatens his wife and other family members with his own death.

That old man got some beef. [A neighbor woman] was going to cook it, but he had other ideas. "But what about wood?" "No, I'm a lively fella for wood," he said. And he was sitting there by the house looking at that beef where he put it. But then he said, "Who is going to get my wood?" [My two daughters and son] just sat there. We didn't say anything. Then that old man said, "If you

:t my wood I'm going to tell the council to open up the gate, and I am
o climb the water tower and fall dead and then you will be happy." Then
e laughing and I said to that old man, "You silly fool, why didn't you
let [the neighbor] cook that beef for you?"

Women attack men verbally and physically but not, as a rule, with
supernatural weapons. Of the following examples, the first represents
the most extreme kind of violence done to men by women.

Last night [a woman] and her husband had a fight over [another woman]. He
has been running around with her. [The wife] was very angry and got a [metal
spear] and speared her husband in the leg. Then he took the spear and speared
her in the hand.

One time when my brother was drunk, he was kicking sand, and my little
daughter was there. We had that big cashew tree then, before the white ants
ate it. And I told him not to kick sand, it might get in her eyes and hurt her.
And he kicked sand again and I pushed him over. And I told him, I will hit you
with my nulla nulla next time you kick sand. So he stopped.

[A married couple] had a little argument at [a settlement with a pub nearby].
She was growling at him. He told us we couldn't go back [to Mangrove] because the plane was broken, but it was really because he wanted another drink.
Someone gave him $150. He gave $60 to me and kept $80. His wife was
growling at him, "You like to drink too much."

In some cases, men initiated aggression by growling or swearing, and
women responded with physical actions or threats.

Yesterday [a married couple] had a row. She gave her son tucker but her husband didn't see her and growled at her to do so. She told him that she had. She
went and got a nulla nulla and said she was going to hit him. "I'm tired of your
grumbling and cheek all day. You go to [the outstation]. I'll come behind. I'm
going to [another settlement] first where I've been growing up."

Social scientists are beginning to pay some attention to women's
aggression against men in American households (Flynn 1990). A 1975
survey of 2,143 American families conducted by the Family Violence
Research Program at the University of New Hampshire found that
women directed nearly as much "violence" against men as men directed
against women. The authors of this study and a follow-up survey conducted in 1985 concluded, however, that much of women's aggression
against men is self-defense. They also concluded that the consequences
of women's actions are relatively minor compared to the consequences

of violence inflicted on women by men (Straus 1980; Straus and Gelles 1986, 1990*b*). For example, Murray Straus writes,

Except for the rare instances when a desperate or enraged woman seizes a knife or gun and is effective in using it, the *effects* of this violence are far from equal. *She* may cast the first coffee pot, but he generally casts the last and most damaging blows. If one could tally the number of men and women who require medical attention because of marital violence, the rate would be many times greater for women. The reasons for this start with the greater size and strength of men. (1980:681–682)

Others looking at women's attacks on men in American households have come to similar conclusions. For example, speaking of the aggression that fifty-two battered women directed against men, Daniel Saunders (1988:108) states, "A shove by a woman may enrage her partner; a shove by a man can knock a woman down and cause a concussion. A woman's punch may only cause laughter, whereas a man's can cause a full range of injuries." Similarly, Lenore Walker (1984:30) concludes that the data from her study of over four hundred battered women do not support the idea of "mutual combat": "Women may react to men's violence against them by striking back, but their actions are generally ineffective at hurting or stopping the men." In contrast, Jan Stets and Murray Straus (1990) suggest that the differences between men and women who sustain severe assaults in domestic violence are small, though they are in the direction of women sustaining greater injury.

It has been observed of "domestic violence" among Aborigines that women's attacks on men are sometimes less direct than men's attacks on women (Bolger 1991). As the examples from Mangrove indicate, however, women's attacks on men are not always minor or reactive. In twenty-nine cases, they led to what I have categorized as a "fight." Looking at this subset of the cases, I find that women's attacks consisted of a direct assault in eighteen instances; women pushed, speared, struck, or threw objects at men. In ten cases, women attacked with verbal aggression, by destroying an object, or by making a physical threat. In one instance, it was not possible to determine the precise nature of the assault. In well over 50 percent of these cases, women's actions consisted of direct physical assaults on men. In chapter 2, I presented sex differences in actions taken and injuries sustained; men attack and injure women more frequently and more severely. Recall that no woman, to my knowledge, has ever killed a man but that two women have died at the hands of men. Nevertheless, women directly assault men on occasion.

Aggression and Gender Relations

Male aggression and gender relations have long been juxtaposed in Western thinking. Consider all those cartoon cavemen, club in one hand, supine woman in the other—graphic illustrations of what Carol Mukhopadhyay and Patricia Higgins (1988:472) have called the "the basic caveman theory of gender." Ideas linking male aggression and female subordination provide a conceptual legacy both for feminists and their opponents. For example:

> Historically it has been woman's lesser capacity for violence as well as for work, that has determined her subordination. . . . Man not only has the strength to assert himself against nature, but also against his fellows. . . . Women have been forced to do "women's work." (Mitchell 1973:103)

According to Susan Brownmiller's thesis in *Against Our Will* (1976:5), male aggression, in its sexual manifestation of rape, "is nothing more or less than a conscious process of intimidation by which *all men* keep *all women* in a state of fear." In contrast, the argument of Steven Goldberg's *The Inevitability of Patriarchy* (1973) is that women's oppression is the incidental outcome of biologically based sex differences in aggression; the male "advantage" of greater aggressiveness inevitably leads to male domination in positions of leadership and status.

In the social sciences, the relationship between aggression and gender relations has also been considered, if sometimes only briefly, by many (see Mukhopadhyay and Higgins 1988 for an overview of anthropological ideas). In some cases, the proposed relationship is a relatively straightforward one. "If women never seem to have exercised coercive dominance over males as a socially established behavior, we believe it is because they lacked the physical ability to enforce their will" (Hayden et al. 1986:460). Peggy Sanday (1981:164) uses male aggression as one of her two indicators of male dominance, including in her definition of male aggression "the expectation that males should be tough, brave, and aggressive; the presence of men's houses or specific places where only men may congregate; frequent quarreling, fighting, or wife beating; the institutionalization or regular occurrence of rape; and raiding other groups for wives."

For others, the proposed relationship depends less on strength and ferocity and more on socially defined motives and goals. Rosaldo, for example, has observed of hunting and gathering societies that "women typically find their autonomy constrained by threats of masculine rape and violence" (1980a:412). Collier and Rosaldo (1981) say that in "brideservice societies"—a category that includes many hunting and gathering groups—men's readiness to fight over women underscores "women's status as objects." Because conflict between men over women is feared by the group, women's behavior is constrained by it. For example, wife beating for real or supposed infidelity may be "justified" insofar as it prevents violence between men.

Kathleen Gough (1975:71) has suggested that what little power men have over women in hunting and gathering societies is due to their control of weapons (or superior weapons) giving them "an ultimate control of force." William Divale and Marvin Harris (1979:328) have elaborated a similar proposition in their theory of "the male supremacist complex." They say that where warfare exists in band and village societies, people will prefer boys and raise them to be fierce and aggressive warriors. The advantage in establishing "a male monopoly over military weapons" and war as the "exclusive prerogative of males" is that "sex can be used as the principle reinforcement for fierce and aggressive performances involving risk of life." Unlike deprivation of food or shelter, sexual deprivation does not lead to physical impairment. But as the reward for military prowess, women must be menaced and intimidated into a passive and submissive role.

The psychologists Eleanor Maccoby and Carol Jacklin (1974:369) reject a simple relationship between men's greater physical strength, aggressiveness, and social dominance when they assert that only "apes and little boys" dominate primarily through aggression. As a "relatively primitive means of exerting influence over others," they continue, aggressive behavior will "be superseded by alternative forms of interaction." They recognize the female disadvantage in intergender encounters but observe that all societies protect women and girls from male aggression. They do consider, however, the potential for male domination through aggression in male/female relationships and speculate on the extent to which women may simply not produce behaviors "that will stimulate male aggression" even in situations in which men may never attack women (ibid.:264). Understanding associations between women's perceptions of men's aggressive potential and their experiences of subordination may be critical for understanding relations between men and women in specific cultural contexts. I return to this point below.

Quinn (1977:221) has identified the domestic realm as one in which women are often isolated. It is, therefore, one in which their autonomy is "threatened by men's greater strength and aggressiveness." With respect to studies of family violence, Wini Breines and Linda Gordon (1983:508) tell us that violence against women is a feminist "discovery." Whether or not researchers embrace an explicitly feminist framework, they are "responding in many aspects of their work to the challenges of feminism, and the new concepts and social analyses it has thrown up in the last decade." There are, however, many "feminisms" (Moore 1988), and thus Michele Bograd's (1988:13) comment that "there is no unified feminist perspective on wife abuse" comes as no surprise. She observes, nevertheless, that all feminist approaches are characterized by the theoretical stratagem of embedding individual or collective acts of violence in a framework of gendered power relations.[2] This approach is important here as well.

In Aboriginal Australia, many anthropologists have witnessed men's attacks on women and have interpreted these as indicators of male dominance and female subordination. Bronislaw Malinowski, for example, infers a husband's authority over his wife by the "excessive harshness and bad treatment, wounds, blows" he inflicts upon her without social interference (1913:78). Hiatt (1965) sees the reluctance of men to support women in fights, when their interests are in opposition to those of men, as an indication of women's inferior jural status. Myers (1986) interprets aggression in Aboriginal society more as an assertion of autonomy than as an attempt at dominance. Nevertheless, he suggests that men's control of the most important rituals is linked to their greater potential for the more injurious forms of violence. In Hamilton's view (1981a:74), the power of men over women in Aboriginal society, a power that "interpenetrates all the realms of interaction between the sexes," is based on the threat of physical force. Cowlishaw (1978, 1986) has characterized the more aggressive aspects of the brother/sister relationship (discussed later in this chapter) as "violence" that constructs the "power relations of gender"; it is, she says, the threat of male violence that teaches women caution.

Aggression and Authority in Aboriginal Australia

Elsie Begler (1978) gives us one of the earliest and most detailed and thoughtful studies of aggression and gender relations in Aboriginal Australia. She begins her investigation of women's status in "egalitarian society" with Morton Fried's definition of "power" as "the ability to channel the behavior of others by threat or use of sanction" (Fried 1967:13 in Begler 1978:574). Begler defines "authority" as the legitimate use of power and asks if one sex has authority over the other. On the basis of her examination of cases largely derived from the ethnographies of Hiatt (1965) and Meggitt (1962), she concludes,

It thus seems evident that in many Australian societies, men, by virtue of their sociocentric status as men, have authority over women, although this authority may be limited to certain areas of behavior. The precise limits of male authority over females among the Australians is, for the moment, difficult to define because of the paucity of good behavioral data. However, the fact of that authority stands; the socially accepted legitimate use of power by the members of one sex to compel the behavior of members of the opposite sex is evident in the frequent lack of support of male kin for a woman who is being overpowered by a male, the similar lack of support of female kin for a woman in a similar position, and the occasional, but analytically important, unprotested ganging up of men against a woman in certain culturally accepted situations (e.g., intrusion into men's country or being the center of an intracommunity dispute between men). The fact that none of the above statements remain valid if the position of the sexes is reversed seals the case. (1978:582)

It will be seen later that this "case" is not as airtight as Begler assumes. But let me first address her assumptions about legitimacy. In an attempt to circumvent the problem of arbitrary and culturally irrelevant evaluations of "status," Begler relies exclusively on behavioral observation, apparently seeing this as the only alternative to a reliance on normative statements. That is, she attends to what observers have written about behavior between Aboriginal men and women rather than what observers say Aborigines have said about relations between men and women. She assumes that people who do not assist a man's victim think that his attack is legitimate. But can legitimacy be inferred from behavior alone? This assumption fails to take into account a number of possibilities; among these, it neglects the understanding and experiences Aboriginal people have of aggression and the rules and responses they have developed for managing it in their communities (see also Counts 1990*b*, 1990*c*).

The Concepts of Status and Gender Relations

As Begler (1978) indicates, authority must not be treated in a global fashion. Kaberry (1939:142) warned decades ago that at least for an analysis of gender relations in Aboriginal society, "the problem of [male] authority cannot be discussed apart from the particular sphere in which it is exercised—those of residence, economics, property, sex, and children" (see also Lee 1979). In recent years, we have learned to expect aspects of what we regard as women's status to vary within a society (Mukhopadhyay and Higgins 1988; Quinn 1977; Whyte 1978), and, as Kaberry remarked, it must be anticipated that the degree of men's authority over women in Aboriginal Australia will vary from sphere to sphere.

During the 1980s, feminist anthropology shifted its focus away from questions about women's "status" or "sexual asymmetries" and toward analyses of "gender relations" (e.g., Lamphere 1987; Ortner and Whitehead 1981). The analysis of gender is, however, a means of understanding women's position in society (Moore 1988). For example, summarizing recent reworkings of "gender relations," Susan Gal (1991:176) writes that "gender is better seen as a system of culturally constructed relations of power, produced and reproduced in interaction between and among men and women"—a formulation that works equally well for this exploration of aggression at Mangrove. In the final analysis, "gender" is of importance to us because of inequality. Thus whether we use words like "status," "dominance," and "subordination," or "power," "resistance," and "contestation," our concepts reflect our concerns with women's position vis-à-vis others.

There are two facets of "status" as it is conceptualized in Rosaldo and Lamphere's seminal book, *Women, Culture, and Society* (1974): asymmetries in the value and authority associated with men's and women's activities and roles, and asymmetries in the amount and kinds of authority that one sex holds over the other (Rosaldo 1974). The concept of status is associated with goals, political motives, social conditions, and an imbalance in obligations and rewards (Collier and Rosaldo 1981). The language of "women's status" includes words like "dominance," "subordination," "power," "authority," "autonomy," and "sexual asymmetries" (see, e.g., Sanday 1981; Reiter 1975; Rosaldo and Lamphere 1974).

My understanding of "gender relations" as an anthropological construct is based in great part on the work of Rosaldo and is illustrated by the following quotation.

> It now appears to me that woman's place in human social life is not in any direct sense a product of the things she does (or even less a function of what, biologically, she is) but of the meaning her activities acquire through concrete social interactions. And the significances women assign to the activities of their lives are things that we can only grasp through an analysis of the relationships that women forge, the social contexts they (along with men) create—and within which they are defined. (Rosaldo 1980a:400)

Discussions of gender relations are discussions of "symbols," "context," and "meaning" (see, e.g., Ortner and Whitehead 1981).

As I have said earlier, the concept of "status" is central to the interpretation presented here. This analysis, however, shares the general orientation of those who would focus on gender relations. My analyses do not lead immediately to an explication of gender at Mangrove; the route is more circuitous. The manner and extent to which aggression affects relationships between men and women at Mangrove is explored through an attempt to understand the significance that women place on specific acts of male aggression. An example of this analytic strategy is found in the work of Thomas Gregor (1990) who has suggested that Mehinaku and Western women experience rape differently because each society constructs human sexuality differently. Here I utilize my understanding of Aboriginal constructions of aggression. This approach allows me to ask what men's acts mean to women and how they affect their self-concepts, their perceptions of the relationships with the men who may or may not attack them, and their behavior in the context of these relationships.

In spite of a commitment to the idea of "cultural relativity," I occasionally encounter ethnographic "facts" that both puzzle and alarm me. One of these is an observation made by Napoleon Chagnon about Yanomamo women.

> Women expect this kind of [aggressive] treatment and many of them measure their husband's concern in terms of the frequency of minor beatings they sustain. I overheard two young women discussing each other's scalp scars. One of them commented that the other's husband must really care for her since he has beaten her on the head so frequently! (1968:83; see also Heelas 1982)

My first reaction to this report was to wonder if "care" is really the best translation of this Yanomamo woman's words. But on reflection, is this so different from American women who say that they deserve to be beaten by their husbands (Fedders and Elliott 1987; NiCarthy 1987; Straus 1980)? The Marxist's concept of "false consciousness" leaps to mind as a kind of explanation but one that too easily dismisses the experiences of these women's lives (Abu-Lughod 1990*b*). These ideas are worthy of study in their own right, and more systematic efforts to understand them are crucial. As Liz Kelly (1988) has argued, attention to women's experience and understanding of male aggression is essential if we are to understand how women's perceptions of their own victimization are ordered—a necessary step when changing these perceptions becomes critical for women's well-being.

Domestic Aggression and Women's Autonomy at Mangrove

How might men's aggressive behavior affect aspects of women's lives at Mangrove? I address this question by beginning with my understanding of the concepts "autonomy," "subordination," and "dominance." By autonomy, I mean the ability to act in one's own interest; by subordination, the loss of autonomy; and by dominance, the ability to subordinate the interest of another in pursuit of one's own interest (see Leacock 1978; Schlegel 1972, 1977).

By far the largest category of relationships represented in these cases of aggression between men and women is that of actual, former, classificatory, or desired spouse, or men and women with a sexual or romantic interest in each other, for example, a woman and the man she wants as a lover. In conformity with police files and social agencies in the United States, I might term this "domestic aggression" or "family violence." Insofar as I wish to compare intergender aggression at Mangrove with acts of domestic violence in our society, this is appropriate (cf. Bolger 1991). I remind the reader, however, that seemingly domestic or personal matters may, at least in this community, have more widespread social or political ramifications.

The reasons given for aggressive interactions between men and women of Mangrove reflect the intimacy of these relationships and tell us something of the concerns of the people in them. Reasons that are significantly associated with intersexual aggression include the acquisition or divorce of a spouse, jealousy of a married partner including suspicion or knowledge of adultery, the delinquent behavior of a child, swearing, and subsistence goods. It is worth noting here that aggression attributed to intoxication is not significantly associated with male/female aggression and is the attributed cause of aggression in only twenty-five cases.[3]

How might male aggression effectively reduce women's autonomy? I can think of several scenarios, each of which begins with mutually exclusive goals or interests. For example, a man wants to take a second wife, but his wife does not want a co-wife; a woman wants to take a lover, but her partner wants to be her only sexual companion. In the ensuing conflict, the man may literally beat the woman into submission. After a beating she says, "All right, take another wife." Or the man may threaten the woman, frightening her into submission; fearing promised retaliation, she abstains from taking a lover. In both cases, the woman's interests are subordinated to those of the man, and her autonomy is, at least momentarily, reduced. Here Peggy Sanday's (1981) observation that the presence of male aggression does not necessarily indicate the presence of female subordination is important. A man may beat his wife, and she may still try to prevent his acquisition of a second wife. He may threaten to spear her, and she may still take a lover. Only if male aggression physically incapacitates a woman, thus preventing her from pursuing an intended act, is female loss of autonomy a necessary outcome of male aggression. Otherwise, it must be viewed simply as a potential cost of a chosen course of action.

A third possibility is that raised by Maccoby and Jacklin (1974) and, with specific reference to women in Aboriginal Australia, by Francesca Merlan (1988): in fearful anticipation of male aggression, a woman does not act in her own interest. For example, although she does not want a co-wife, a woman acquiesces when her husband obtains one, protesting in no way. Here two mutually exclusive goals may be said to exist, but they are never juxtaposed in conflict. Female subordination is an integral part of this scenario, but, perhaps somewhat ironically, observable male aggression is not, only feminine fear or anticipation of its eventual manifestation. Such constructs as the nonpursuit of unstated goals and the anticipation of unobserved male aggression present some problems of documentation. Nevertheless, I include them in the following analysis, as just such a scenario is implied in writings on the relationship between male aggression and female subordination (e.g.,

Hamilton 1981*a*) and is, I believe, an implicit but central part of our thinking about aggression and gender relations.

Perceived Sex Differences in Aggressive Behavior

|The proposition that the male potential for aggression may subordinate women does not require that male aggression toward women be manifest. It is necessary, however, to demonstrate that women perceive the potential for male aggression and that they perceive it as a danger to be avoided. |

Women at Mangrove are certainly aware of the possibility that a man may attack a woman. They see or hear of these attacks if they do not actually experience them themselves. Indeed, when they speak about women and aggression, they often speak about male attack. For example, in 1988, I asked six women to visualize a fight in which an adolescent girl was being beaten and asked who they thought might be doing this. Three of the women (and perhaps significantly the three youngest) answered, "young boy" (i.e., adolescent boy), "lover," or "boyfriend." I also asked these six women if they could tell me about one of their own fights. Two chose to tell me about fights with their husbands. A third woman, Rosalind, said she had never been in a fight. She attributed this, among other things, to the fact that she had followed the advice of the European minister who married her. This is her account of what he said: "Love your husband, take care of your husband, if your husband says anything to you, do it. And don't go running around with anyone, mind your husband as long as you live."

The following account of an Aboriginal practice at one time current among the people of Mangrove indicates that at least some women anticipate a greater male potential for aggressive behavior.

Emu and bush turkey have strong power. If you eat them and somebody is fighting, the spear will come to you. They make you deaf and you fight. [Younger boys] can eat and women can always eat, but when a man is young neither he nor his mother will eat things like emu, turkey or fat from the dugong and turtle. . . . If he does eat emu, when somebody throws a spear he won't run away. He will throw back and kill that man. When a man becomes old, gets gray hair or has children, then he can eat.

The women do this because this is the Law. They help the boy. If a boy ᴄ
will be cranky and fighting. If his mother eats she won't get cranky, but hᴇ

At least some women also see male aggression as more dange
than female aggression. I asked four women who would get "really
hurt" in a fight between men and women. "The woman," answered all
four. It is not clear, however, that all women see men as more aggressive than women. For example, in 1978 and in 1988, I asked women if
they thought men or women are more "cheeky." Men are, according to
six women. For example:

Men are more cheeky than women, because men get spears and want to kill
men. Women only get sticks and pull each other's hair. Women never murder
their husbands, only men murder their wives.

Men get more angry than women. They have lots of muscle. They are stronger
than women. They get spears, [metal spears], [spear throwers].

But one group of five women said, "Some women are cheeky, just like
men." Three other women also thought that men and women are both
cheeky. I asked this question of one of Lily's sisters, the first woman
quoted above, again in 1988. In the intervening years, she had changed
her mind or was thinking of "cheeky" in a different way. Women, she
said this time, are more cheeky: they start the fights. As we have seen,
the Kriol word "cheeky" is used in the sense of "angry," "aggressive,"
or "dangerous," and in most of the women's responses to my question
about sex differences, it is difficult to tell which meanings, or combinations of meanings, respondents were using. Again I find the ambiguity
of Aboriginal women's words thought-provoking; here, because they
remind us of the parallel ambiguity with which our concept "aggressive" is often used.

What significance do women at Mangrove assign to the sex differences in aggression they appear to perceive? To what extent and in what
manner do they see male aggression as a threat to their well-being?

Some of the aggression at Mangrove is conceptualized as what we
might call "dominance attempts." For example, here is a description of
fighting between adolescent schoolgirls.

We used to gang up, like me, [girl], [girl], [girl], and [girl]. The rest of the
girls were the other gang. We were always fighting. Sometimes we didn't agree,
like to go out to the beach. They didn't agree with what [we wanted to do], so
that's why we fought. We used to fight at the beach or at the water tank at the
shop—hair fight, not stick fight. We thought someone might get hurt. The

group that lost, they followed the other group. It happened day after day, night after night.

Women sometimes talk specifically about male aggression as a means of dominating women. For example:

Some women are frightened of cheeky men. . . . When women are married to a cheeky man they know they had better be careful.

And,

[A woman] is running off to another man, I don't know why, her husband is a young man. She keeps running around because he doesn't strike her. If he did, she would stop.

But while women may experience male aggression as a form of attempted domination, at least some women may also see it as a rather ineffective means of accomplishing this. For example, Tina's sister told me about a married woman who ran off with a boyfriend on a number of occasions; the woman's husband would beat her, but, as the account went, she would just go to the clinic and then run off again. Following up this theme in women's conversation, I asked six women, "If a married woman got a hiding from her husband because he heard she has a friend [lover], should she go meet her friend again?" Only two women answered that she should not. Two of the remaining four urged caution. One woman said that she should wait until her husband left the settlement, and the other suggested that she wait a few months before resuming her affair. But none of the four thought that a "hiding" would deter a woman from meeting her lover.

Women make many statements about male aggression as a response to women's behavior. But often it is not at all clear that the acts of male violence are interpreted as dominance attempts.

When girl friends can't do what they are told, their boyfriend strikes them with a stick or a stone.

A woman sleeps with her husband. If she didn't, he would chase her with a shovel spear.

Those men don't drink, fight, steal for nothing. They want women. Mothers might even get speared by them if they don't give their daughters in marriage.

In these statements, aggression follows male displeasure. But dominance is not identified as the motive for these acts. One could as easily say that men's violence is interpreted by these speakers as an expression of anger.

Myers describes a Pintubi man who "wreaked havoc" in his efforts to obtain a wife. He threw spears, dragged the girl he desired out of a vehicle, threatened her supporters, and disrupted an entertainment program at the school. Myers's (1986:162) interpretation of these acts as "rooted more in self-regard . . . than in a desire for power" is pertinent here, for it suggests that male aggression may not necessarily be employed or interpreted as dominance in other Aboriginal communities. Roheim's (1933:255) remarks about domestic violence in Central Australia are also of interest, for he emphasizes male violence as an expression of anger. The men, he says, are not "sadists who deliberately torture their wives." Instead their aggression is caused by a "lack of inhibitory control," on the one hand, and "a sudden outburst of anger," on the other.

I remind the reader of the argument, presented in chapter 3, that aggressive behavior is often experienced, by aggressors and targets alike, as an expression of anger. When aggression is seen as a dominance attempt, there are two likely responses: submission or defiance. But when aggression is seen as an expression of anger, other responses may be appropriate. One may still, for example, submit to or defy an angry person. But one may also ignore an angry person, at least once the display of anger has passed. I suggest that male aggression is relatively ineffectual in changing women's attitudes and behavior at Mangrove because women do not see this as its primary goal. Instead, they see it largely as a means by which men display and express their anger. And they see male aggression this way not because men do not attempt to dominate women through aggression (though I do not know that they do)[4] but because of the cultural emphasis on aggression as an expression of anger.

The Legitimacy of Male Aggression

In chapter 2, I discussed the possibility that at least some aggression may be viewed as legitimate expressions of anger by people at Mangrove. There remains the question, however, of the extent to which men and women share perspectives on what constitutes legitimate aggression.

er the years I have recorded a number of fights and other aggres-
:idents precipitated by women's failure to provide food for their
ids and children. I have also recorded a number of statements
ııυıı women who have said that men would attack women who would
not cook. In 1988, knowing this to be a commonly perceived reason
for male aggression and wishing to pursue the topic of male aggression
as coercion or dominance, I posed this scenario to six women: "A married woman got a hiding from her husband. He was angry because she
didn't cook any food for dinner. If you were this woman, what would
you do?" Three woman said they would cook for him after being
beaten, though one said she would first fight back. A fourth woman
said she would feel like hitting him back but would not because she was
in the wrong for neglecting her domestic duties. These replies indicate
that some women may accept men's aggression as legitimate—a sanctioned means of correcting women's perceived failings—and change
their behavior accordingly. However, a woman who did not answer
this question once volunteered that men should not hit women.

Men shouldn't bash women. Growling is OK, when he is right. Like if a
woman doesn't cook or do his washing. But sometimes there is no baking
powder [to make bread with] and no money. So unless family can give [food
or money, a woman can't cook]. My husband is like that, he doesn't hit me, he
only growls.

The women I know rarely talked to me about the legitimacy of various acts of aggression. Could I assume, as Begler (1978) has, that the
extent to which others interfere in a fight, either to stop an aggressor
or to help him, is a measure of their acceptance of his action? For example, I was told that one man had made the following remark to his
clan "son."

Don't fight when you are drunk. Only when you are sober. [My clan brothers,
your fathers] won't take partner with you if you fight when you are drunk.

In an earlier analysis of aggressive behavior at Mangrove (Burbank
1980a), I examined accounts of eleven fights attributed to intoxication
and counted the number of individuals who either helped in the fights
or tried to stop them. In these cases, thirteen people tried to stop the
fighters, whereas only four people helped them in their aggressive efforts. While this analysis suggests that people at Mangrove tend to do
what they say they do, at least where incidents related to intoxication
are concerned, I cannot say with certainty that people interfered in

these fights because they saw the fighters' actions as illegitimate. Other explanations are possible. For example, the precept of stopping fights to prevent serious injury may account for the willingness of people to stop rather than join in drinkers' fights. A fear of drunkenness and an anticipation of danger is present at Mangrove. Very likely this has been created by violent deaths occurring on nearby settlements in which alcohol was clearly a precipitating factor.

Behavior alone appears to be a poor indicator of the perceived legitimacy of an aggressive act. Are there other ways of addressing this issue? One could ask participants and observers about the legitimacy of each aggressive act. But I was rarely able to do this. And I suspect that the degree of consensus would vary with any given event. What is viewed as legitimate action by some is probably not viewed as such by others. Structural and personal relationships to aggressors and victims undoubtedly affect perceptions of legitimacy (see Heelas 1982; Reid 1983; Riches 1986). There are clear indications that some women do not accept male aggression directed toward them whatever the reason and its perceived legitimacy.

But what of the women who said that a hiding from her husband would not deter a woman from seeking out her lover on subsequent occasions? Clearly, responses to aggression are not only based on the perceived legitimacy of an act. A woman whose son-in-law has beaten her daughter for infidelity may recognize his right to strike her but may still be unhappy about his action. Similarly, the women who would continue to see their lovers after a beating may recognize the legitimacy of their husband's attacks but nevertheless resist them. For example, two women responding to the question about cooking said they would not cook for their husband following the beating. One said that she would not cook for her husband because she had another man and she would continue to run away with him. The other said that she would leave her husband and stay with her family for a while. Some women, it appears, might not submit even to legitimate rebukes.

LEGITIMATE MALE AGGRESSION: *MIRRIRI*

Mirriri has been described as a ritualized form of aggression in which a man throws spears or otherwise attacks his sisters on violation of brother/sister etiquette, particularly its avoidance components.

Olden times, somebody eloped. I came here [to Mangrove] from a long way. I came by canoe and was staying here. When they eloped, the woman's brother looked around. "My sister has eloped." He picked up his spears and chased all his sisters into the bush. I saw that. I was a little girl. Their brother hunted those women away. Well they stayed in the bush. Then in a little while when the sun went down they came back to their husbands.

At Mangrove, women speak of mirriri as an emotion like "shame" that intensifies when etiquette associated with the brother/sister relationship is violated. When attention is called to a real or classificatory sister's sexuality, reproductive capacities, or eliminatory functions, a man's mirriri increases, and he is expected to behave aggressively toward her (Burbank 1985). Should a man see his sister going to one of the public toilets, for example, women say he might throw a stick or tin (can) at her. Or if he hears anyone, even a small child, swear at her—almost all swearing at Mangrove refers to sexuality—he would chase her and any other of his sisters who might be around. In consequence, as Rosalind put it, "women are very careful of brothers."

The sexual asymmetry of this etiquette is one of its most striking aspects. It is the sister who must assume responsibility for proper conduct (Cowlishaw 1978). It is women who must avoid their brothers and who suffer from their own and other's indiscretions. And to judge from the following, women do suffer. I asked six women how a woman would feel after being chased by a brother who had heard somebody swear at her. Their answers included the words, "shame," "frightened," "shaky," "sick," and "settling down." No one said that a woman would feel angry with her brother, although one woman said that a brother would be "sorry" afterward for chasing his sister. I have also been told stories of the discomfort that women suffer when they need to urinate but their brothers are present.

Mirriri has been described elsewhere in the literature (see Burbank 1985; Cowlishaw 1978, 1979, 1986; Hiatt 1964, 1966; Maddock 1970; Makarius 1966; Warner 1937). Critiquing most of these efforts, Cowlishaw (1986:10) observes that they all "focus attention on the attacker," while the "sister who is the target of the spears receives no empirical or analytic attention." This leads, she argues, to a failure to recognize that "the most significant aspect of the mirriri . . . is that it is an illuminating expression of the relationship between men and women" (ibid.:8). She, in contrast, views mirriri as an event "in the ongoing reproduction of social forms" (ibid.:10) and as "the most powerful sexually differentiating experience a child has in Arnhem

Land" (1979:119). An example from her fieldwork provides a coi
ing illustration of these possibilities.

An eight-year-old girl sat down near her visiting eighteen-year-old "brother"
near the fire. He turned suddenly and shouted furiously "Get away from me
rubbish." . . . This is unheard of behaviour in other contexts. The trauma this
little girl suffered was evident in her long period of whimpering. (ibid.:120)

Mirriri, says Cowlishaw, does not just teach girls to be careful in the
presence of men. It carries a message to all women "about the sensitiv-
ity of men to certain situations and the necessity therefore to always be
alert to their presence" (1986:11). Whatever male motives in mirriri
might be and however consonant with etiquette and other aspects of
social relations, Cowlishaw's analysis of this ritualized behavior underlines its effects on women and allows us to consider its implications for
gender relations in Aboriginal society.

The women I talked to at Mangrove have said little about mirriri;
rarely is an act of male aggression described as mirriri motivated. But
at least some of what the women say tends to support Cowlishaw's
(1986) contention and, indirectly, Begler's (1978) argument about
male aggression and female subordination. I do not think, however,
that the relationship between this form of male aggression and its effects on women at Mangrove is quite so straightforward.

Elsewhere (Burbank 1985) I have discussed the similarities between
mirriri-motivated aggression and displaced aggression. To summarize
briefly: Sometimes men and women at Mangrove perform acts that
resemble aggressive behavior and are recognized as such (e.g., such activity is often described as "fighting") but attack objects rather than
people. The young man described in chapter 2 who "skidded" a stolen
vehicle and rammed a house provides an example of this kind of action.
Here are two additional examples of what I call "displaced aggression."

The other night it was really late and we saw [a woman] walking with a stick.
And you know that little house that [a man] built? She went up to that house
and she was striking it, bang, bang, bang. And she lit a match and there was
[her former husband] and [another man] with no clothes on sleeping. And she
banged on the house and they woke up. "Waah! don't hit me, don't hit me,"
[her former husband] said. And [the woman] was crying in the road and we all
felt sorry. [Her former husband] said, "You got your new fella." "Only because
the young girls were always taking you away," she replied.

[A man] bought some batteries for that new tape recorder. And he was fixing
it and [his three-year-old grandson] was there and [the man] told him, "Don't

push all the buttons." And his grandson just dropped the tape recorder [from about 2 feet above the ground] and went away. So [the man] picked up the tape and went to the toilet and you know that round bowl, he just smashed the tape against it and smashed it again and again. And his son came but he was too late, the tape recorder was finished. And [his grandson] didn't stay with [his grandmother and grandfather] that night.

I have suggested that aggressive acts such as these permit the expression of anger without hurting others and possibly jeopardizing important social relationships. For instance, in the examples above, the people who could have been the targets of attack were clearly important to their potential aggressors. The woman who did not attack her former husband was attempting a reconciliation with him at the time. The man who destroyed the tape recorder avoided attacking a child, his grandson. He also probably avoided a fight with his son who could be expected to come to his son's defense, even against his father. I have also argued that mirriri-motivated aggression is a form of displaced aggression. Although a woman is certainly not an object, when attacked by her brother, she is not expected to stand and fight; she is expected to run away. I recorded no case, past or present, in which mirriri-motivated aggression resulted in serious injury to women at Mangrove. And a survey of the literature on mirriri in Arnhem Land suggests that in other Aboriginal communities such injury is rare. When it does occur, it is condemned (Burbank 1985).

I do not wish to dispute Cowlishaw's assertion that mirriri teaches women to be careful of male sensibilities. The few comments from women about their responses to mirriri indicate that these are feelings of caution and fear. What I do want to suggest is that the complex of mirriri-motivated aggression carries an additional message to women: that others will protect them from their brothers; that the people around them will act to ensure that mirriri-motivated aggression will neither be directed against them nor harm them. For example, I asked a question about brother/sister etiquette: If a brother of that girl came up and said, "What are they fighting for?" could they say, "They are fighting because that man thought that girl slept with that other man"? The answer was:

No! [laugh] And they can't hear that you have been eloping. They won't listen. "What are they fighting for?" "I don't know," somebody says to them. They know but they won't tell those brothers.

There is even an indication here that brothers may also collude to protect women by pretending not to hear what is being said. Hiatt (1964) has suggested that some men are less willing to attack their sisters than others and that the small number of cases of mirriri-motivated aggression that he recorded at Maningrida may be due to this. Men, he suspects, leave situations in which they might hear someone swear at their sisters. Elsewhere (Burbank 1985) I have suggested that the prescribed form that mirriri-motivated aggression takes—that of throwing spears at a group of women—is likely to prevent any one woman from actually being speared.

At Mangrove, people intervene when brothers are attacking sisters on mirriri-motivated grounds. Maddock (1970) and Hiatt (1966) report cases elsewhere in Aboriginal Australia in which others act to prevent women's injury. This is further evidence that behavior alone is not a good indicator of the perceived legitimacy of an act. Mirriri-motivated male aggression is culturally patterned and culturally prescribed aggression. It is clearly legitimate aggression, yet people attempt to stop it and prevent injury to women.

It may be that people wish to avoid the male displeasure that violations of the brother/sister etiquette bring.

Like if someone wants me somewhere, like they want to have a talk, and if my husband is going to look for me. "Where has so and so gone?" And if my brother is going to be there, those women say "Oh, so and so has gone to get wood." But they can't say, "Oh, she's going to have a talk with that man." They can't say that because my brother is going to be there. He doesn't like to hear that bad news.

Still, such restraint protects women, and some are clearly aware of this.

It may be, as Cowlishaw (1978, 1979, 1986) has suggested, that mirriri provides a model of gender relations in Aboriginal society. Here I want to propose a further possibility—that at Mangrove, at least, mirriri provides a paradigm of social response when male aggression is directed against women.

The Protection of Women

Indications are that women at Mangrove generally see men as stronger than themselves and if not more aggressive, then at least more dangerously so. These perceptions are undoubtedly created and reinforced by the greater amount of injury and death that they

: hands of men. Why, then, do they fight with men? Follow-
· (1976)—whose formulation of sex differences in aggres-
:d earlier—it might be assumed that women's aggression at
s a function of men's aggression; the preponderance of
work on family violence in America certainly would encourage such a
conclusion (e.g., Straus and Gelles 1990b). But it is clear that women's
attacks on men sometimes represent motives other than self-defense. I
suggest that women at Mangrove initiate aggression against men because the norms of their community permit and encourage such behavior. Women, like men, have learned that anger is appropriately expressed through aggressive behavior (see also Straus 1980). They know
that women are sometimes hurt or even killed by men, but they do not
think that they will be seriously injured. Hence, when they get angry at
men, they attack them.

The women I know recognize that the public nature of fighting provides them with an important safeguard. As knowledge of its occurrence is almost instantaneous, steps can be taken to minimize the effects
of aggressive behavior. In a discussion in which we compared wife beating in America and at Mangrove, Tina observed that on the settlement
people fight "outside," and there is always somebody to stop a fight.
When a woman in a nearby community was fatally stabbed by her husband, Rosalind explained how this was possible:

That man and woman were fighting in front of everybody on Monday and she
was alright. But yesterday when they were alone, he stabbed her. He locked the
door of the house and then stabbed her with a spear.

After a neighbor recounted her husband's aggressive displays of jealousy, Tina advised her not to "go bush" with him. "By and by he'll
strike you." She then explained to me that a man who wishes to give
his wife a beating without interference may attempt to isolate her. One
means of doing so is on the pretext of a hunting or fishing trip.

It is not only women at Mangrove who say that the public nature of
fighting provides women with protection. Draper (1975) tells how
!Kung women compare the lot of Bantu women, whose husbands can
beat them behind locked doors, to the protection they are afforded by
the openness of their camps. With Robert Burgess (Burgess and Draper
1989; see also Erchak 1984, 1987), she suggests that the absence of
such "safeguards" in contemporary settings contributes to the brutality
of family violence in Western society, where there is seldom anyone

present to interfere when aggression becomes excessive or life threatening.

But it is not simply in the public nature of aggressive interactions that the women of Mangrove find reassurance. They are also cognizant that others will interfere on their behalf. No matter what a woman's transgression might be, she knows that family members will come to her assistance if they perceive imminent injury. "If her husband is too rough, marking her, making her sick, killing her, then we take partner." I suggest that the public nature of fighting at Mangrove in conjunction with a widespread concern that no one be seriously injured largely compensate for any imbalance in size, strength, and ferocity in men's and women's battles. The women of Mangrove recognize this and expect others in their community to protect them from serious harm.

An examination of assistance rendered in the cases of intersexual aggression suggests that such confidence is not misplaced. Men's attacks on women account for about 17 percent of the cases in which the sex of targets and victims is known. But the help women receive in these encounters accounts for about 32 percent of all help given by men and about 29 percent of all help given by women. In their attacks on women, male aggressors are also stopped at a disproportionately high rate. About 21 percent of all such interference by men takes place within these cases; about 24 percent of all such interference by women takes place within these cases. When men are the targets of female aggression (a category that accounts for about 9 percent of all cases in which the sex of target and aggressor is known), male targets are also stopped at a disproportionately high rate. Men's activity in these cases accounts for 75 percent of all such male activity; women's activity accounts for about 54 percent of all such female activity.

The willingness of at least some of the women of Mangrove to attack men on occasion indicates that at least some of the women in this community are willing to risk male attack. I suggest that this willingness is based on women's realistic evaluation of their social circumstances. Men have killed women, and the women of Mangrove know this. But the frequent help and protection that women see or receive from neighbors and kin is likely to have much more salience than two deaths that occurred many years ago. These experiences remind them that people will attempt to prevent serious injury to a woman who is fighting with a man. Male aggression is seen as potentially dangerous but rarely so in actuality. It is not an experience to be avoided at any cost. Thus, if women at Mangrove do not always act in their own interests, it is likely that they do so for reasons other than a fear of men's physical aggression.

Wife Beating and Wife Battering

What effects do such perceptions have on women's behavior vis-à-vis the men in their lives? How do they interact with the realization of women's aspirations and interests? I begin to address these questions with the suggestion that women at Mangrove do not experience male aggression in the same manner that many women in American society do. In preface, I relate a remark that Aboriginal women from a community in northern Australia made to the anthropologist Elizabeth Povinelli (pers. commun.). Following a television program on domestic abuse in the West, they turned to her and asked, "Why don't white women fight back?" I believe that women at Mangrove would have made a similar remark to me had we watched the program together.

Looking at men's attacks on women, some anthropologists have distinguished between "wife beating" and "wife battery." According to Judith Brown (1988:3, 1992), wife beating is "the intentional inflicting of pain" that is, in some societies, "frequent, humdrum, unremarkable, routine." Wife battering, in contrast, is violence that is "out of the ordinary," violence in which a woman is "seriously injured, incapacitated, or even killed" (see also Campbell 1992). In much of the writing on wife abuse in Western society, however, any kind of physical aggression directed toward women is considered to be out of the ordinary. Walker's (1984:26) description of wife battering, for example, includes low-grade violence—relatively harmless acts like "pushing," "slapping," and "spanking"—that might be regarded in some settings as "humdrum" or "unremarkable."

Western attitudes about the male victimization of women are complex. The social sciences are just beginning to discover how very widespread such violence is in modern society (Counts 1990a). The disapproval manifest in much of the writing on the topic may reflect the values of middle-class academics as well as the fact that wife abuse was first brought to their attention by activist women who saw male aggression as an attack on women's rights and well-being (Bograd 1988; Breines and Gordon 1983). But researchers have found that male aggression directed against women (not to mention aggression directed against children) has a degree of acceptance (e.g., Straus 1980). A Louis Harris poll for the National Commission on the Causes and Prevention of Violence conducted in 1968 found, for example, that "one-fifth of all Americans approve of slapping one's spouse on appropriate occasions" (Stark and McEvoy 1970:52). Some family violence researchers (e.g., Straus 1980) have even come to talk about the marriage license as a "hitting license" (see also Walker 1979).

There is, undoubtedly, a range of attitudes about wife abuse, just as there are a range of abusive acts and a variety of individual abusers and victims. As Murray Straus, Richard Gelles, and Suzanne Steinmetz (1980:35) have observed, there are some who regard their acts of violence within the family as normal, whereas for others, these same acts elicit feelings of guilt and shame. Nevertheless, I think it can be argued that for many, if not the majority, of Western aggressors and victims, there is some sense that any form of physical aggression directed against wives or girl friends is wrong. Wife beating is, after all, against the law. For many years, at least some women have called the police, even though the law enforcement establishment has not always responded to their pleas for help (Martin 1976). Many of the accounts of violence against women include a male apology and a pledge of "never again" (e.g., NiCarthy 1987; Switzer and Hale 1984; Walker 1979). According to James Ptacek, men in treatment programs for wife abusers commonly explain away their violence as a loss of control.

We used to argue about picayune-ass things anyway. And a lot of this was building and building. And I was keeping it all inside. All of the frustration and anger. You're supposed to sit there and take this stuff from your wife. And, like I say, I'd take it for awhile, but then *I'd lose my head*. (Anonymous man quoted in Ptacek 1988:143; my emphasis)

In America, the use of physical aggression against women is regarded, at least by many, as deviant.

According to Walker (1979), battered women generally accept the myths of our culture that define battered women as a crazy, masochistic minority of women who get what they deserve. Walker has presented a thought-provoking analysis of why women stay in a battering relationship for as long as they often do. These women, she says, may be much like the laboratory rats who are trained to be helpless, so helpless that they will drown without a struggle when placed in a bucket of water (see Seligman 1975). It is the sociocultural circumstances of women's lives that teach them "helplessness."

I suggest that our beliefs about aggression also contribute to the experiences of battered woman. These women live in a society where messages about aggression, especially physical aggression, are mixed. On the one hand, many, if not most, acts of aggression are taboo. If they are not actually outlawed, they are shameful departures from expected behavior. Aggression, according to this perspective, is something that should be suppressed whenever it arises. Ideally it should not be aroused in the first place. We may, in certain circumstances and fashions, express our angry feelings but never physically and interpersonally. However, just such aggression is lauded in movies, on television, and in sports. As capital punishment, it is enthroned in the law of many states. At home, it is how some of us teach our children right from wrong. But observe that with the exception of the corporal punishment of children, prosocial aggression is largely the domain of adult males: they are the Rambos, the boxers, the police; "hangperson" is not yet a word in our vocabulary. Aggression in Western society is thus both normal and deviant, shameful and heroic, and the experience of both men and women, yet largely the prerogative of adult males.

Therefore, when a woman becomes a victim of physical aggression, it is not only a painful experience but it may also be a shameful or strange one. Among other things, it may be this very strangeness or shamefulness that feeds a battered woman's assumptions that there is something wrong with her (see, e.g., Fedders and Elliott 1987; Switzer and Hale 1984; Turner 1984). Hence, perhaps, her willingness to accept a man's attempt to discipline and dominate her and the extreme form his behavior takes.

> He said he wouldn't hit me because I wasn't a bad person, but then he did. What was this thing I had done? I could never find it, but there must be something really bad. You don't go around hitting people for no good reason. I didn't know that it was something, within him. (Anonymous woman in NiCarthy 1987:29)

Many women who observed battering in their family of orientation may see a man's abuse as something they deserve. For those women from homes where they were pampered by fathers "who treated their daughters like fragile dolls" (Walker 1979:35), the first experience with male violence is probably something for which they are completely unprepared.

THE CASE OF HEDDA NUSSBAUM

To compare women's experience of male aggression at Mangrove with women's experience in the West, I briefly consider a

case of male brutality and female subjugation in American sc
has shocked and disturbed many, that of Joel Steinberg ar
Nussbaum. In November 1987, Steinberg and Nussbaum
rested after their illegally adopted daughter, Lisa, was beati
coma. Later, the six-year-old died. Nussbaum was released by me pros-
ecutors, who determined that she was "physically and emotionally unable to harm—or save—Lisa" (*People* magazine, Feb. 13, 1989, 83). A
common response to the story was to ask how a woman could fail to
save a child. How could she allow the child to lie unconscious for
twelve hours without summoning help? A list of Nussbaum's own injuries at the time of her arrest is the answer for many (Summers 1989;
Walker 1989). She had a splayed nose, a cleft lip, sixteen broken ribs,
and a leg so ulcerated that amputation was considered (Weiss 1989).
Steinberg's batterings and torture of Nussbaum were accompanied by
her increasing isolation.

Embarrassed to be seen with so many black eyes and bruises, Hedda kept taking
time off from her job at Random House until finally, in 1982, she was fired.
Without a job, which had provided her with a source of income and contact
with the outside world, Hedda became increasingly isolated and dependent on
Steinberg. "Slowly, Joel convinced me that my friends weren't good enough
for me," she says. "So I stopped seeing them and became friends with his
friends." . . .
　　In order to separate Hedda from her family, Joel took a different tack. He
told Hedda that they were part of a group of dangerous people, a "cult" that
could hypnotize them both and destroy him. He also said they had a terrible
effect on Hedda's behavior, and he forbade them from coming to the apart-
ment. "I missed my parents," she says. "But I was actually relieved when they
stayed away because I began to believe the things Joel told me about them."
(Weiss 1989:89)

　　Assuming that this account reflects "what really happened," I find
Nussbaum's isolation the most striking aspect of her circumstances,
especially after my years at Mangrove. The words of the psychiatrist
who examined Nussbaum after her arrest are significant in this context.

If you don't have much sense of who you are, anything is possible. People like
Hedda are totally dependent on their circumstances. If you have no ability
to decide who you are independently, the other person can decide for you.
(Michael Allen in Brownmiller 1989:63)

Clearly, Nussbaum is a woman of great vulnerability, as are we all. This
vulnerability along with the effects of cocaine and violence must have
contributed to her subjugation to a male psychopath (Walker 1989).

But her isolation sealed her fate. There were no co-workers, neighbors, friends, or relatives to witness her deterioration and try to save her when she could not save herself.

THE CASE OF SUNNY

I now turn to an account of the abuse of a woman from Mangrove. Sunny is a woman who was in her late twenties in 1988. She was married, had three children, and like many of the women at Mangrove today, lived with her mother and married sisters and brothers. This account is somewhat atypical insofar as the incident took place when Sunny was living away from Mangrove at the time, her husband was drinking, if not intoxicated, and the injury she suffered was more severe than that which is usually inflicted, though she is not the first woman at Mangrove to be stabbed. This is her account of the incident.

When I was married, not to this husband, to the other one, [my daughter's] father, when he was drunk, he always fought and argued with me. One day, Sunday afternoon, we went to the beach. He was drinking. We went crabbing and fishing and got a lot of fish. After we went out fishing, we came back home and we went down to the river and we were swimming but he was still drunk. I was carrying [my son] Timmy. My husband went and asked one of his cousins for a car, a white Falcon. And they gave him the key and then we went down to the top crossing and I didn't know he had a beer. He was hiding it. And then we got off and he told me, "I've got beer." "Well," I told him, "don't drink, you might hit me and Timmy." He had a gun but that gun didn't have any bullets. "I'll hit you," he said to me. "No." "I'll hit you." "No." And we ran away and we were walking down by the side of the river, and he was following us with the car, but he didn't walk down by the riverside. He was driving on the road, looking for our tracks but he didn't find us.

He got home first and we came last. The door was wide open and we went inside. I was carrying Timmy and I put him on the bed. Timmy was crying and my husband woke up and shut the door and he said, "I'll stab you with the knife." He was coming closer and closer and I was shouting and screaming and I opened the door and took Timmy outside and my husband's cousin's son heard us and went and got Timmy and said, "I'll take Timmy to my father's house. I'll take him." "OK," I said. "He's full drunk, he might hit him." After I gave Timmy to his cousin's son, I went back inside. My husband told me to shut the door. I wouldn't shut it so he did. I sat down on the bed. He started arguing more and got a knife and stabbed me. [Here Sunny shows me six scars on her arms and two on her legs.] And I was crying and I started to bleed, blood was all over the floor, bed, I was jumping, screaming, crying. My blood was on the wall. I ran outside now screaming and crying and his cousin's wife saw me. "What's wrong?" "He stabbed me with the knife." And he was fighting with his [other] cousin now and her husband. And they started arguing about me and I was running and I saw him chasing me with that same knife. His cousin was there and she asked her husband, "What's wrong?" They looked down the road and they saw him chasing me. I ran to [my uncle's] house. I saw [my uncle] there. He said, "You stand behind my back," and he said to my husband, "You come close, I'll hit you." But my husband didn't listen. He came forward and punched me and when he punched me I bled more. [My uncle] told his eldest sister, my sister-in-law, "Take her to the hospital." And she did. First he told her to wash me and she washed me, but the blood was still running and after that we went. And he had a fight, [my uncle] hit [my husband] from the step, and [my husband] fell down and he was bleeding then and [my uncle's] two wives talked for their cousin, growled at [my uncle], but my uncle said, "He is wrong, he stabbed her."

I was in hospital and we rang the police and the police came there and checked up. They didn't fix me at the mission, they fixed me at the mining town. [My sister-in-law] and I were in front of the police car and my husband was in the back of the same car and we went to the hospital and the [nursing] sister fixed me and did the stitches. The police took me to the police station to put the statement and I put the statement and I didn't go to court. He went to trial for stabbing me and they gave him one more chance.

That was on Sunday afternoon that one. And on Monday morning a charter came from here, the pilot came to get me, me and my kid. [My two fathers] sent it for me. And they told me, "Don't go back to him." And I said, "OK," and I didn't. I didn't go back. And maybe I stayed here at Mangrove for three or four months time. Then I went to [another settlement]. And I stayed there a couple of weeks. And [one of my fathers] went with a charter to get me from [that settlement]. Because [my husband] came from his settlement. He came from his settlement and I didn't know he was at Mangrove. So I came back and some girls told me "Your husband is here." And I said, "I don't want to go back to him. I've been having trouble and arguing, I don't want to go back now."

After a while I made up my mind again and I went back with that man. And that was his last chance. I told him, "You do that again, you do that again, and I'll leave you forever." I told him. But he still kept drinking. He kept going to [the other settlement] for beer and I heard the news now for him. He was mucking around with another girl there and they told me. And I just rolled his swag [bedding and personal belongings] and sent it over to him. But his cousin was here, she came to get his clothes, too. But she told me, "It's alright, you can leave him, because he is tricking you and always drunk, arguing." And I told her, too. After that I went, three months later, to my aunties. I went to [an outstation]. And I stayed there maybe one month only. And my aunties sent me back and I stayed here now. And I was staying with my other aunties and I didn't have a problem now that I left him.

When I got back I started looking around now for another man and I made friends with [my new husband]. So we were making friends with each other and we had a little talk. I wanted to marry him and he told me "You ask your family, if they say OK you can tell me." And I talked to them and they said OK and I told him, "Now you go ask your family, too." So he flew over to [the other settlement] and talked to his family and they said "OK, you can get her." And we started living together now and we stay here now. And my family told me, "He doesn't argue with you, he stays with you and he doesn't drink much." They asked me, "He argue with you?" "No, he doesn't. But when I got married to that other one, I had a big problem. That one I got now, he's a good man. He doesn't run away or tease me or drink. When he feels like going away to drink he goes only for one day and comes back." "That's a good man you've got." I don't have a problem now. We are living together good now.

Social Support for Victims of Male Aggression

Unlike Hedda Nussbaum, there were many people to help and protect Sunny from the worst effects of her husband's attack. Her husband's cousins and members of their households and Sunny's uncle and sister-in-law were immediately aware of the fight and willing and able to punish Sunny's husband and protect her. The only people mentioned in this account who might have been willing for Sunny to return to her husband were the "European" police who gave him "one more chance." Sunny's family was not willing for her to remain with her husband, however, and backed up their advice to leave him with a chartered airplane to bring her and her son back to Mangrove. When Sunny talks about the pilot coming just to get her and Timmy, we catch a glimpse of what it must mean to have kin send such a strong, clear message of protection and support.

Even Sunny's husband acted to protect her. According to her account, he was alone with her in a house with a closed door, he had a knife, and he was drunk. Yet he did not stab her in any vital spot; he chose instead to strike at her arms and legs, areas of the body that are prescribed targets according to the rules of fighting (chap. 4). Even drunk and with no one to remind or restrain him, Sunny's husband followed the rules.[5] What rules was Steinberg following when he ruptured Nussbaum's spleen?

Mangrove's "European" nursing sisters have treated a number of women with stab wounds like Sunny's, so many, apparently, that they have come to call the upper arms and legs "punishment places." When other women have been abused by husbands or lovers as Sunny was, reactions are similar. Neighbors and relatives restrain the man, protect the woman, and advise her to leave. When, like Sunny (and Hedda), these women return to men who abuse them, others are still there to help. Here is a another example of help and advice given to women whose husbands attack them.

[A woman and her second husband] had a fight on Friday. He cut her on her mouth and then [a man] growled at him and hunted him away. They are close family. [She] was sent to the hospital but she came back and went back to [her husband]. We told her not to go back to him. "Next time he will kill you dead."

Like Sunny and this woman, women at Mangrove do not always follow the advice of kin who tell them to leave an attacker. At least, not right away. One of the most disturbing—and controversial—questions about wife battering in America, for it can be interpreted as a form of "blaming the victim" (Bograd 1988), is why women stay with men who batter. As NiCarthy (1987) has pointed out, this question requires many different kinds of answers, answers that focus on such diverse areas as institutionalized sexism in the political or economic realm and individual psychology. It has been obvious to many activists and researchers in America, however, that first such women must have some place to go.

The women of Mangrove do have some place to go. They are often already there—living in the homes of their parents or other close relatives. They need only get their husbands to leave; like Sunny, they can simply roll up the man's swag. Nor is life without a husband necessarily bleak, as I have argued. Economically, the men of Mangrove seem to make little difference in the lives of their wives and children. Leaving a husband may, nevertheless, be a difficult experience for women at Mangrove. Like women elsewhere, fear may be a factor affecting a woman's decision to leave a husband who attacks her (Martin 1976). For example:

The other day [a woman] came to see her son. She is staying at [an outstation] now with [her second husband]. [Her first husband] was drunk and was trying to shoot her and the children. She ran to [a neighbor's] house and someone grabbed the rifle. He is in jail now for a long time. They let him out to go to his father's funeral. But the policeman was there with him. She is afraid he will come back here. That is why she stays away.

But the women of Mangrove do not appear to stay for long in relationships in which they are continuously attacked. During each visit, I recorded a number of fights between couples—many in which women were attacked by their husbands. But from one trip to the next, these were almost never the same men and women. On each subsequent visit, couples who had fought a great deal had either separated or were no longer fighting. Myrna Tonkinson (1985) has made this point about violence between Aboriginal men and women across Australia. But when a woman stays and the fights cease, what does this mean? Fearing male aggression, some women may modify their behavior, though it may be no coincidence that the following words were spoken by a woman discussing not herself and her husband but her brother and sister-in-law.

[My sister-in-law] used to always be like that, growling at her husband. But then her husband cut her on the leg. She had to go to the hospital. She learned her lesson, and now she doesn't growl at him. She's good now.

Women also say that as men grow older, they are less likely to become jealous and get angry with their wives (Burbank 1988). But a conversation that I had with a young married woman suggests a third alternative.

AW: I used to have fights with my husband, before we had [our children]. He used to think about other men staring at me and he used to see them and get jealous and we used to fight inside the house. . . . He used to hit me and I used to grab him by the hair or sometimes scratch his face, sometimes hit him with a stick, not a nulla nulla, but just any stick. . . . He used to lock me up in the house. Tell me not to come out. These days I have free time and go out with other girls, talk, tell stories. Before he used to never let me go with other girls.

VKB: Why is he not locking you up now?

AW: Maybe he's giving up. He knows I know how to fight back. When I get a stick I just go ahead, I don't pull back, I just let go.

Mangrove is a community like any other insofar as it is made up of diverse individuals with their own unique powers of understanding, motives, needs, strengths, and weaknesses. Some women, at least during some periods in their lives, may be more willing than others to stay with men who attack them. But even when women are willing to stay and risk attack, their attitude is not necessarily colored by submission or masochism. Sometimes male aggression makes women angry. For example, after a woman fighting with another was attacked by the brother of her opponent, she threatened to really fight with him, with a nulla nulla, if he did not leave her alone. Sometimes women even find male aggression funny.

On Friday night [two women] bathed and dressed and polished [their finger-nails]. When Rosalind asked them where they were going and they said, "Out," she said if they went near that hill, [the former husband of one of the women] would strike them. And sure enough, they were walking along and he came at them with a [fence picket]. He tried to hit [his former wife] on the head, but he missed. Then he hit her backbone. Then he tried to stab her on the top of the head with the picket, but [the other woman] grabbed it and hit him in the chest with it and he fell down and they ran away. [The two women] were crying and screaming and when Rosalind heard them she started to laugh. And the next day when [the former wife] saw Rosalind, she was laughing and told her, "You told us it would happen."

Men, Women, and Supernatural Aggression

In addition to attacking women physically and verbally, men at Mangrove also attack women using supernatural means. Men may "curse" women. They do so if their advances are rejected by a woman they desire as a wife or sexual partner. They may also curse a wife who runs off with another man.

A man wanted to take [a woman] as a second wife. She told him, "No, I don't want you." And maybe she swore at him. He cursed her, to that country. That meant she might die. She cried and cried.

The act of cursing appears simple. I am told that an aggressor simply says that a woman is cursed to a ceremony or to a certain sacred area in a country. By this act, the cursed woman is removed from the world of the ordinary. She becomes sacred and by association "dangerous," as does everything she might touch. She cannot sit, stand, or lean on any-thing without spreading the sacred domain. She must, consequently, stay by herself and not come in contact with areas, objects, food, or water used by other people. She uses only her own clothing, blanket, and cup—much like a person in quarantine. She is in danger of im-pending death, and almost anyone who might touch her is similarly threatened.

Not only women are targets; objects like buildings and vehicles, ani-mals, and places may also be cursed. Something can be "put the way of" a dead person, a ceremony, or the sacred area of a country. The presence of the dead or sacred has been called to the person, animal, object, or place and must be treated accordingly.

The act of cursing replicates conditions associated with death, ceremonies, and sacred areas. Similarly, the rules for dealing with cursing replicate rules governing death, ceremonies, and sacred areas. For example, when an adult dies, people who call the deceased by certain kin terms (including those for "mother," "father," "mother's brother," and "father's sister") can manipulate the body, place it on a platform for desiccation, or prepare it for burial. Only such people can dispose of or use the dead person's possessions. However, people whom the deceased called by certain terms (including "mother," "father," "mother's brother," and "father's sister") cannot approach the body. When something is put the way of a dead person, these same rules apply. Similarly, as adult men may approach and witness a certain ceremony, so may they come into contact with something cursed with that ceremony. Such men, for example, may drink water that has been "put ceremony way." Younger men, women, and children who cannot see the ceremony cannot drink the water either. Men who call a country "mother," "mother's mother," or "father's mother" are regarded as its *junggayi*, or "boss," and may approach sacred areas there (see Biernoff 1978; Maddock 1974). They may also approach objects, people, and places that have been cursed with this country. Men and women may use a dead person in a curse. Only men, specifically junggayi, should put something the way of a ceremony or a country.

The same categories of people who can put a curse on something can remove it. This may or may not be the same individual. Seniority comes into play when a curse has been placed and people want to clear it away. If it has been placed by a very senior man, it cannot be removed without his permission. If a more junior man has placed it, however, his seniors may remove it without his permission.

A woman who has been cursed can be cleared by being washed in fresh water, rubbed with red ocher and white paint, and placed in the smoke of a fire. I was told that this is done by a woman who calls the country or ceremony used in the curse "mother" or "mother's mother," that is, a female junggayi of the ceremony or country. However, in several cases, men were said to have cleared curses from women. I was told that the clearing takes place inside a circular enclosure made of blankets or canvas. This is not necessary if the woman who has been cursed is given as a wife to a man who calls the ceremony or country "mother's mother." By "sleeping" with her, he removes the curse, though one woman said he may also rub her with red ocher.

Cursing, employed as it is at Mangrove today, is, according to Aboriginal people, an innovation of settlement life. Once, said an older man, the only things cursed were dugong, large manateelike aquatic mammals hunted by men at Mangrove. Cursing took place when a man danced "really beautifully" at a ceremony.[6] A woman told me that a man might also curse the dugong after a dream. The junggayi would eat the first animal caught after the curse had been placed; after this, all could eat dugong flesh.

According to mission journals and reports, the first curse employed at Mangrove occurred in 1971 when a "spell" was placed on the shop and cistern. In 1972, another spell was placed on the water. In 1973, following the theft of a tractor by some of the young men and misbehavior on the part of some adolescent girls, a member of the Aboriginal "Security Force" that then patrolled the settlement placed a curse on the outdoor movie area. The curse remained from May 13 to 18. Then it was lifted. In the meantime, the area was unusable, and the scheduled movie could not be shown. The use of this curse as punishment, for so it was intended according to the man who placed it, highlights one aspect of Aboriginal social control that is useful for understanding something of the present-day context of aggression at Mangrove. Recognized means of coercion, control, and punishment, whether supernatural devices or physical actions, are not the monopoly of a few. I have argued throughout this chapter that it is this quotidian and, in a sense, egalitarian aspect of aggressive behavior that contributes to women's relative fearlessness when faced with male aggression. It is unlikely that there is any adult at Mangrove, male or female, who cannot legitimately place a curse. Nevertheless, as a rule, cursing is something that men do to women, not vice versa.

Men do not curse women very often. Over the years that I have been visiting Mangrove, I have been told of thirteen occasions when women have been cursed, but some of these occurred before 1977, and in one instance a woman was cursed by her mother. The women of Mangrove were cursed by men residing on the settlement and by men of nearby communities. The desire to take a woman as a wife is a predominant reason for cursing women. This reason was attributed to seven cases. In two instances, women were cursed because men were intoxicated; in the three other cases, women were cursed for reasons I have summarized as "premarital sexual behavior," "misbehavior," and "jealousy of a married partner."

No woman was cursed in 1988. This may be a chance occurrence, or it may represent a change in men's tactics. In none of the cases that I recorded were women given to the men who cursed them, though in many instances this was the stated motive for placing the curse. It may be that the men of Mangrove are learning that cursing does not lead to getting what they want, at least when what they want is a specific woman.

It is ironic that the one instance in which a curse resulted in a marriage that was not of a woman's choosing occurred when she was cursed by her mother. Women may use curses, but when they do, they usually curse objects and places rather than people. I have never heard of a woman cursing a man. There is no indication that women even regard this as a possibility. The woman who was cursed by her mother had been seeing an inappropriate marriage partner, a young man whom her mother did not want her to marry. As the account goes, the mother "put" her daughter to her own country in order to force her to marry a man of the mother's choosing. This strategy worked, but it is "dangerous." Not only are women not supposed to employ country in their curses, no one is supposed to use their own country in a curse. This is something that could lead to "trouble," and it seems no other woman has thought it a precedent worth following.

Although women do not curse men, they may cause them annoyance and inconvenience by cursing objects and places. One woman told me that women may also curse their own hands. Husbands are then unable to eat food that they cook. The women can cleanse the curse from their hands by rubbing them in red ocher and then hitting them with a leafy branch that has been held in the smoke of a fire. I did not hear of any actual cases of this.

"MURDER" AND "TROUBLE"

In chapter 4, I discussed aspects of women's theories of aggressive behavior that embrace the supernatural as a source of cause and effect. A man, this theory would hold, who was apparently killed by a shark was really murdered by another's manipulation of supernatural elements. "Trouble" or "murder," as this form of aggression is generally called, is seen largely as a male activity (see Reid 1983; Kaberry 1939). A man might enlist the aid of his wife in a murder. By pretending desire, she can entice a victim into the bush where her husband is waiting to kill him. Otherwise, women do not usually murder. As Lily explained, "Women can't kill, they might cry and be sorry."

Women may, however, be the victims of this kind of supernatural aggression. When a woman died in 1988, people recalled that shortly before her death she had returned late from a favored fishing spot.

Yesterday all the men looking into the death went to the place she had been fishing. They found the place where they were fighting, two men and her. They saw her footprints, how she tried to get away, and they saw blood. They saw where the bushes were broken when she grabbed a hold of them, mangroves. They hit her with a big stick. I don't know how they can take away a woman's life. She has kids to look after.

Men's ability to manipulate the elements may also be used against women. For example, when his son's head was cut by another child, a man "rowed" with several mothers, presumably those of the children he thought had harmed his son. He cursed the playing cards and threatened to break a stone he had taken from his "uncle." This latter act would bring thunder and, as Tina exclaimed, "kill us all."

Often when supernatural aggression is being discussed, the word "someone" is used, as in "Maybe someone murdered her." From the context of women's remarks about this kind of aggression, I assume that most of the time they were talking of a male "someone." In a few instances, however, supernatural aggression has been attributed to women. Two women were accused of using fighting sticks that had been sung to bring illness or death to whomever might be struck. In neither accusation, however, was it explicitly stated that the wielder of the fighting stick had actually done the singing. In one case it was said that the woman's mother and father knew that kind of song. Three other women were said to have used a Dreaming site of which they were junggayi to harm women with whom they had been fighting.

Once, an old woman announced that she had brought the rain of a previous day because a neighbor's son had been hurt in a fight. She had stopped the rain, she said, because the young man's assailant was not at Mangrove at the time. This woman possesses a number of songs and other means of manipulating disease, body functions, and the elements. I know that at least one other woman regards her as exceptional because she has such knowledge. I expect other people at Mangrove would agree with this assessment. Unlike most of the women at Mangrove, her ancestors come from a country some miles to the south of the settlement. She is the only women I ever saw called on to cure illness.

But in only one of these cases—the old woman's rain—were men the targets of aggression. I do not know if other women at Mangrove ever consider working what little supernatural ills they may know on male victims.[7] In the literature on Aboriginal Australia, there are occasional references to women's use of the supernatural against men. Myers (1986), for example, reports an incident in which Pintupi men worried that a man might become the target of women's sorcery. According to Bell (1983:37), Warrabi women, though no longer able to "send men up in a 'puff of smoke' " as they no longer have access to the sites where this power resides, can "still inflict a lingering illness and death." In the Kimberleys, if a menstruating woman is angry, she may touch a man's belongings and thus bring illness to him (Kaberry 1939).

It is said that Central Australian men who accidentally stumble on women's secret rituals risk illness or even death (Hamilton 1981a). It is not clear if illness and death result from women's active agency with the supernatural or simply as a result of contact with the power of the Dreaming. But this raises an important question: To what extent is the ability to manipulate the supernatural in mundane contexts a function of an individual's ritual status and knowledge of the sacred? Discussions of sorcery at Mangrove often include mention of ceremony. For example, "trouble" may come to a person or a member of his close family if he makes a mistake during a ritual or breaks the Law during or after its performance. However, it is not clear if the techniques for bringing illness or death necessarily derive their power from the Dreaming.

Multiple sources of supernatural power are found in other Arnhem Land communities. Speaking of supernatural forms of aggression among the "Murngin," for example, Warner (1937:218–219) distinguishes "ritual power" from "magic." The former is derived from the sacred totemic well and its associated rituals and objects; the latter, from the equally sacred dead. At Yirkalla, Aboriginal people told Janice Reid (1983) that such power is derived from spirits, some of whom are from the Dreaming and some of whom are not.

Reid has observed that sorcery accusations at Yirkalla are statements about social relations. Insofar as discussions of supernatural aggression at Mangrove make similar kinds of declarations, the message seems clear: men "murder" women, but women do not "murder" men. What is not clear is why women do not murder. Is it because they "feel sorry," as Lily tells us? Or is it because they do not have equal access to the power to do murder, excluded as they are from major sources of supernatural power—the totemic mysteries, rites, and sacred objects—controlled by men?

WOMEN'S FEAR OF SUPERNATURAL AGGRESSION

People at Mangrove, men and women alike, appear to be frightened of supernatural aggression. For example, following a death attributed to sorcery, a number of people apparently thought they might be next. One young man was reportedly walking around with a "tomahawk" tucked in his belt. Elder kinsmen had sent another away from the settlement and, they hoped, the danger. Rosalind said that she did not like to visit me after dark because she saw a man lurking in the shadows of a nearby community building. The context in which this remark was made suggested that she was afraid of "murder," not a physical attack. One of my neighbors told his wife that if she must open the door at night, she should stand back from it in case someone was waiting outside to "murder" her. A young mother expressed a desire to leave Mangrove for a European center where they do not "murder secret way."

At least some women may fear supernatural aggression more than physical attack. In 1988, I asked five women if seven kinds of aggressive acts frightened them "not at all," "a little bit," or "a lot." Being cursed frightened them all a lot. In contrast, only one woman said that being hit with a stick would frighten her a lot. None of the women said that someone wrestling with them would frighten them a lot.[8] I also asked which of the seven acts would be most frightening. Only one women did not include being cursed in her answer. Two of the other four who included being cursed also said that a gun being fired in the air and being chased with a spear frightened them the most. I think the equation these women made between guns, spears, and curses, all of which are usually men's weapons, indicate how frightening the supernatural can be; their answers suggest that being cursed is seen as a matter of life and death.

Women at Mangrove are not the only people in the world to draw parallels between physical and supernatural aggression. Laurence Carruci (1990:108; see also Carruci 1992) has said of the Marshallese, "In indigenous terms malevolent magic and physical violence are equatable." The language used to speak of the two kinds of aggression is the same. There, however, it is women who possess the means of magic, and people fear this magic more than they fear men's violence.

Women's talk at Mangrove also indicates that they anticipate supernatural attacks as a consequence of displeasing men. Here, for example, Lily speaks about the potential dangers of widowhood.

A good woman is one that never goes away, who stays with her husband when he is old, never goes away. If a woman leaves a *mardayin* man, especially when he is old, and the man dies she won't get a string [a fiber necklace worn by widows]. She will die. That is really dangerous. That string keeps the widow from dying. A mardayin man has gray hair, he is one that follows the Law, he has everything, not just gray hair. . . . [A woman] left one and she won't get a string. People will remember a woman who stays with her husband. A widow who runs around with men when she has a string will have murderers sent to her. If she runs around they will kill her. Two or three men will go away and kill that woman or the man she is with. They kill her with a [metal spear] but we don't know how. They use a special kind of thing to kill.

Once I asked Rosalind, "If a young girl wants to get married and have kids and three men want to marry her—a young boy, one who is a little bit older, and an old man—which should she marry?" Rosalind chose the "young boy." But her answer included the following reservations.

Sometimes, if a young boy takes a girl away, maybe an old man makes a fight, just because that girl doesn't like him and maybe that man says, "Oh, she doesn't like me, I'm going to do something to her," get her dress or thongs [sandals] and put them somewhere [use sorcery on them] to take that girl's life away, maybe.

In the 1980s, people at Mangrove seemed to be getting tired of cursing. Some individuals were taking steps to minimize the inconvenience it caused. For example, in 1981 when one of the health workers was cursed by a man in a nearby settlement, because he hoped to take her as a wife, a junggayi at Mangrove rubbed her from finger to elbow so that she could continue treating patients. Such steps seem to lessen the psychological impact of being cursed, at least for some women. Just a few months after the health worker was cursed, a local man cursed three adolescents whom, people said, he hoped to marry. For reasons that were not explained to me, the girls were rubbed, like the health worker, from their fingers to their elbows. Perhaps this is why the curse did not appear to frighten or intimidate at least two of the girls.

[The two adolescent girls] keep walking around. They don't have sense. They don't think about their mother and father. They just think about boys. They think it's funny. [One girl] is still seeing [her boyfriend]. [A woman] was talking to those two yesterday. They just keep walking around. [The woman] told them that Dreaming is for that old man and if they keep walking around he won't block for them. They will die. He will just let them kill them. Lots of women have talked to them, but they don't have ears.

One day in 1978, I accompanied a group of women into the bush to hunt goanna, a large lizard with succulent meat. As we sat by our evening fire following the day's hunting, Tina told us that this was the place of a "devil devil," what we might call a "ghost." Her sister and a friend had heard it cough on a previous visit. But another in our party said, "Don't think about devil devil, think about God." The incident suggests why cursing and other forms of supernatural aggression may not hold the same fear for all woman at Mangrove. The effects of Western ideologies on the cognitive salience and emotional internalization of the Dreaming have been discussed by many (see, e.g., Myers 1980; Reid 1983; Sackett 1978; Stanner 1966). Christianity, of course, has its own long history as a belief system that has been, and still is, used to frighten and intimidate. But, currently, the teaching of Christianity and the beliefs of non-Christian whites provide alternatives that may lessen the intellectual impact of precontact ideologies. It is not surprising that after more than thirty years of being told that "devil devils" and "murderers" do not exist, some women at Mangrove may not believe in them. What is more interesting is that so many people on the settlement apparently continue to fear supernatural aggression (see Reid 1983, for a discussion of this topic at Yirkalla).

As I mentioned above, few women have been cursed. Similarly, few of the illnesses and deaths of women have been attributed, at least in my presence, to the supernatural. I have heard people attribute many more men's deaths to sorcery. This leads me to believe that more suspicion attaches to male death, reflecting, I suggest, not a greater concern with male mortality but a greater association between men and violent death. Nevertheless, at least some women at Mangrove may fear supernatural aggression as much as or more than some forms of physical attack. Men, more than women, that is, are associated with supernatural aggression. This translates into a fear of male aggression and leads to a question similar to that asked in the case of physical aggression: To what extent do women subordinate or abandon their own interests when these conflict with those of men, because they fear that men will use supernatural means to bring about their injury or death?

Evidence of such fear is abundant, but evidence that fear actually changes or inhibits women's behavior is not easy to find. Still, an occasional comment indicates that this may happen.

That old man was fighting with [his two sisters] because [one of their daughters] was running around [with boys] too much. He hit [one sister] and she was crying, but she didn't hit him back because he does a lot of "business" [ritual activity].

Speaking of a woman who had left an old man and the supernatural penalties that might follow, Tina remarked, "He is blind and weak in the knees. I'd mind that kind [of man] all the way."

Conclusion

I have argued that the women of Mangrove, though targets of male aggression, are not necessarily subordinated or victimized by male physical attack. There may be "batterers" at Mangrove, but there are not many, if any, "battered women" (in the sense that writers like Walker [1979, 1984] have portrayed them); the women I know at Mangrove have not learned "helplessness." These women see men's aggressive behavior not as a means of dominating them but as expressions of anger, expressions that are an expected and accepted part of daily life for both men and women. And women are prepared for male attacks; they know how to fight back. Perhaps most important, they also know that others are there to protect them if there is any danger that men may seriously hurt them.

Cowlishaw (1979:236) has said of male aggression in Aboriginal Australia that it is "neither the cause nor the condition of the continued subordination of women." Instead, she argues, it is "the sign of the weakness in the pattern of male hegemony." In a similar vein, Judith Okely (1989:6) interprets Aboriginal women's fights with men "as a momentary *resistance* to their fundamental subordination" (see also Lateef 1990, 1992). Cowlishaw, along with others (e.g., Bern 1979; Hamilton 1981a; Hiatt 1985; Maddock 1972), identifies the source of men's domination in their control of the religious mysteries of Aboriginal society. That is to say, it is the male monopoly of a body of ideas, not male possession of a body of superior strength and force, that underlies Aboriginal women's subordination. In Aboriginal Australia it may be, as Maccoby and Jacklin (1974) have suggested of people in general, that brute force has always been superseded by subtler means of domination.

Westerners might see the harm that physical attack can do as more "real" than any sorcerer's magic. But at Mangrove, ideas can be at least as frightening, if not more, than a physical assault. Returning to Western women, it has been argued that ideas—even more than physical injury—are what keep some women in bondage to abusive partners. In the Western case, it is not ideas about the supernatural but ideas about relationships between men and women that bind women to the men who hurt them (e.g., Hirsch 1981).

Hamilton (1981a:75) links men's superior physical power with their superordinate position in at least some domains of Aboriginal society when she says, "This power of men over women is expressed ultimately in physical force. Women who violate the secrecy of men's ritual, even inadvertently, may be punished by gang rape or death. Women have no equivalent power of punishment over men." The question remains, however. Can men punish women because of their superior physical powers or because of their superior ritual powers—the creation not of brute strength but of culture (see also Mukhopadhyay and Higgins 1988; Smuts 1992). Or to put this another way, is male social superiority merely a reflection of biology? Is bigger really better? There is, in fact, intriguing evidence that humans perceive what is biggest as what is best (Handwerker and Crosbie 1982; Kohlberg 1966). We must listen, however, to a commonplace of today's feminism (e.g., Connell 1987; Errington 1990; Fausto-Sterling 1985; Flax 1987a, 1990): much is missed if what seem to be "natural" facts are not examined in social terms. Rosaldo (1980a:397) was one of the first to decide that biological sex is more of an excuse than a cause of sexual asymmetries—asymmetries, she asserts, that are not "natural" but rather "a by-product . . . of nonnecessary institutional arrangements that could be addressed through political struggle." When it is so unclear (as it is in the case of Mangrove) whether ideas or raw strength give male aggression an edge, we can afford to ignore neither the biological nor the power of culture and the ways in which human perception is channeled.

Ideas about what should and should not happen to people, and the behavioral expressions of these ideas, create an environment at Mangrove in which the superior physical strength of men has less effect than it might in other social circumstances. The fact that women of Mangrove willingly attack men or fight back—which, I argue, makes a difference to the physical and psychological integrity of these women—can be seen as a creation of these social circumstances. These women know that the actions of others will compensate for their relative lack of strength in physical contests with men.

At Mangrove, ideas also have the potential to protect women from other ideas—ideas that supernatural forces may be set in motion to harm or kill. I close this chapter with the words of the old and knowledgeable woman. Her sister had told her that there was a devil devil near her camp. This was her response.

I am not afraid. I have lots of songs and I have never seen a devil devil. I have been all over the bush and I have never been killed by one. I don't have to move camp even though a devil devil has been here because I have lots of songs. I also have a lot of dogs. If you are frightened, you can die at anytime. If you are not frightened, you live until you just grow weak. I'm not frightened, I can go anywhere.

7

Conclusion

The Cultural Construction of Anger and Aggression

I have described aggressive behavior displayed by men and women in a small Aboriginal community in Arnhem Land, Australia; I have explored women's experiences of aggression both as aggressors and as victims; and I have looked at ways in which Western theories, metaphors, and stereotypes channel our understanding of gender and aggression. This effort has taken place largely within a framework based on the idea that gender is a system in which unequal power relations are constructed, maintained, and challenged by mundane interactions between and among the sexes (Connell 1987; Flax 1990; Gal 1991; Gordon 1990; Rosaldo 1980*a*).

My analyses of "fight stories" at Mangrove suggest that aggression in this community springs from a multiplicity of motives and represents a variety of strategies for both the situationally powerful and the situationally powerless. Relying heavily on the words of many woman and a few men, I have interpreted various aggressive acts in this community as examples of competition, dominance attempts, or attempts to resist domination; I have interpreted them as a means of punishing others, of taking revenge, and of defending self or other. I have interpreted aggressive acts as instruments of authority and as instruments for the violation of authority. Most important, I have interpreted acts of aggression as expressions of anger.

Over the years since I first visited Mangrove, I have come to understand aggression as an intrinsic part of anger. My interpretations of Aboriginal women's experiences of aggressive behavior rest on this conceptual confluence. I have argued that it is this construction that underlies the rules and expectations that guide aggressive manifestations and protect its victims. It is also in this construction of anger and aggression that women's stance as aggressors rather than as victims has its genesis.

In my white middle-class version of Western society, anger is a resource only for the powerful (see Frost and Averill 1982, for an overview of this perspective). "Anger"—the emotion we associate with aggression—stands in a peculiar relationship to "the emotional woman"; it is an emotion she is denied (Lutz 1988, 1990). As Stephanie Shields (1987:235) puts it, "the emotional female is not the angry female." This is not to say that women in our society do not experience anger; there is considerable evidence that they do (e.g., Frost and Averill 1982; Kopper and Epperson 1991; Shields 1991). It can be said, however, that the legitimacy of their experience—particularly the manner in which they might express this emotion—is more likely to be called into question, if not by others, then by themselves (Lerner 1985). For example, women politicians agreed that similar displays of anger in men and women are judged differently; in men, anger is interpreted as a sign of conviction, whereas in women, anger is interpreted as a sign of instability (*New York Times*, February 12, 1979, in Hochschild 1983). Another example is provided by a study of sex differences in anger (Frost and Averill 1982). Its authors conclude that the "results lend only modest support to the notion that women and men differ markedly in their everyday experience of anger" (291). However, they also report that "women were more likely to report that their anger was greater than the incident called for" (290) and that women were less likely to be "overtly aggressive in the expression of their anger" (297).

In scientific and political realms, our society's denial of women's anger has been explained in terms of biological sex differences (Lutz 1990). A growing literature proposes that we look at women's anger, or lack of anger, with reference to women's subordinate position in American society—an alternative with clear feminist implications (Frost and Averill 1982). It has been observed that insofar as American women are "*culturally* inhibited from expressing anger," they are constituted as " 'less equal' than men" (Myers 1988:600). According to Carol Tavris (1982:198), women have an "anger problem," not because they do not get angry but because they are more likely to occupy a position subordinate to that of the people with whom they are angry. "Most people," she continues, "have difficulty expressing anger to others of high status, especially when those others have the power to administer raises, pink slips, tickets, or contempt-of-court citations." Jean Baker Miller (1991:183) suggests that processes suppressing the anger of subordinates are both violent and insidious. Those in positions of dominance fear this anger, she says, and repress it with violence by threatening to withhold economic and social resources and by saying there is "something *wrong*" with a subordinate who feels anger. According to Lutz (1990:78), because we accept emotions as "natural," "emotion discourses may be one of the most likely and powerful devices by which domination proceeds." She has also observed a feminist strategy of reconceptualizing emotions as "a discourse on problems" (88) and has interpreted the suppression of emotions as the suppression of political discourse. Insofar as we constitute anger as a means of perceiving "that something is wrong—something hurts—and needs changing" (Miller 1991:188), we can say that our constructions of gender and anger deny women an important means of perceiving their relationship to the world (Lutz 1990).

Is overt aggression also a resource to which the white middle-class woman is denied legitimate access?[1] Some might argue that women are no more denied the use of aggression than are men. For example, Jan Stets and Murray Straus (1990:162–163) claim that "probably millions of girls have been told by their mother, 'If he gets fresh, slap him.' There is hardly a day in which such ritualized 'slap the cad' type of behavior is not presented as an implicit model to millions of women in one television show, movie, or novel." Presenting a small and predominantly female group of students with a scenario in which aggression begins when a husband criticizes his wife's cooking, then escalates to the point of physical attack, Linda Harris, Kenneth Gergen, and John Lannamann (1986) found that participants thought the woman's aggression both probable and desirable. Certainly, many would say, our society expects, if not demands, that women punish children (e.g., Straus 1980).

But we must also ask how women experience their use of overt aggression. Here some of the findings of a recent meta-analysis of sex differences research are relevant.

[This meta-analysis] demonstrates that women and men think differently about aggression and suggests that these differing beliefs are important mediators of sex differences in aggressive behavior. Women reported more guilt and anxiety as a consequence of aggression, more vigilance about the harm that aggression causes its victims, and more concern about the danger that their aggression might bring to themselves. (Eagly and Steffen 1986:325; see also Frodi, Macaulay, and Thome, 1977)

What are the sources of the unease women feel about their own aggression? Assuming here, as I have in the case of Aboriginal women, that our ethnotheories about gender and aggression are a critical part of our experience, the importance of rendering these beliefs explicit becomes apparent (see Lutz 1985, 1988). Acknowledging the epistemological interplay between popular stereotypes and empirical research on gender and aggression, Jacqueline Macaulay has derived a list of our ideological constructs about women and aggression from the research literature, conversations with psychologists and "nonpsychologists," "fiction, women's magazines, the Sunday papers," and other unspecified sources. Her list is as follows.

1. Women are innately nonaggressive. . . .
2. Women express their anger in "sneaky" ways. Their aggressive behavior is "indirect" and verbal, meaning that women aggress without using physical violence or that women cover up their aggression with prosocial explanations. . . .
3. Women are unable to express anger because they have been trained to repress anger, or because they are innately passive, or both. . . .
4. Women are prone to sudden, unexpected bursts of "fury"—with fury defined as near-violence or actual violence. . . . These bursts are sometimes viewed as irrational overreactions to minor slights, teasing, etc. There is a hydraulic analogy being made here, possibly related to the belief that women are trained to "repress anger." . . .
5. Angry women are sick and in need of psychological treatment, especially if "passive aggressive" (a clinician's epithet for a style of aggression involving mild verbal aggression and deprivation that can sometimes amount to psychological torture). This follows from both (1) and (3): Angry women are having identity problems, are rejecting their proper sex role, are being poisoned by bottled-up anger, or are being destroyed by aggression turned inward—or all of these things at once. . . .
6. Women are fiercely aggressive in defense of their children. . . . This is a biological trait. A woman who could condone sexual or physical abuse of her child, then, is barely human.
7. Jealousy is a common source of women's aggression because women are very possessive of the men that they are attached to. This, too, may be a biological trait, related to women's biological role as child-bearer and child-nurturer. (Macaulay 1985:199–200)

The reader must, of course, judge the extent to which this list captures his or her ideas. It probably reflects white middle-class beliefs to a greater extent than those of other classes or ethnic groups.

Although women who kill or attempt to kill are sometimes sensationalized by the popular press, the topic of women's aggression is not one that often generates serious attention in Western society (Brown and Schuster 1986; Schuster 1983). Though our ideology often denies it, we "know" that women are aggressive, yet the magnitude of male aggression—it is men who usually kill—has largely allowed us to ignore women's potential for violence (Björkqvist and Niemelä 1992a). Mukhopadhyay and Higgins (1988) have observed that the Euro-American folk model discourages us from questioning gender scenarios that feature violent dominant males and passive female victims. There is a tendency to assume that because men are aggressive, women are not. The manner in which the "aggressive/passive" distinction "colonizes" (Strathern 1980 cited in Merlan 1988) other domains of our gender ideology suggests the centrality of this gender construct. For example, teenagers in the Midwest describe men's speech as "aggressive" and "forceful," while women's speech is described as "gentle" (Kramarae 1982 cited in Gal 1991). As is the case with anger, this dichotomy has largely been explained in terms of biological sex differences (see Lutz 1990; Macaulay 1985). Given our misunderstandings of what that means—for example, we misperceive biological attributes as immutable (Klama 1988)—women who display behavior defined as "aggressive" are seen as "unfeminine" or "unnatural" (see Flax 1987b, 1990; Jones 1980; Lutz 1990; Miller 1991). This ideological casting of women as nonaggressive victims can have practical ramifications, as when sympathy and support for battered women are threatened by a recognition of their own potential for violence (Breines and Gordon 1983; Gordon 1986). Yet the "passive," "gentle" female is an image that is hard for us to maintain; one needs only to look at the inconsistencies in Macaulay's list for examples of our difficulty (see Macaulay 1985). It begins with the assertion of innate female passivity but shortly afterward describes female "fury" and the fierce aggressiveness of women protecting their children.

The description and analyses that I have presented throughout these pages join those of others[2] in providing an empirical base, outside the research laboratory, that requires us to challenge our constructions of women as passive beings and to question the priorities of an ideology that renders them so. One of the most important contributions this exploration of anger, aggression, and gender can make is to emphasize how our understanding of gender and aggression is socially constructed. Women at Mangrove are, from time to time, angry and aggressive. But they are not regarded as "sick" by their community. Nor are their aggressive acts seen as "unexpected," "irrational," "unnatural," or "unfeminine" (see Cook 1993). For the most part, their anger is accepted as justified and its aggressive expression viewed as predictable. These are not women deviating from societal norms, "rejecting their proper sex role," or "having identity problems." Rather, they are women who are displeased with a turn of events and express their displeasure in culturally prescribed, culturally expected ways. Why are women at Mangrove so able to express their anger with aggressive acts? And what does this ability say about gender relations in this community? Are these women "more equal" than we are? I cannot say that I know why the women at Mangrove are not denied anger and aggression. But clearly Aboriginal constructions of anger, aggression, and gender must be a critical part of any answer to this question.

Aggressive Women, the Battered Husband Controversy, and "the Victim's Viewpoint"

What I have learned from women at Mangrove is this: women can be aggressive, and in being aggressive, they potentially augment rather than diminish themselves. But this is a message that is received and interpreted in the context of American gender relations toward the end of the twentieth century. Most critically, it is a message that is received by women isolated in the single parent and nuclear family households that characterize our "advanced" capitalistic society.

One of the most painful domains of Western gender relations—in a literal sense—is that of domestic violence. As the discussion of Lisa Steinberg and Hedda Nussbaum illustrates (chap. 6), the pain and injury suffered by women and children in the American household can be horrendous. I am sensible of the controversy that accompanied the publication of Steinmetz's (1977) work on "the battered husband syndrome" (see Breines and Gordon 1983; Flynn 1990; Saunders 1988 for overviews of this controversy). It is important to deflect those who might use the materials I have presented in these pages to undermine support for the victims of family violence or to justify violence against women (see Flynn 1990; Straus and Gelles 1986). To say that women can be aggressors is not to say they cannot also be victims. It must also be very clear that the sociocultural context in which Aboriginal women's aggression is enacted is radically different from the context in which an American woman faces a male aggressor.

Straus and Gelles (1990*b*:105) have said that women's violence "is a critically important issue for the well-being *of women*." I agree. Women's violence in our society is dangerous for women, they continue, because it "sets the stage" for severe male violence against them. With women's well-being in mind, I would add two further reasons for attending not just to women's violence but to women's aggression in general. I introduce these two reasons with the words of Jane Flax, who, warning us against the dangers of succumbing to "the victim's viewpoint," says, "We need to avoid seeing women as totally innocent, acted upon beings. Such a view prevents us from seeing the areas of life in which women have had an effect, are not totally determined by the will of the other, and the ways in which some women have and do exert power over others" (1990:181–182).

To begin with Flax's last point, women are often victimized by the aggression of other women. My cross-cultural survey (Burbank 1987*b*) of 317 societies in the Human Relations Areas File suggests how widespread this pattern may be. In 91 percent of the 137 societies in which women's aggression was found, women attack other women. Schuster has taken a detailed look at the harm women can do to each other. In a series of papers on this theme (Glazer 1992; Schuster 1983, 1985; Schuster and Hartz-Karp 1986), she discusses ways in which women's aggressive interactions harm women beyond the immediate hurt of the actions themselves. For example, the "political harassment" that elite Zambian women direct at others "sanctions, and may even be said to provoke, male violence directed against subelite women" (Schuster 1983:329, 1985). On an Israeli kibbutz, she and Hartz-Karp (1986:192) identify "verbal violence," that is, "bickering, quarreling, gossiping, criticism, and ostracism," as the "spiteful" vehicle by which women prevent others from occupying prestigious positions and from rising in the gender hierarchy. With Wahiba Abu Ras (in press), she contends that women's "aggressive gossip" invites the murder of a young bride in an Arab village. Though her theoretical focus lies elsewhere, Caroline Bledsoe (1984, 1993) writes in a similar vein of the multiple effects of women's aggression in two African societies. For example, she suggests that the often aggressive competition between

Mende co-wives has enabled men to avoid providing their wives and children with economic support (Bledsoe 1993). Jane Collier (1974) and Karen Sacks (in Brown 1992) have suggested that patriarchal power is preserved by hostility between women and their daughters-in-law.

Attending to women's aggressive potential not only attunes us to the potential harm women can do each other but also allows us to nurture what I have come to think of as an "aggressive stance." I again use the work of Flax (1987b) to elaborate my meaning; here I use her discussion of gendered repression. Intrapsychic conflicts, she says, with reference to psychoanalytic theory, especially those between individual attributes and cultural prohibitions, are resolved by "repression." This is an ongoing process whereby unacceptable aspects of the self become and remain unconscious. We can think of repression as more than an individual or personal experience insofar as there exist gender-specific patterns in the kinds of material that are repressed. Flax (1987b:105) argues that the "autonomous self," the self that "would enjoy mastery, aggression, competition, and define its desires independently of, even against, the wishes of others" cannot exist in our male-dominated society. The concept of "repression" is useful even though one rejects, as I do, the Freudian idea that the source of aggression is within us (e.g., Freud 1920b). What some women in our society may be said to "repress" is their potential to employ aggressive means, even when circumstances are such that aggressive acts would be beneficial, if not moral. In failing to use this "resource," or to see that they are using it, many Western women impoverish their own existence as well as the existence of others (cf. Tavris 1982).

Taking an Aggressive Stance

Let me say more about what I mean by an aggressive stance by describing what it is not. I do not mean here to advocate further violence. There is more than enough of it in our society already; indeed, I see the adoption of an "aggressive stance" as a means of opposing violence. Let us learn, for example, from a Sri Lankan woman who "had a husband who physically assaulted her from the beginning of their marriage. . . . She sent him away, but allowed him to return twice. His behavior improved, she says, because she has threatened to strike back if he assaults her again" (Miller 1992:180). Or from women in the English city of Leeds: "Shortly after my door-to-door study was done, a flasher was seen in the area. Immediately, spray-painted slogans appeared: 'Flasher do not expose yourself to women's anger'; 'Watch out Flasher about'; 'Flasher beware. We will get you. Angry Women.' The flasher has not been seen since" (McNeill 1987:108).

An aggressive stance may well be opposed to one of the few forms of violence that is associated with women in our society—child abuse (e.g., Breines and Gordon 1983; Frodi, Macaulay, and Thome 1977; Steinmetz and Lucca 1988). The idea that individual illness is the cause of "the battered child syndrome" (Kempe et al. 1962) has long been superseded in our models of family violence. Ecological, structural, and cultural factors are so greatly implicated in its etiology (e.g., Gelles and Lancaster 1987; Korbin 1981; Scheper-Hughes 1987; Straus and Smith 1990) that no proposed solution can focus solely on individual psychology. Nevertheless, it is inescapable that it is individuals who abuse children (cf. Breines and Gordon 1983; Hirsch 1981). Miller (1991:185) has observed that when unacknowledged anger "is finally expressed, it often appears in exaggerated form, perhaps along with screaming or yelling, or in ineffective form, with simultaneous nega- tions and apologies." At the same time, a review by Raymond Starr (1988) suggests that just such a state of emotional arousal may be asso- ciated with child abuse. Here it should be noted that for the most part the women of Mangrove do not appear to abuse their children.[3] Anger employed as a means of perceiving "that something is wrong and needs changing," however, may prevent child abuse. For example, there is considerable evidence that disturbances in caretaker/child relation- ships—disturbances that may contribute to child abuse—are transmit- ted across generations (e.g., Egeland, Jacobvitz, and Popatola 1987; Parkes, Stevenson-Hinde, and Marris 1991). Significant correlations have been found between less optimal attachment behaviors on the part of infants and ratings of "the mother's rejection by her mother in child- hood." This pattern was unlikely to occur, however, when the mother had "expressed anger and resentment about rejection by her mother in childhood" (Ricks 1985:220). Again, material from Mangrove should be recalled, specifically, the number of incidents precipitated because of the perceived neglect or mistreatment of children.

Finding gender inequality linked to family violence, Murray Straus and Christine Smith (1990:515) have advocated "sexual equality" as a "prophylactic" for both child and spouse abuse. If the inequalities encapsulated by our concept "gender" are indeed produced and reproduced in the daily interactions of women and men, then the possibility of an aggressive stance becomes particularly important for women's well-being. Women are picked on in large and small ways. For example, Caroline Ramazanoglu (1987:64) describes the "violent academic situation" experienced by many women "as one of diminishing other human beings with the use of sarcasm, raised voices, jokes, veiled insults or the patronising put-down." This is not to say that men are never the victims of such treatment. Women, however, may be less able than men to respond or retaliate. Though men tend to be aggressed against more often than women in the psychologists' laboratories (e.g., Eagly and Steffen 1986; Frodi, Macaulay, and Thome 1977), in some "real life" circumstances women may be targeted more frequently than men. For example, women drivers who are blocking an intersection are more likely to be honked at than men drivers (Deaux 1971 and Unger, Raymond, and Levine 1974 in Frodi, Macaulay, and Thome 1977; see also White 1983). In a study involving male and female flight attendants, Arlie Hochschild (1983:177–178) found that "frustrations were vented more openly toward female workers," a finding she explains with reference to women's lower status and authority. Additionally, women in many walks of life may be picked on for the simple reason that aggressors justifiably assume they will not retaliate.

Here we may have much to learn from women in various African societies. When, for example, the "dignity of their sexual identity" is insulted, Bakweri women are

supposed immediately to call out all the other women of the village. The circumstances having been recounted, the women then run and pluck vegetation from the surrounding bush, which they tie around their waists. Converging again upon the offender, they demand immediate recantation and a recompense. If their demands are not met they all proceed to the house of the village head. The culprit will be brought forward, and the charges laid. If the insult is proved to have been made, he will be fined a pig of a certain size for distribution to the group of women, or its money equivalent, plus something extra, possibly salt, a fowl, or money, for the woman who has been directly insulted. The women then surround him and sing songs accompanied by obscene gestures. (Ardener 1975:30)

In the context of this discussion of an aggressive stance, Shirley Ardener's interpretations of these acts are particularly apropos. She suggests that such practices serve as "templates" for women's acts of political protest (see also Ifeka-Moller 1975; Kanogo 1987; Van Allen 1972) and observes their parallels with techniques employed by Western feminists in the 1970s (e.g., Germaine Greer's [1971] discourse on the vagina and bra burning). In both cases, women demand respect for their femininity by calling public attention to the very body parts others have labeled obscene.

An aggressive stance is not taken simply by substituting verbal for physical aggression. The findings of Straus and Smith that child abuse is correlated both with verbal aggression directed at children and with verbal aggression between husband and wife is crucial here. This verbal aggression, they suggest, creates "additional animosity, which makes it even more difficult to deal with the original source of the conflict" (1990:254). Just what an aggressive stance might be is, however, adumbrated in a discussion of the links between being a victim of violence and perpetrating violence. In a summary of some of the findings of the 1975 National Family Violence Survey, Straus reports that

the more violent husbands are toward their wife, the more violent the wife is toward her children. Wives who were victims of violence that is sufficiently severe to meet the popular conceptions of wife-beating had the highest rate of child abuse. Even those who were subjected to minor violence such as pushes and slaps had more than double the rate of frequent severe assaults on their children than did wives whose husbands did not hit them. (1983:229–230)

An aggressive stance begins as a sense of self-protection. How that stance is expressed must depend to a great extent on the individual abilities and vulnerabilities of each woman. It must also depend on the kinds of psychological and structural support that neighbors, friends, kin, and community members are able and willing to give to women in conflict with others.

Breines and Gordon remind us that domestic violence is more than an outcome of sociocultural factors.

No act of violence is simply the pitting of one individual against another; each contains deep cultural and psychological meanings. At the same time, no act of violence is merely the expression of a social problem (or a culture) such as poverty or un-employment or male dominance; each is also the personal act of a unique individual. (1983:530)

Similarly, while victimization is no doubt structured by sociocultural factors, it is a personal experience of a "unique individual" (see Hirsch

1981). A number of authors have noted that women as targets of male abuse are not always "passive victims" (e.g., Hanmer and Maynard 1987*a;* Lateef 1990, 1992; McDowell 1990; Smuts 1992). From around the world, the diversity of women's responses to violence against them bespeaks the diversity of their experiences. These range from acceptance of violence as a sign of their imperfection or guilt (e.g., Miller 1992) to the kinds of response we might expect of women at Mangrove. Dorothy Counts (1992:70) says, for example, that a woman in Kaliai may feel "so strongly about achieving a goal or asserting her rights that she persists in behavior even though she knows she will be beaten as a result." Other women leave abusive partners (e.g., Kerns 1992; Lambek 1992). And some women, again like women at Mangrove, literally fight back. The following example is provided by a Venezuelan woman.

When I was a young woman, I worked for a rich man who was the owner of commercial fishing boats. At the time, I was with a man named Juan. We were not married but he was my man at that time. One time, he slapped me on the top of the head. He was very disrespectful and used to smart-mouth me. I was young, and the owner of the commercial fishing boats said to me: "You don't have to take that from him. The next time he does that to you, take this stick and give him a good blow." So the next time he did it, I warned him. Then I went and got a pole and hit him real hard across the forearm. I broke it and it was bleeding. He cried. I had really injured him. (Cook 1992:155)

While there is no doubt that a responsible society should work to change the sociocultural factors associated with domestic violence, men's violence toward women clearly arises from a multiplicity of sources and is a problem that will long be with us. In the meantime, it may be that there are better and worse ways of experiencing victimization. One of our tasks is the identification of the varying ways, and the varying circumstances associated with them, in which women's experiences of victimization are less likely to intensify their hurt. There are probably circumstances in which being beaten is the best alternative. For example, a woman might rather be beaten than see her child beaten. There may also be circumstances in which "acceptance" is the best psychological course. Referring to the work of K. Huston (1984), Dee Graham, Edna Rawlings, and Nelly Rimini (1988:231) say of battered women's "denial," "If this anger and rage erupt while the victim is at the mercy of the abuser, it could further escalate violence, resulting in more severe injury or death." The examples provided by women at

Mangrove make it clear that in order for women's aggression not to backfire into harm against them, it must be expressed in circumstances in which they can be defended and protected. It remains for others to develop the no doubt myriad ways of taking an aggressive stance. It remains for us all to work for the circumstances in which this stance can be taken.

Notes

1. Introduction

1. Mangrove and the names of all individuals used in this work are pseudonyms. I have told the people of Mangrove that I would not use their names in anything that I publish. I use a pseudonym for the community to provide some privacy from the outside world.

2. Though some construe the words "action" and "behavior" to signify a different order of things (e.g., Harré and Secord 1973 and Reynolds 1976 in Klama 1988; Taylor 1964 in Gergen 1984), I use them synonymously. In using either word, I intend to indicate that I am talking about something that people do rather than something they only feel or think, but I never mean to imply that thoughts and feelings are not a part of specific human behaviors.

3. There is a growing literature that attempts this kind of self-reflection. For a recent example, see Kondo (1990).

4. Speaking of "human conflicts," Martin Daly and Margo Wilson write,

Self-report methods, so often adopted out of expediency, are of dubious validity at the best of times, and perhaps especially so for studying conflict. People may or may not be prepared to discuss their hostilities and affections, and they may or may not be willing to predict their own behavior in various hypothetical situations, but even if we could be sure that our subjects were being forthcoming, we would not have much reason to trust their introspections. (1988:11–12)

Not only did I find Aboriginal people willing to discuss their "hostilities" and "predict their own behavior in various hypothetical situations" but I also found many reasons, which should be evident in these pages, to "trust their introspections" (see also Burbank 1988). Indeed, Aboriginal "introspections" have provided the impulse and much of the substance of this book's presentation.

Daly and Wilson go on to say that "homicide, by contrast, is drastic action, with a resultant validity that all self-report lacks" (1988:12). It should be noted, however, that insofar as they did not observe at firsthand the homicides they discuss, they too rely to some extent on the reports, predictions, and introspections of others. Undoubtedly, the majority of homicides are reported to the police rather than witnessed by them. The obvious role of report, predictions, and introspection in the collection of any kind of "case" is underlined when Daly and Wilson mention that they include in their analyses cases of homicide in which the "police have identified the killer to their own satisfaction, regardless of prosecution or conviction" (1990:85; 1988). While the police may be regarded as "experts" with regard to Western homicides, so may Aboriginal people be recognized as knowledgeable authorities on the kinds of aggressive behavior manifest in their community.

5. Of interest here is Susan Abbott's (1983:173–174) discussion of conflict with a Kikuyu woman that she experienced during her fieldwork in rural Kenya. According to Abbott, it was precisely because the women perceived Abbott to be powerful that she attempted to thwart her research project, competing with her "to gain influence among local women." While I think I share the motives of writers who characterize ethnographic subjects as "oppressed," I must agree with Diane Bell who points out that this stance can be "both misleading and demeaning for all parties" (1990:158–159). It strikes me that in characterizing other women in this manner, we deny both the ways in which they can be powerful and the ways in which we can be powerless, two possibilities that must be considered in discussions of ethics and responsibility.

6. Some might argue that my access to such items as Land Rovers, fans, and refrigerators bespeaks the "very existence of privilege that allows the research to be undertaken" (Patai 1991:137). In my experience, however, possession of these items did not give me power over Aboriginal people. Such power depends on very specific constructions of material objects and concepts of "possession," constructions that are not necessarily shared by Aboriginal people (Gerrard 1989). I should also point out that while my material circumstances in 1977–1978 and 1981 were unlike those of many Aboriginal people, by 1988 they were quite similar insofar as people at Mangrove had gained much greater access to Western material goods, including refrigerators and vehicles.

7. I believe that this participation is also based on some knowledge of what I do. I have from the beginning of my work at Mangrove told people that I am an anthropologist and have talked with them about the general nature and substance of my work. As is the case with any Aboriginal community today, to work at Mangrove, it is necessary to obtain permission from Mangrove's Aboriginal Council and from the Northern Land Council. In addition to writing to the council at Mangrove about my proposed research, I tried to discuss it in general terms with as many people as possible. Following the guidelines of the Australian Institute of Aboriginal and Torres Strait Islander Studies (formerly the Australian Institute of Aboriginal Studies), the Australian research institute that has sponsored my work at Mangrove, I have sent copies of reports (Burbank 1980*b*, 1987*c*), a paper (Burbank et al. 1989), and my previous book *Aboriginal Adolescence* (1988) to the council, clinic, school, and specific people

in the community, providing them with an opportunity to see what I do with what I learn. Many people at Mangrove read, often for pleasure, and several have told me that they have received, read, and found what I write of interest.

8. It is within this largely integrated community that I formed my primary relationships, and it was from men and women in this integrated community that I came to learn about Aboriginal life. Discussions of past social forms are confined to those of the predominant language group at Mangrove.

9. Deborah Rose reminds us that the American Anthropological Association statement of *Professional Ethics* (1973:1) includes the following: "[Anthropologists] bear a professional responsibility to contribute to an 'adequate definition of reality' upon which public opinion and public policy may be based" (quoted in Rose 1986:28). While Rose would focus on the "physical, economic, and political deprivation which people suffer" (ibid.), she also acknowledges "that not all Aboriginal communities are experiencing such distress and there may be much to be learned from comparative studies" (ibid.:24). I would add that an "adequate definition of reality" must also include the identification of factors that ameliorate suffering and engender well-being.

10. Bronislaw Malinowski's book on the Aboriginal family in Australia includes the following statement:

Ill-treatment [of wives] is—in the primitive state of the aboriginal society—in most cases probably a form of regulated intra-family justice; and that although the methods of treatment in general are very harsh, still they are applied to much more resistant natures and should not be measured by the standards of our ideas and our nerves. (1913:82)

I wish to make it absolutely clear that my argument bears no resemblance to Malinowski's assertions about Aboriginal senses and sensibility. When I propose differences in the experiences of American and Aboriginal women with male aggression, I focus on differences in meaning and social context, creations of social experience, not of putative differences in physiology.

2. Aggression at Mangrove

1. I occasionally recorded Aboriginal speakers on tape. My transcription of this account reads as follows.

[Man speaker]: All the Aborigines been here. [Woman speaker]: Here we been only on top, ceremony, we've been dancing in olden days. [Man]: Aborigine been all over, Billy Macoy story, before, shooting olden day. Used to come in a helicopter and shoot people. They used to hate them, white fellow used to shoot black people. Him [refers to woman speaker] husband working on those boats. [Woman]: My husband, I been little girl yet, I no been married, spear, this way [name], him been get killed. One girl him been taking. [Man]: No more one girl, big mob prisoners. [Woman]: All the prisoners they been taking. [Man]: Billy Macoy, they speared him and let the people go. . . . [VKB]: What for those whitefellas been coming shooting everybody? [Man]: Long time ago, before like me been coming, white like you skin but black like me . . . colored man . . . came here and made a lot of trouble. . . . Billy Macoy and Mr. McCall.

Keith Cole mentions that in 1932, Aboriginal people killed five Japanese pearlers at Caledon Bay, an area to the north of Mangrove. He also reports that Aboriginal people then killed the police investigator of these murders, Constable McColl. Soon after these deaths, two "white beachcombers were also killed." According to Cole, members of the Church Missionary Society's "Peace Expedition" persuaded the "self-confessed killers" to return with them to Darwin to stand trial, thus averting "a demand for a police punitive party to go and 'teach the Caledon Bay Aborigines a lesson' " (1977:194; 1982). According to Nancy Williams (1987:1), news of the planned punitive expedition reached the south, and a "public outcry" resulted. A consequence of the outcry was the establishment of a mission by the Methodist Missionary Society at Yirkalla in 1935. The mission was conceived as a "buffer" between Aboriginal and non-Aboriginal people.

2. This group of people, described by Warren Shapiro (1977), had only a minimal presence at Mangrove in 1977 and 1978. According to Cole (1982), almost all of them had left the settlement by 1981. In March 1988, however, according to my residence survey, there were approximately three dozen people from this group living at Mangrove. I had very little contact with them.

3. H. C. Coombs, B. G. Dexter, and L. R. Hiatt (1980) have described the events and policies leading to the establishment, in 1974, of a federal program that provides financial support for outstations. In 1977, groups of Aboriginal people were leaving Mangrove to set up small communities on their clan lands. By 1981, eleven outstations had been established. In 1988, the outstations seemed to hold little attraction for most of the people I knew. One young woman periodically took supplies to her father who along with his wife were the sole inhabitants of one station. Others were visited occasionally at best. I only visited two in 1988. One of these was deserted by all but the occasional visitor, its garden abandoned, its tin houses empty and falling down. I was told that a third outstation, one that had previously held the largest year-round population, had recently been devastated by a cyclone.

Natural disasters aside, there are many possible reasons that the outstations have not provided more of a long-term alternative to settlement residence. Among these are both the attractions and compulsions of Mangrove. In 1978, for example, when parents took school-aged children to the outstations during the school year, there was talk of fines for absenteeism and withholding of "child checks," a government allowance paid to the parents of schoolchildren. I do not know if such financial penalties were ever actually imposed. The perceived threat, however, may have contributed to the smaller outstation population in subsequent years. Though outstation life can be seen as a means of regaining autonomy and preserving Aboriginal practices (Altman 1987; Burbank 1988), their residents, nevertheless, continued to depend on many of the goods and services provided at Mangrove. Trips to the settlement were made, for example, to obtain foodstuffs from the shop and medicine from the health clinic. The outstations' relatively small populations and lack of popular entertainment may also contribute to their small population. In 1988, the people I knew expressed much more interest in visiting "town" or other settlements to attend such events as Bible meetings, dance festivals, or rock concerts. Alcohol may also be a factor affecting outstation residence. Like Mangrove, its surrounding outstations are legally "dry." Thus Aboriginal people who want to drink, as a number do, are more likely to visit towns or settlements where alcohol is available than an outstation where it is not. The use of outstations as "punishment" for adolescents who misbehave may also reduce the desire of young people to visit them voluntarily (Burbank 1988).

Abandonment of Mangrove and a permanent exodus into town, while an option taken by some, does not appear to be seen as an attractive alternative by the majority of the settlement's residents. Attachment to land and kin, in and of themselves, are probably sufficient reasons for people to remain on or near the settlement.

4. According to Nancy Williams, Aborigines have always been "fully subject to Australian law," although their status as Australian citizens has varied over the years since 1788. Her work on law at Yirkalla suggests how the "two laws" have worked at Mangrove.

> Just as Yolngu consistently associated big troubles with Australian intervention, so they linked little troubles with the legitimacy of Yolngu modes of dispute settlement. Their creation of these categories represented a prediction that white intervention would occur in big troubles but would be unlikely in little troubles. (1987:129)

In 1986, the Australian Law Reform Commission recommended limited recognition of Aboriginal customary law. Marcia Langton (1988) notes that in most areas of remote Aboriginal Australia two systems of law have been in operation. She also observes that in some parts of Australia police tolerate the Aboriginal "law maintenance devices" of swearing and fighting. Other recent anthropological discussions of the relations of the "two laws" are to be found in Williams (1988) and Bell and Ditton (1980).

5. My determination of a "case" is guided by my own definition of an "event" as well as the perceptions of Aboriginal people. Generally, when I observed or was told of an aggressive event such as a "fight" or an "argument," I counted this as one case of aggression. Sometimes, however, a series of aggressive events that would, say, be described as a "fight" by Aboriginal speakers include an act that can be regarded, either according to Aboriginal categories or mine, as another form of aggression. For example, in the course of fighting with his wife, a man might strike her, then throw a spear at the shop. In order not to "lose" the act of spear throwing (an act we might conceptualize as displaced aggression) by subsuming it in the fight, I have scored two cases, noting, however, that the act of throwing a spear was related to the fight. In 145 instances of the 793, I have coded aggressive cases as "related." The number and content of aggressive cases, then, are as much a reflection of how Aboriginal people and I have chosen to slice up a stream of action as they are of that stream itself. This scheme should be compared to those employed by others, such as Pilling's "trouble cases" (1957) and Hiatt's "dispute cases" (1965), before any intercommunity comparisons are made.

Beyond defining "aggression" and "cases," I have also made a series of methodological decisions, necessary in any research, about what to include and what to exclude in the total number of cases. I have, for example, not included cases of sorcery, sexual violence, vandalism and juvenile delinquency, or the punishment of children—all acts that could be regarded as aggressive. During the years that I have visited Mangrove, I have been told of many cases of vandalism and juvenile delinquency and perhaps four or five cases, both past and present, that might be defined as rape, attempted rape, or sexual molestation. I have excluded these cases from my analysis because at the time of my fieldwork they seemed to be regarded as a different order of things. I remind readers that the specific acts detailed in these pages must be kept in mind when discussing "aggression" at Mangrove (Macaulay 1985).

The reader should also note that these cases of aggression are not a random sample. It must be asked if the women who told me of the vast majority of these cases tended to talk more about their own aggressive acts, thus introducing a form of sex or gender bias into the data. I examine this possibility elsewhere (Burbank 1992a). To summarize briefly, a series of statistical tests have suggested that the possibility of gender bias is negligible.

6. A major division made by Aboriginal women in their categorization of aggression is between physical and verbal acts. I also use this categorization but go beyond it for theoretical reasons that are evident in the various discussions of aggressive behavior in this book. For example, the Aboriginal women I know tend to call any kind of physical aggression a "fight." I make further distinctions; for example, I have coded acts of physical aggression into six different categories: "fights" (where physical aggression is threatened or used between at least two adults), "displays" (where an object rather than a person is attacked; see chap. 6), "displays within fights" (where the attack of an object takes place during a fight or appears to be a substitute for attacking a person in a fight), "discipline" (adult aggression directed against an adolescent who occupies a "child" relationship to the aggressor; see chaps. 2 and 3), "murder" (at least one person is killed), and "mirriri" (the aggression of a "brother" against a "sister" following a breach of etiquette; see chap. 6). In addition, I use the category "fight?" for cases where people use the word "fight" in an account but it is not clear if physical aggression actually was threatened or took place. In organizing types of aggression, I have also created categories for "miscellaneous acts" (including abduction and destroying property but not in a display), "cursing" (as described in chap. 6), "threats" (both verbal and physical), "suicide attempts," and acts that are "not clear."

7. All z scores are derived from one-sample proportion tests (Hintze 1990).

8. These cases probably include less verbal aggression than occurred because of a coding artifice. For reasons of economy, I coded only one action—the one judged to be the most severe or destructive—for each participant in a case. For example, if an aggressor both picked up a rock and struck her target with her hand, the latter action would be scored. Thus, in cases in which verbal aggression precedes physical aggression, the verbal aggression is "lost."

9. I use the word "girl" to indicate that I am talking about an immature female, one who is not regarded as a "woman" by her community (see Burbank 1987a, 1988). I also use the word "girl" in my conversations with Aboriginal women because they use this word to talk about themselves.

10. These numbers should be regarded as an approximation because ages, necessary for calculating the number of adults in residence, were not in all cases

known. Following the Department of Aboriginal Affairs' census practice, people age 15 and over are counted as adults.

3. The Cultural Construction of Anger and Aggression

1. Though I tend to follow the spelling of Heath (1982), I do not use his orthographic system for the sake of readability.

2. As I understand this speaker, the husband would "get jealous" because the women's laughter indicates that they are talking about lovers. I was not aware of lesbian relationships at Mangrove. Women's homosexual practices in Aboriginal Australia are discussed, if only briefly, by Berndt (1965), Reay (1970), Kaberry (1939), and Roheim (1933).

3. For accounts of trysting in Arnhem Land, see Shapiro (1981), Warner (1937), Berndt and Berndt (1951), and Burbank (1988).

4. The word "tease" in Aboriginal English lacks all connotations of playfulness. I think it is best understood to mean "attack," either verbally or physically. I find this understanding of a word borrowed from the English vocabulary particularly interesting with respect to Miller's (1991) supposition about the construction of masculine anger in Western society. Briefly, she proposes that particular constructions of anger and aggression develop in interactions that fathers have with their sons. The boys are teased but not allowed to express anger and hurt, because it is, after all, "just teasing." If boys express their anger, the father withdraws from the "game" and may punish the child. This leads, says Miller, to a more general masculine stance in which, "the game is played with the pretense that no one really is hurt" (191). If we say that Aboriginal constructions of anger allow greater recognition of potential harm, are we not also saying that some constructions better reflect human experience than others?

4. The Control of Aggression

1. Others have made similar observations about aggressive events in Aboriginal Australia (see Langton 1988; Macdonald 1988; Sansom 1980; Stanner 1968; Warner 1937) and elsewhere (e.g., Bohannan 1960*b*; Cummings in press; Fox 1968, 1975; LeVine 1961).

2. Other observers of Aboriginal social life have postulated a relationship between patterns of aggressive events and aspects of the childhood environment. Hamilton (1981*b*) has drawn a parallel between the "violent and unreasonable demands" that men make of women and temper tantrums displayed by

children over food. Myers (1988) sees children's anger as "paradigmatic" of that expressed in adult life. Grayson Gerrard (n.d.:17) sees wife beating by adults and mother beating by children as "part of the same continuum." David McKnight has made the following remarks about links between childish and adult aggression.

Although I do not hold that the violent behaviour of the Mornington Islanders can be attributed simply to their childhood experience, nevertheless there is some connection and it is plain that the aggressive behaviour of children and adults is all of a piece. Children are continuously exposed to violence and they soon learn to regard violence as a way of life. Initially when I observed children screaming and crying when their parents were involved in fights I thought the children were terrified. I eventually learnt that I had misinterpreted their reactions, for they in fact often enjoyed the spectacle. This was borne out by people's comments and by the children's animated and carefree accounts. Most children seemed to have strong egos and they would stubbornly assert themselves. The were apt to strike out when thwarted. They frequently threw tantrums, smashed things and took sulk (*bunme*). The children fought each other and took sides in the traditional windward and leeward manner—even my five-year-old son was recruited. *The* childhood game was throwing tin lids at one another which the children blocked with sticks, or else they rolled the lids on the ground and tried to hit them, using their sticks as spears. . . . Needless to say these games are excellent training for hunting and fighting. (1986:156)

3. Some of the people known by any individual at Mangrove are described as "close" or "full" "relations." We might call this segment a "kindred" (Shapiro 1979, 1981). Individuals are said to be "full relations" on the basis of perceived genealogical links (e.g., a woman might say, "We are all one mother's mother"), shared clan membership, or a shared "Dreaming." The totality of an individual's "full relations" are described as "family."

4. According to Warner's (1937; see also Williams 1987) accounts of *makarata*, a very similar form of ritual revenge, a spear thrust through the offending party's thigh indicates forgiveness, but a shallow wound or no wound at all indicates a lack of forgiveness and/or intentions to take further vengeance. What may be a contemporary deviation from the earlier form might represent a modification designed to placate the legal concerns of the larger Australian society.

5. Past and present forms of these body operations include circumcision, scarification of chest and upper arms, and nose and ear piercing.

5. Women and Aggression

1. In 736 of the 793 cases, I have been able to ascertain the sex of the aggressors and targets. I have devised seven categories for a variable I call "Sex of Aggressors/Targets." These include cases where (1) men attack women (MAW); (2) women attack men (WAM); (3) men and women are aggressors, but it is not clear which sex began the attack (MWAG); (4) men attack other men (MAG); (5) women attack other women (WAG); (6) a male aggressor

does not have a specific human target (SMAG) (see chaps. 3 and 6); (7) a female aggressor does not have a specific human target (SWAG).

The cross-tabulation of "Sex of Aggressor/Target" with the variable "Reason" is significant (chi-square with 90 degrees of freedom = 240.2872, p < .0001). The chi-square value in the cell in which MWAG and "Subsistence" intersect is 4.1, that is, greater than 3.0, a number conventionally accepted to indicate significance (Fienberg 1977). I interpret significance to indicate characteristic reasons for aggression for the various gender combinations of aggressors and targets.

It should be noted that this use of cross-tabulation is intended as a close heuristic rather than as a direct test of the significance of the differences. The chi-square is approximately z^2 and therefore approximates a difference of proportions test for the hypothesis that the particular cell does not differ from its expected proportion under an equal distribution. The chi-square value of 3 is approximately a z of 1.73 with a one-tailed probability of .05. This value is sufficiently close to acceptable levels of significance to warrant further evaluation of the relationship (see Fienberg 1977).

2. The actual phrase used in my question was "young boy," the Kriol and Aboriginal English words for adolescent males.

3. This is not to say that men's contributions are not important to the well-being of women and children. See Burbank and Chisholm (1990) for a discussion of this issue.

4. This statement reflects the old adage, "It is a wise child who knows its own father." Men cannot always be sure that the child their wife bears is their own. Women, however, unless their children are removed at birth and placed in the hospital nursery, know that they are the mother of their child. Similarly, relatives of a woman can be more certain than relatives of a man that their kin's children are indeed their genetic relatives. The potential difference in "paternity certainty" is an important theoretical issue in sociobiological discussions of gender relations (e.g., Daly, Wilson, and Weghorst 1982; Burgess and Draper 1989).

5. Aboriginal women at Mangrove use the words "find" and "found" to speak of a child's mother and presumed genitor. According to Shapiro (1979), this terminology reflects the practice of dreaming the child. In a dream, a man encounters the spirit of the child and directs it to its mother. At Mangrove, people dream children, but fathers do not usually dream their own children (Burbank 1988).

6. Women, Men and Interpersonal Aggression

1. Maccoby and Jacklin include in their summary of an early review of the research on "sex differences" the following passage:

We have seen that the greater aggressiveness of the male is one of the best established, and most pervasive, of all psychological sex differences. We have also seen reason to believe there is a biological component underlying this difference. (1974:368)

There have been rebuttals of their conclusion that there is a biological substrate to this difference (e.g., Tieger 1980; Fausto-Sterling 1985) and discussions that cast doubt on the quality of data derived from experimental psychology (e.g., Deaux 1985; Frodi, Macaulay, and Thome 1977; Macaulay 1985). However, aggression manifest in observed "real world" patterns of male and female experience continues to be "one of the best established and most pervasive" gender differences. For example, cross-cultural explorations find that men are, with few exceptions, the warriors in any given society (Adams 1983; Ember and Ember 1971; Ember 1981; Whyte 1978). There is also consistent evidence that killers are usually men (e.g., Bohannan 1960a; Daly and Wilson 1988; Fry 1992; Knauft 1985, 1987b; Lee 1979).

When the focus is on nonlethal interpersonal aggression, however, the question of difference becomes more complex (see Frost and Averill 1982). There is evidence both for and against our perceptions that men are more aggressive, and we must always specify what we mean by "more" (Burbank 1987b, 1992a; Björkqvist and Niemelä 1992a). David Levinson, for example, in a cross-cultural study of family violence, finds wife beating "the most common form of family violence around the world," occurring in 84.5 percent of the societies surveyed; husband beating, in contrast, occurs in far fewer societies (26.9%) and generally occurs less often than does wife beating (1989:30–31). Similar cross-cultural distributions of spousal violence have been found by Broude and Greene (1983) and Whyte (1978). Cross-cultural comparisons have also found boys to be more aggressive than girls (Ember 1981; Maccoby and Jacklin 1974, 1980; Rohner 1976; Whiting and Edwards 1973). However, Rohner's (1976) cross-cultural survey did not find that men were significantly more aggressive than women. Some reviewers of the largely experimental psychological literature have found few consistent or robust sex differences in aggression (e.g., Epstein 1988; Frodi, Macaulay, and Thome 1977; White 1983). Differences, however, always in the direction of greater male aggression, continue to be found (e.g., Eagly and Steffen 1986; Hyde 1986, 1990).

2. Overviews of feminist studies of woman abuse are provided by Breines and Gordon (1983), Bograd (1988), and Liddle (1989). Feminist thought characterizes studies done within psychological, sociocultural, and sociobiological frameworks. Examples of psychological approaches are provided by the work of Walker (1979, 1984); examples of sociocultural approaches, by Campbell (1992) and by the papers edited by Counts (1990b) and Counts, Brown, and Campbell (1992). Examples of feminist approaches within sociobiology are provided by Burgess and Draper (1989) and Smuts (1992).

3. In 606 cases, I have been able to code a reason for an aggressive event. (See table 3, p. 99, for details of the coding categories; see chap. 5, n. 1, for a discussion of my use of statistical procedures.)

4. Liddle has said that feminists make a series of assumptions about "individuals, consciousness, and interests" when they attribute the motive of dominance to men's use of violence against women. He also points out that "feminist

characterizations of 'male interests' or 'the interests of men' are quite undeveloped" (1989:764). Gregor has used a similar strategy for interpreting rape in our society. He argues that there is little to support the idea that it is intended by men as a political act. He says with reference to women's experience, however, that "the implications for gender politics are far-reaching" (1990:482).

5. Yengoyan's (1990) analyses of 29 dreams of aggression from Pitjantjatjara men suggests the extent to which cultural constructions may be internalized in the individual psyche.

6. I asked this speaker why the dugong would be cursed when a man danced "really beautifully." He replied that it was because people thought it was a really good ceremony.

7. Several women at Mangrove have told me that women do use supernatural means to woo men as lovers or husbands. One woman labeled some of these acts *jarrada*. In the literature on women's ritual activity, the term "jarrada" is more commonly used to refer to a complex of women's rituals that may include attempts to manipulate male/female relationships (see Burbank 1989, for an overview of the literature on women's ceremonies in Aboriginal Australia). One older woman who attempted to introduce jarrada of this kind at Mangrove told me that some of the older men told her to stop after a couple of performances. The ceremonies were too successful, and young women were running off with inappropriate partners. Currently, women's attempts to entice men through supernatural means appear to be isolated, individual acts.

Although this is clearly manipulation of the supernatural and an attempt to compel someone to do something they might otherwise not do, I do not think that jarrada should be included in a discussion of aggression. Neither the means nor the ends of these acts are intended to harm another. Although magically separating a woman from her husband, or a man from his wife, could be described as an aggressive act insofar as it leaves an injured spouse, the purpose of jarrada seems to be that of obtaining a spouse or lover rather than of hurting the previous husband or wife.

8. Before phrasing this question, I had heard Aboriginal people using the word "frightened" to describe their reactions to seeing things like spears, snakes, and fights (see Burbank 1988). The seven kinds of aggressive events I asked about were "gun fired in the air," "you are hit with a stick," "you are chased with a spear," "shop is cursed," "you are cursed," "someone wrestles with you," "someone swears at you."

7. Conclusion

1. Anne Campbell (1982, 1984*a*, 1984*b*) and Marsh and Paton (1986) have found overtly aggressive behavior to be accepted and employed by British working-class schoolgirls, "lower-class teenage girls," and American black and Hispanic gang members, girls and women ranging in age from 15 to 30.

2. Many of these studies can be found in the volume edited by Björkqvist

and Niemelä (1992*b*) and in a special issue of *Sex Roles* edited by Fry (in press). Other references include Browne (1987, 1988), Burbank (1987*b*, 1992*b*), Campbell (1982, 1984*a*), Cook (1993), Marsh and Paton (1986), Schuster (1983, 1985), and Schuster and Hartz-Karp (1986).

3. At Mangrove, children are sometimes hit, but physical aggression that is injurious is proscribed and punished:

If a mother hits the child for something too hard or makes it bleed the father will hit her.

If a father hit [a child] too hard, the child's brother, uncle, or [grandfather] would make a big fight and tell the man not to hit hard.

According to these criteria, there is little child abuse apparent at Mangrove. In 1981, for example, a "European" nursing sister, who had worked on the settlement for just under two years, reported that no cases of child abuse had been brought to her attention. In 1988, an Aboriginal health worker reported that one mother had "bruised" her daughter but also said that she had ceased this behavior after the health worker and other women spoke to her.

References

Abbott, S.
   1983   "In the End You Will Carry Me in Your Car": Sexual Politics in the Field. *Women's Studies* 10:161–178.

Abu-Lughod, L.
   1990*a*   Shifting Politics in Bedouin Love Poetry. In *Language and the Politics of Emotion,* ed. C. Lutz and L. Abu-Lughod, 24–45. Cambridge: Cambridge University Press.
   1990*b*   The Romance of Resistance: Tracing Transformations of Power Through Bedouin Women. In *Beyond the Second Sex: New Directions in the Anthropology of Gender,* ed. P. Sanday and R. Goodenough, 311–337. Philadelphia: University of Pennsylvania Press.
   1991   Writing Against Culture. In *Recapturing Anthropology: Working in the Present,* ed. R. Fox, 137–162. Santa Fe, N.M.: School of American Research Press.

Abu-Lughod, L., and C. Lutz
   1990   Introduction: Emotion, Discourse, and the Politics of Everyday Life. In *Language and the Politics of Emotion,* ed. C. Lutz and L. Abu-Lughod, 1–23. Cambridge: Cambridge University Press.

Adams, D.
   1983   Why There Are So Few Women Warriors. *Behavior Science Research* 18:196–212.

Agar, M.
   1973   *Ripping and Running: A Formal Ethnography of Urban Heroin Addicts.* New York: Seminar Press.

Altman, J. C.
   1987   *Hunter-Gatherers Today: An Aboriginal Economy in North Australia.* Canberra: Australian Institute of Aboriginal Studies.

Altmann, J.
    1974   Observational Study of Behavior: Sampling Methods. *Behavior* 49:227–267.

Ames, D. W.
    1953   Plural Marriage Among the Wolof in the Gambia, with a Consideration of Problems of Marital Adjustment and Patterned Ways of Resolving Tensions. Ph.D. dissertation, Northwestern University, Evanston, Ill.

Ardener, S.
    1975   Sexual Insult and Female Militancy. In *Perceiving Women*, ed. E. Ardener, 29–53. London: Dent.

Atkinson, J.
    1990a   Violence in Aboriginal Australia: Colonization and Gender. Pts. 1 and 2. *Aboriginal and Islander Health Worker* 14(2):5–21 and 14(3):4–27.
    1990b   Violence Against Aboriginal Women: Reconstitution of Community Law—The Way Forward. *Aboriginal Law Bulletin* 2:6–9.

Attili, G., and R. Hinde
    1986   Categories of Aggression and Their Motivational Heterogeneity. *Ethology and Sociobiology* 7:17–27.

Axelrod, R., and W. Hamilton
    1981   The Evolution of Cooperation. *Science* 211:1390–1396.

Ayres, B.
    1976   Marriage Systems as Reproductive Strategies: Cross-Cultural Evidence for Sexual Selection in Man. Paper presented at the Society for Cross-Cultural Research.
    1983   Intra-Societal Variation in the Incidence of Polygyny. Paper presented at the Society for Cross-Cultural Research.

Bauer, F.
    1964   *Historical Geography of White Settlement in Part of Northern Australia. Pt. 2: The Katherine-Darwin Region.* Canberra: Commonwealth Scientific and Industrial Research Organization.

Begler, E.
    1978   Sex, Status, and Authority in Egalitarian Society. *American Anthropologist* 80:571–588.

Bell, D.
    1980   Desert Politics: Choices in the Marriage Market. In *Women and Colonization: Anthropological Perspectives,* ed. M. Etienne and E. Leacock, 239–269. New York: Praeger.
    1983   *Daughters of the Dreaming.* Sydney: McPhee Gribble/George Allen and Unwin.
    1990   A Reply to "The Politics of Representation," by Jan Larbalestier. *Anthropological Forum* 6:158–166.

Bell, D., and P. Ditton
    1980   *Law: The Old and the New.* Canberra: Aboriginal History.

Bell, D., and T. Nelson
1989   Speaking about Rape Is Everyone's Business. *Women's Studies International Forum* 12:403–416.

Berkowitz, L.
1969   The Frustration-Aggression Hypothesis Revisited. In *Roots of Aggression,* ed. L. Berkowitz, 1–28. New York: Atherton Press.

Bern, J.
1979   Ideology and Domination: Toward a Reconstruction of Australian Aboriginal Social Formation. *Oceania* 50:118–132.

Berndt, C.
1965   Women and the Secret Life. In *Aboriginal Man in Australia,* ed. R. Berndt and C. Berndt, 236–282. Sydney: Angus and Robertson.
1978   In Aboriginal Australia. In *Learning Non-Aggression: The Experience of Non-Literate Societies,* ed. A. Montagu, 144–160. Oxford: Oxford University Press.

Berndt, R.
1951   *Kunapipi.* Melbourne: Cheshire.
1965   Law and Order in Aboriginal Australia. In *Aboriginal Man in Australia,* ed. R. Berndt, 167–206. London: Angus Robertson.

Berndt, R., and C. Berndt
1951   *Sexual Behavior in Western Arnhem Land.* New York: Viking.

Biernoff, D.
1974   Pre and Post European Design of Aboriginal Settlements: The Case of the Nunggubuyu of Eastern Arnhem Land. *Man-Environment Systems* 4:273–282.
1978   Safe and Dangerous Places. In *Australian Aboriginal Concepts,* ed. L. Hiatt, 93–105. Canberra: Australian Institute of Aboriginal Studies.
1979   Traditional and Contemporary Structures and Settlement in Eastern Arnhem Land with Particular Reference to the Nunggubuyu. In *A Black Reality: Aboriginal Camps and Housing in Remote Australia,* ed. M. Heppell, 153–179. Canberra: Australian Institute of Aboriginal Studies.

Björkqvist, K., and P. Niemelä
1992*a*   New Trends in the Study of Female Aggression. In *Of Mice and Women: Aspects of Female Aggression,* ed. B. Björkqvist and P. Niemelä, 4–16. New York: Academic Press.
1992*b*   (eds.). *Of Mice and Women: Aspects of Female Aggression.* New York: Academic Press.

Björkqvist, K., K. Österman, and A. Kaukiainen
1992   The Development of Direct and Indirect Aggressive Strategies in Males and Females. In *Of Mice and Women: Aspects of Female Aggression,* ed. K. Björkqvist and P. Niemelä, 51–64. New York: Academic Press.

Bledsoe, C.
  1984   The Political Use of Sande Ideology and Symbolism. *American Ethnologist* 11:455–472.
  1993   The Politics of Polygyny in Mende Education and Child Foster-age Transactions. In *Sex and Gender Hierarchies,* ed. B. Miller, 170–192. Cambridge: Cambridge University Press.

Bligh, V.
  1983   Study into the Needs of Aboriginal Women Who Have Been Raped or Sexually Assaulted. In *We Are Bosses Ourselves,* ed. F. Gale, 100–104. Canberra: Australian Institute of Aboriginal Studies.

Bograd, M.
  1988   Feminist Perspectives on Wife Abuse: An Introduction. In *Feminist Perspectives on Wife Abuse,* ed. K. Yllo and M. Bograd, 11–27. Beverly Hills: Sage.

Bohannan, P.
  1960*a*   Patterns of Murder and Suicide. In *African Homicide and Suicide,* ed. P. Bohannan, 230–266. Princeton: Princeton University Press.
  1960*b*   Theories of Homicide and Suicide. In *African Homicide and Suicide,* ed. P. Bohannan, 3–29. Princeton: Princeton University Press.

Bolger, A.
  1991   *Aboriginal Women and Violence.* Darwin: Australian National University, North Australian Research Unit.

Bond, M., and S.-H. Wang
  1983   China: Aggressive Behavior and the Problem of Maintaining Order and Harmony. In *Global Perspectives on Aggression,* ed. A. Goldstein and M. Segall, 58–74. New York: Pergamon Press.

Brady, M.
  1985   *Children Without Ears: Petrol Sniffing in Australia.* Parkside, South Australia: Drug and Alcohol Services Council.
  1991   Drug and Alcohol Use Among Aboriginal People. In *The Health of Aboriginal Australia,* ed. J. Reid and P. Trompf, 173–217. Sydney: Harcourt Brace Jovanovich.

Breines, W., and L. Gordon
  1983   The New Scholarship on Family Violence. *Signs: Journal of Women in Culture and Society* 8:490–531.

Brenner, C.
  1957   *An Elementary Textbook of Psychoanalysis.* Garden City, N.Y.: Doubleday.

Broude, G., and S. Greene
  1983   Cross-Cultural Codes on Husband-Wife Relationships. *Ethnology* 22:263–280.

Brown, D.
  1991   *Human Universals.* Philadelphia: Temple University Press.

Brown, J.
  1988   Sanctions and Sanctuary: Cross-Cultural Perspectives on Violence
          Toward Women. Paper presented at the American Anthropologi-
          cal Association meetings.
  1992   Introduction: Definitions, Assumptions, Themes, and Issues. In
          *Sanctions and Sanctuary: Cultural Perspectives on the Beating of
          Wives,* ed. D. Counts, J. Brown, and J. Campbell, 1–18. Boulder:
          Westview Press.
Brown, P., and I. Schuster
  1986   Introduction. *Anthropological Quarterly: Culture and Aggression*
          59:155–159.
Browne, A.
  1987   *When Battered Women Kill.* New York: Free Press.
  1988   Family Homicide: When Victimized Women Kill. In *Handbook of
          Family Violence,* ed. V. Van Hasselt, R. Morrison, A. Bellack, and
          M. Hersen, 271–292. New York: Plenum Press.
Brownmiller, S.
  1976   *Against Our Will: Men, Women and Rape.* New York: Simon and
          Schuster.
  1989   Madly in Love. *MS* (April):56–64.
Burbank, V.
  1980a   Expressions of Anger and Aggression in an Australian Aboriginal
          Community. Ph.D. dissertation, Rutgers University, New Bruns-
          wick, N.J.
  1980b   Some of the History, Custom and Law of the People. Unpub-
          lished report, Australian Institute of Aboriginal and Torres Strait
          Islander Studies, Canberra.
  1985   The Mirriri as Ritualized Aggression. *Oceania* 56:47–55.
  1987a   Premarital Sex Norms: Cultural Interpretations in an Australian
          Aboriginal Community. *Ethos* 15:226–234.
  1987b   Female Aggression in Cross-Cultural Perspective. *Behavior Science
          Research* 21:70–100.
  1987c   Young Boys and Young Girls: Some Issues of Adolescence in the
          1980s. Unpublished report, Australian Institute of Aboriginal and
          Torres Strait Islander Studies, Canberra.
  1988   *Aboriginal Adolescence: Maidenhood in an Australian Community.*
          New Brunswick: Rutgers University Press.
  1989   Gender and the Anthropology Curriculum: Aboriginal Australia.
          In *Critical Reviews of Gender in Anthropology: Implications for Re-
          search and Teaching,* ed. S. Morgen, 116–131. Washington, D.C.:
          American Anthropological Association.
  1992a   Sex, Gender, and Difference: Dimensions of Aggression in an Aus-
          tralian Aboriginal Community. *Human Nature* 3:251–278.
  1992b   Fight! Fight!: Men, Women, and Interpersonal Aggression in an
          Australian Aboriginal Community. In *Sanctions and Sanctuary:
          Cultural Perspectives on the Beating of Wives,* ed. D. Counts, J.
          Brown, and J. Campbell, 33–42. Boulder: Westview Press.

in press   Women's Intra-Gender Relationships and "Disciplinary Aggression" in an Australian Aboriginal Community. *Journal of Cross-Cultural Gerontology.*

Burbank, V., and J. Chisholm
1989   Old and New Inequalities in a Southeast Arnhem Land Community: Polygyny, Marriage Age, and Birth Spacing. In *Emergent Inequalities in Aboriginal Australia,* ed. J. Altman, 85–94. Sydney: Oceania Monographs.
1990   Adolescent Pregnancy and Parenthood in an Australian Aboriginal Community. Paper presented at the Association for Social Anthropology in Oceania meetings.

Burbank, V., J. Chisholm, A. Murrungun, and J. Nundhirribula
1989   Parents' Concerns about Child-Rearing Problems in an Arnhem Land Community. Unpublished report, Austrailian Institute of Aboriginal and Torres Strait Islander Studies, Canberra.

Burgess, R., and P. Draper
1989   The Explanation of Family Violence: The Role of Biological, Behavioral, and Cultural Selection. In *Crime and Justice—An Annual Review of Research: Family Violence,* ed. L. Ohlin and M. Tonry, 59–116. Chicago: University of Chicago Press.

Buss, A.
1961   *The Psychology of Aggression.* New York: John Wiley and Sons.

Campbell, A.
1982   Female Aggression. In *Aggression and Violence,* ed. P. Marsh and A. Campbell, 135–150. Oxford: Basil Blackwell.
1984a   Girl's Talk: The Social Representation of Aggression by Female Gang Members. *Criminal Justice and Behavior* 11:130–156.
1984b   *The Girls in the Gang.* Oxford: Basil Blackwell.

Campbell, J.
1992   Wife-Battering: Cultural Contexts versus Western Social Sciences. In *Sanctions and Sanctuary: Cultural Perspectives on the Beating of Wives,* ed. D. Counts, J. Brown, and J. Campbell, 229–250. Boulder: Westview Press.

Capell, A.
1960   Myths and Tales of the Nunggubuyu, S.E. Arnhem Land. *Oceania* 31:31–62.

Caplan, P., and J. Bujra (eds.)
1979   *Women United, Women Divided: Comparative Studies of Ten Contemporary Cultures.* Bloomington: Indiana University Press.

Carruci, L.
1990   Negotiations of Violence in the Marshallese Household. *Pacific Studies, Special Issue: Domestic Violence in Oceania,* 13:93–113.
1992   Nudging Her Harshly and Killing Him Softly: Displays of Disenfranchisement on Ujelang Atoll. In *Sanctions and Sanctuary: Cultural Perspectives on the Beating of Wives,* ed. D. Counts, J. Brown, and J. Campbell, 111–124. Boulder: Westview Press.

Chagnon, N.
    1968   *Yanomamo: The Fierce People.* New York: Holt, Rinehart and Winston.

Chagnon, N., and P. Bugos
    1979   Kin Selection and Conflict: An Analysis of a Yanomamo Ax Fight. In *Evolutionary Biology and Human Social Behavior: An Anthropological Perspecitve,* ed. N. Chagnon and W. Irons, 213–238. Belmont, Calif.: Wadsworth.

Chisholm, J.
    1992   Putting People in Biology: Toward a Synthesis of Biological and Psychological Anthropology. In *New Directions in Psychological Anthropology,* ed. T. Schwartz, G. White, and C. Lutz, 125–149. Cambridge: Cambridge University Press.

Clifford, J., and G. Marcus (eds.)
    1986   *Writing Culture: The Poetics and Politics of Ethnography.* Berkeley, Los Angeles, and London: University of California Press.

Colby, B.
    1966   The Analysis of Cultural Content and the Patterning of Narrative Concern in Texts. *American Anthropologist* 68:374–388.

Cole, K.
    1977   A Critical Appraisal of Anglican Mission Policy and Practice in Arnhem Land, 1908–1939. In *Aborigines and Change: Australia in the '70s,* ed. R. Berndt, 177–198. Canberra: Australian Institute of Aboriginal Studies.

    1982   *A History of Numbulwar: The Story of an Aboriginal Community in Eastern Arnhem Land, 1952–1982.* Bendigo, Victoria: Keith Cole Publications.

Collier, J.
    1974   Women in Politics. In *Woman, Culture, and Society,* ed. M. Rosaldo and L. Lamphere, 89–96. Stanford: Stanford University Press.

Collier, J., and M. Rosaldo
    1981   Politics and Gender in Simple Societies. In *Sexual Meanings: The Cultural Construction of Gender and Sexuality,* ed. S. Ortner and H. Whitehead, 275–329. Cambridge: Cambridge University Press.

Collier, J., and S. Yanagisako
    1989   Theory in Anthropology Since Feminist Practice. *Critique of Anthropology* 9:27–37.

Collmann, J.
    1988a   "I'm Proper Number One Fighter, Me": Aborigines, Gender, and Bureaucracy in Central Australia. *Gender and Society* 2:9–23.

    1988b   *Fringe-Dwellers and Welfare: The Aboriginal Response to Bureaucracy.* St. Lucia: University of Queensland Press.

Connell, R.
    1987   *Gender and Power: Society, the Person and Sexual Politics.* Stanford: Stanford University Press.

Cook, H.
1992   Matrifocality and Female Aggression in Margariteño Society. In *Of Mice and Women: Aspects of Female Aggression*, ed. K. Björkqvist and P. Niemelä, 149–162. New York: Academic Press.

1993   *Small Town, Big Hell: An Ethnographic Study of Aggression in a Margariteño Community*. Antropologica, Suplemento 4. Caracas: Fundación La Salle de Ciencias Naturales, Instituto Caribe de Antropología y Sociología.

Cook, J., and M. Fonow
1990   Knowledge and Women's Interests: Issues of Epistemology and Methodology in Feminist Sociological Research. In *Feminist Research Methods: Exemplary Readings in the Social Sciences*, ed. J. Nielsen, 69–93. Boulder: Westview Press.

Coombs, H., B. Dexter, and L. Hiatt
1980   The Outstation Movement in Aboriginal Australia. *Australian Institute of Aboriginal Studies Newsletter, New Series* 14:1–8.

Coser, L.
1956   *The Functions of Social Conflict*. New York: Free Press.
1967   *Continuities in the Study of Social Conflict*. New York: Free Press.

Counts, D.
1990a   Conclusion. *Pacific Studies, Special Issue: Domestic Violence in Oceania*, 13:225–254.

1990b   (ed.). *Pacific Studies, Special Issue: Domestic Violence in Oceania*, 13.

1990c   Domestic Violence in Oceania: Introduction. *Pacific Studies, Special Issue: Domestic Violence in Oceania*, 13:1–5.

1992   "All Men Do It": Wife-Beating in Kaliai, Papua New Guinea. In *Sanctions and Sanctuary: Cultural Perspectives on the Beating of Wives*, ed. D. Counts, J. Brown, and J. Campbell, 63–76. Boulder: Westview Press.

Counts, D., J. Brown, and J. Campbell (eds.)
1992   *Sanctions and Sanctuary: Cultural Perspectives on the Beating of Wives*. Boulder: Westview Press.

Cowlishaw, G.
1978   Infanticide in Aboriginal Australia. *Oceania* 48:262–283.
1979   Women's Realm: A Study of Socialization, Sexuality, and Reproduction among Australian Aborigines. Ph.D. dissertation, University of Sydney.

1986   Broken Promises: Aboriginal Traditions. Paper presented at Australian Institute of Aboriginal Studies Seminar: Hierarchial and Egalitarian Tendencies in Traditional Aboriginal Society.

1988   *Black, White or Brindle: Race in Rural Australia*. Cambridge: Cambridge University Press.

Crawford, M., and J. Marecek
1989   Psychology Reconstructs the Female: 1968–1988. *Psychology of Women Quarterly* 13:147–165.

Cummings, L.
in press   Fighting by the Rules: Women's Street-Fighting in Chihuahua,

Chihuahua, Mexico. *Sex Roles, Special Edition: Multicultural Perspectives on Aggression in Women and Girls,* ed. D. Fry.

Daly, M., and M. Wilson
1983   *Sex, Evolution, and Behavior.* 2d ed. Boston: Willard Grant Press.
1988   *Homicide.* New York: Aldine de Gruyter.
1990   Killing the Competition: Female/Female and Male/Male Homicide. *Human Nature* 1:81–107.

Daly, M., M. Wilson, and S. Weghorst
1982   Male Sexual Jealousy. *Ethology and Sociobiology* 3:11–27.

D'Andrade, R.
1984   Cultural Meaning Systems. In *Culture Theory: Essays on Mind, Self, and Emotion,* ed. R. Shweder and R. LeVine, 88–122. Cambridge: Cambridge University Press.

Daylight, P., and M. Johnstone
1986   *Women's Business: Report of the Aboriginal Women Task Force.* Canberra: Australian Government Publishing Service.

Deaux, K.
1971   Honking at the Intersection: A Replication and Extension. *Journal of Social Psychology* 84:159–160.
1985   Sex and Gender. *Annual Review of Psychology* 36:49–81.

di Leonardo, M.
1985   Morals, Mothers, and Militarism: Antimilitarism and Feminist Theory. *Feminist Studies* 11:599–617.

Divale, W., and M. Harris
1979   Population, Warfare, and the Male Supremacist Complex. In *Issues in Cultural Anthropology: Selected Readings,* ed. D. McCurdy and J. Spradley, 322–340. Boston: Little Brown and Company.

Dollard, J., L. Doob, N. Miller, O. Mowrer, and R. Sears
1939   *Frustration and Aggression.* New Haven: Yale University Press.

Douglas, M.
1973   *Natural Symbols.* Harmondsworth, England: Penguin.

Draper, P.
1975   !Kung Women: Contrasts in Sexual Egalitarianism in Foraging and Sedentary Contexts. In *Towards an Anthropology of Women,* ed. R. Reiter, 77–109. New York: Monthly Review Press.
1978   The Learning Environment for Aggression and Anti-Social Behavior among the !Kung (Kalahari Desert, Botswana, Africa). In *Learning Non-Aggression: The Experience of Non-Literate Societies,* ed. A. Montagu, 31–53. Oxford: Oxford University Press.

DuBois, C.
1944   *The People of Alor.* New York: Harper.

Eagly, A., and V. Steffen
1986   Gender and Aggressive Behavior: A Meta-Analytic Review of the Social Psychological Literature. *Psychological Bulletin* 100: 309–330.

Edwards, A.
1987   Male Violence in Feminist Theory: An Analysis of the Changing

Conceptions of Sex/Gender Violence and Male Dominance. In *Women, Violence and Social Control*, ed. J. Hanmer and M. Maynard, 13–29. London: Macmillan.

Egeland, B., D. Jacobvitz, and K. Popatola
1987   Intergenerational Continuity of Abuse. In *Child Abuse and Neglect*, ed. R. Gelles and J. Lancaster, 255–276. New York: Aldine de Gruyter.

Elkin, A. P.
1964   *The Australian Aborigines*. Garden City, N.Y.: Doubleday.

Ember, C.
1981   A Cross-Cultural Perspective on Sex Differences. In *Handbook of Cross-Cultural Human Development*, ed. R. Munroe, R. Munroe, and B. Whiting, 531–579. New York: Garland Press.

Ember, M., and Ember, C.
1971   The Conditions Favoring Matrilocal versus Patrilocal Residence. *American Anthropologist* 73:571–594.

Epstein, C.
1988   *Deceptive Distinctions: Sex, Gender, and the Social Order*. New Haven: Yale University Press.

Erchak, G.
1984   Cultural Anthropology and Spouse Abuse. *Current Anthropology* 25:330–332.
1987   Adaptation and Spouse Abuse: A West African Case and Suggestions for Research. Paper presented at the American Anthropological Association meetings.

Errington, S.
1990   Recasting Sex, Gender, and Power: A Theoretical and Regional Overview. In *Power and Difference: Gender in Island Southeast Asia*, ed. J. Atkinson and S. Errington, 1–58. Stanford: Stanford University Press.

Fausto-Sterling, A.
1985   *Myths of Gender: Biological Theories about Women and Men*. New York: Basic Books.

Fedders, C., and L. Elliott
1987   *Shattered Dreams: The Story of Charlotte Fedders*. New York: Harper and Row.

Fienberg, S.
1977   *Analysis of Cross-Classified Categorical Data*. Cambridge: MIT Press.

Flanagan, J.
1989   Hierarchy in Simple "Egalitarian" Societies. *Annual Review of Anthropology* 18:245–266.

Flax, J.
1987a   Postmodernism and Gender Relations in Feminist Theory. *Signs: Journal of Women in Culture and Society* 12:621–643.
1987b   Remembering the Selves: Is the Repressed Gendered? *Michigan Quarterly Review, Special Issue: Women and Memory*, 26:92–110.

1990   *Thinking Fragments: Psychoanalysis, Feminism, and Postmodernism in the Contemporary West.* Berkeley, Los Angeles, and Oxford: University of California Press.

Flynn, C.
1990   Relationship Violence by Women: Issues and Implications. *Family Relations* 39:194–198.

Fox, R.
1968   *Encounter with Anthropology.* New York: Harcourt and Brace.
1975   The Inherent Rules of Violence. In *Social Rules and Social Behavior,* ed. P. Collett, 132–149. Totorwa, N.J.: Rowman and Littlefield.

Freud, S.
1920*a*   *A General Introduction to Psychoanalysis.* New York: Washington Square Press, 1969.
1920*b*   *Beyond the Pleasure Principle.* New York: W. W. Norton, 1961.

Fried, M.
1967   *The Evolution of Political Society: An Essay in Political Anthropology.* New York: Random House.

Frodi, A., J. Macaulay, and P. Thome
1977   Are Women Always Less Aggressive Than Men? A Review of the Experimental Literature. *Psychological Bulletin* 84:634–660.

Frost, W. D., and J. Averill
1982   Differences Between Men and Women in the Everyday Experience of Anger. In J. Averill, *Anger and Aggression: An Essay on Emotion,* 281–316. New York: Springer-Verlag.

Fry, D.
1992   Female Aggression among the Zapotec of Oaxaca, Mexico. In *Of Mice and Women: Aspects of Female Aggression,* ed. K. Björkqvist and P. Niemelä, 187–199. New York: Academic Press.
in press (ed.). *Sex Roles, Special Edition: Multicultural Perspectives on Aggression in Women and Girls.*

Gal, S.
1991   Between Speech and Silence: The Problematics of Research on Language and Gender. In *Gender at the Crossroad of Knowledge: Feminist Anthropology in the Postmodern Era,* ed. M. di Leonardo, 175–203. Berkeley, Los Angeles, and London: University of California Press.

Gallin, R.
1992   Wife Abuse in the Context of Development and Change: A Chinese (Taiwanese) Case. In *Sanctions and Sanctuary: Cultural Perspectives on the Beating of Wives,* ed. D. Counts, J. Brown, and J. Campbell, 219–250. Boulder: Westview Press.

Geertz, C.
1973   *The Interpretation of Cultures.* New York: Basic Books.

Gelles, R.
1987   *Family Violence.* Beverly Hills: Sage.

Gelles, R., and J. Lancaster (eds.)
1987   *Child Abuse and Neglect: Biosocial Dimensions.* New York: Aldine de Gruyter.

Gelles, R., and M. Straus
    1979   Determinants of Violence in the Family: Towards a Theoretical
            Integration. In *Contemporary Theories about the Family*. Vol. 1, ed.
            W. Burr, R. Hill, F. Nye, and I. Reiss, 549–581. New York:
            Free Press.

Gerber, E.
    1985   Rage and Obligation: Samoan Emotion in Conflict. In *Person, Self,
            and Experience: Exploring Pacific Ethnopsychologies*, ed. G. White and
            J. Kirkpatrick, 121–167. Berkeley, Los Angeles, and London:
            University of California Press.

Gergen, K.
    1984   Aggression as Discourse. In *Social Psychology of Aggression: From
            Individual Behavior to Social Interaction*, ed. A. Mummendey,
            51–68. New York: Springer-Verlag.

    1990   Social Understanding and the Inscription of Self. In *Cultural Psy-
            chology: Essays on Comparative Human Development*, ed. J. Stigler,
            R. Shweder, and G. Herdt, 569–606. Cambridge: Cambridge
            University Press.

Gerrard, G.
    1989   Everyone Will Be Jealous for that Mutika. *Mankind* 19:95–111.
    n.d.   Rape in Arnhem Land: Aboriginal Child-Rearing Practices and
            the Abuse of Women. Unpublished manuscript.

Gilmore, D.
    1987   *Aggression and Community: Paradoxes of Andalusian Culture*. New
            Haven: Yale University Press.

Glazer, I. (see also Schuster, I.)
    1992   Interfemale Aggression and Resource Scarcity in a Cross-Cultural
            Perspective. In *Of Mice and Women: Aspects of Female Aggression*,
            ed. K. Björkqvist and P. Niemelä, 163–171. New York: Aca-
            demic Press.

Glazer, I., and W. Abu Ras
    in press Aggression, Human Rights, and the Multiple Voices of Feminist
            Anthropology. *Sex Roles, Special Edition: Multicultural Perspectives
            on Aggression in Women and Girls*, ed. D. Fry.

Gluckman, M.
    1956   *Custom and Conflict in Africa*. Oxford: Basil Blackwell.
    1965   *Politics, Law and Ritual in Tribal Society*. Chicago: Aldine.

Goldberg, S.
    1973   *The Inevitability of Patriarchy*. New York: William Morrow.

Goodale, J.
    1971   *Tiwi Wives*. Seattle: University of Washington Press.

Goodenough, W.
    1956   Residence Rules. *Southwestern Journal of Anthropology* 12:22–37.
    1970   *Description and Comparison in Cultural Anthropology*. Chicago:
            Aldine.
    1971   Culture, Language and Society. Reading, Mass.: Addison Wesley
            Module #7.

Gordon, L.
1986   Family Violence, Feminism, and Social Control. *Feminist Studies* 12:453–476.
1990   Response to Scott. *Signs: Journal of Women in Culture and Society* 15:852–853.

Gough, K.
1975   The Origin of the Family. In *Toward an Anthropology of Women,* ed. R. Reiter, 51–76. New York: Monthly Review Press.

Graham, D., E. Rawlings, and N. Rimini
1988   Survivors of Terror: Battered Women, Hostages and the Stockholm Syndrome. In *Feminist Perspective on Wife Abuse,* ed. K. Yllo and M. Bograd, 217–233. Beverly Hills: Sage.

Greer, G.
1971   *The Female Eunuch.* London: MacGibbon and Kee.

Gregor, T.
1990   Male Dominance and Sexual Coercion. In *Cultural Psychology: Essays on Comparative Human Development,* ed. J. Stigler, R. Shweder, and G. Herdt, 477–495. Cambridge: Cambridge University Press.

Hallowell, I.
1955   *Culture and Experience.* Philadelphia: University of Pennsylvania Press.

Hamilton, A.
1981*a*   A Complex Strategical Situation: Gender and Power in Aboriginal Australia. In *Australian Women: Feminist Perspectives,* ed. N. Grieve and P. Grimshaw, 69–85. Melbourne: Oxford University Press.
1981*b*   *Nature and Nurture: Aboriginal Child-Rearing in North-Central Arnhem Land.* Canberra: Australian Institute of Aboriginal Studies.
1982   Child Health and Child Care in a Desert Community 1970–1971. In *Body, Land and Spirit: Health and Healing in Aboriginal Society,* ed. J. Reid, 49–71. St. Lucia: University of Queensland Press.

Handwerker, W., and P. Crosbie
1982   Sex and Dominance. *American Anthropologist* 84:97–104.

Hanmer, J., and M. Maynard
1987*a*   Introduction: Violence and Gender Stratification. In *Women, Violence and Social Control,* ed. J. Hanmer and M. Maynard, 1–12. London: Macmillan.
1987*b*   (eds.). *Women, Violence and Social Control.* London: Macmillan.

Haraway, D.
1989   *Primate Visions.* London: Routledge.

Harcourt, A., and F. de Waal
1992   Cooperation in Conflict: From Ants to Anthropoids. In *Cooperation in Conflict: Coalitions and Alliances in Animals and Humans,* ed. A. Harcourt and F. de Waal, 493–510. Oxford: Oxford University Press.

Harré, R., and P. Secord
1973   *The Explanation of Social Behaviour.* Oxford: Blackwell.

Harris, L., K. Gergen, and J. Lannamann
1986   Aggression Rituals. *Communications Monographs* 53:252–265.

Hart, C., A. Pilling, and J. Goodale
1988   *The Tiwi of Northern Australia.* 3d ed. New York: Holt, Rinehart and Winston.

Hasselt, V., R. Morrison, A. Bellack, and M. Hersen (eds.)
1988   *Handbook of Family Violence.* New York: Plenum Press.

Hayden, B., M. Deal, A. Cannon, and J. Casey
1986   Ecological Determinants of Women's Status among Hunter/Gatherers. *Human Evolution* 1:449–474.

Heath, J.
1982   *Nunggubuyu Dictionary.* Canberra: Australian Institute of Aboriginal Studies.

Heelas, P.
1982   Anthropology, Violence and Catharsis. In *Aggression and Violence,* ed. P. Marsh and A. Campbell, 45–61. Oxford: Basil Blackwell.

Herdt, G.
1986   Aspects of Socialization for Aggression in Sambia Ritual and Warfare. *Anthropological Quarterly* 59:160–164.

Hiatt, L.
1964   Incest in Arnhem Land. *Oceania* 35:124–128.
1965   *Kinship and Conflict: A Study of an Aboriginal Community in Northern Arnhem Land.* Canberra: Australian National University Press.
1966   A Spear in the Ear. *Oceania* 37:153–154.
1978   Classification of the Emotions. In *Australian Aboriginal Concepts,* ed. L. Hiatt, 182–187. Canberra: Australian Institute of Aboriginal Studies.
1985   Maidens, Males and Marx: Some Contrasts in the Work of Frederick Rose and Claude Meillassoux. *Oceania* 56:34–46.
1986   *Aboriginal Political Life.* Canberra: Australian Institute of Aboriginal Studies.

Hintze, J.
1990   *Number Cruncher Statistical System.* Kaysville, Utah.

Hirsch, M.
1981   *Women and Violence.* New York: Van Nostrand Reinhold.

Hochschild, A.
1983   *The Managed Heart: Commercialization of Human Feelings.* Berkeley, Los Angeles, and London: University of California Press.

Holland, D., and N. Quinn
1987   *Cultural Models in Language and Thought.* Cambridge: Cambridge University Press.

Holmberg, A.
    1969   *Nomads of the Long Bow: The Siriono of Eastern Bolivia.* Garden City,
            N.Y.: Natural History Press.

Howard, A.
    1985   Ethnopsychology and the Prospects for a Cultural Psychology. In
            Person, Self, and Experience: Exploring Pacific Ethnopsychologies, ed.
            G. White and J. Kirkpatrick, 401–419. Berkeley, Los Angeles, and
            London: University of California Press.

Hrdy, S.
    1981   *The Woman That Never Evolved.* Cambridge: Harvard University
            Press.

Hrdy, S., and G. Williams
    1983   Behavioral Biology and the Double Standard. In *Social Behavior of
            Female Vertebrates,* ed. S. Wasser, 3–17. New York: Academic
            Press.

Huffer, V.
    1980   *The Sweetness of the Fig: Aboriginal Women in Transition.* Seattle:
            University of Washington Press.

Hughes, E.
    1971   *Nunggubuyu-English Dictionary.* Oceania Linguistic Monographs.
            Sydney: University of Sydney Press.

Hunter, E.
    1991   The Intercultural and Socio-Historical Context of Aboriginal
            Personal Violence in Remote Australia. *Australian Psychologist*
            26:89–98.

Huston, K.
    1984   Ethical Decisions in Treating Battered Women. *Professional Psy-
            chology: Research and Practice* 15:822–832.

Hyde, J.
    1986   Gender Differences in Aggression. In *The Psychology of Gender: Ad-
            vances Through Meta-Analysis,* ed. J. Hyde and M. Linn, 51–66.
            Baltimore: Johns Hopkins University Press.
    1990   Meta-Analysis and the Psychology of Gender Differences. *Signs:
            Journal of Women in Culture and Society* 16:55–73.

Ifeka-Moller, C.
    1975   Female Militancy and Colonial Revolt: The Women's War of
            1929, Eastern Nigeria. In *Perceiving Women,* ed. E. Ardener,
            127–145. London: Dent.

Irons, W.
    1983   Human Female Reproductive Strategies. In *Social Behavior of Fe-
            male Vertebrates,* ed. S. Wasser, 169–213. New York: Academic
            Press.

Ito, K.
    1987   Emotions, Proper Behavior (Hana Pono) and Hawaiian Concepts
            of Self, Person, and Individual. In *Contemporary Issues in Mental*

Health Research in the Pacific Islands, ed. A. Robillard and A. Marsella, 45–71. Honolulu: Social Science Research Institute, University of Hawaii.

Jennaway, M.
1991   Paradigms, Postmodern Epistemologies and Paradoxes: The Place of Feminism in Anthropology. *Anthropological Forum* 6:167–189.

Jones, A.
1980   *Women Who Kill.* New York: Holt, Rinehart and Winston.

Joseph, S.
1983   Working-Class Women's Networks in a Sectarian State: A Political Paradox. *American Ethnologist* 10:1–22.

Kaberry, P.
1939   *Aboriginal Woman: Sacred and Profane.* London: George Routledge and Sons.

Kanogo, T.
1987   Kikuyu Women and the Politics of Protest: Mau Mau. In *Images of Women in Peace and War: Cross-Cultural and Historical Perspectives,* ed. S. MacDonald, P. Holden, and S. Ardener, 78–99. Madison: University of Wisconsin Press.

Keen, I.
1989   Aboriginal Governance. In *Emergent Inequalities in Aboriginal Australia,* ed. J. Altman, 17–42. Sydney: Oceania Monographs.

Keesing, R.
1974   Theories of Culture. *Annual Review of Anthropology* 3:73–97.
1975   *Kin Groups and Social Structure.* New York: Holt, Rinehart and Winston.

Kelly, K.
1991   *Nancy Reagan: The Unauthorized Biography.* New York: Simon and Schuster.

Kelly, L.
1988   How Women Define Their Experiences of Violence. In *Feminist Perspectives on Wife Abuse,* ed. K. Yllo and M. Bograd, 114–132. Beverly Hills: Sage.

Kempe, C., F. Silverman, B. Steel, W. Droegmueller, and H. Silver
1962   The Battered Child Syndrome. *Journal of the American Medical Association* 181:17–24.

Kerns, V.
1992   Preventing Violence Against Women: A Central American Case. In *Sanctions and Sanctuary: Cultural Perspectives on the Beating of Wives,* ed. D. Counts, J. Brown, and J. Campbell, 125–138. Boulder: Westview Press.

Kirkpatrick, J., and G. White
1985   Exploring Ethnopsychologies. In *Persons, Self, and Experience: Exploring Pacific Ethnopsychologies,* ed. G. White and J. Kirkpatrick,

3–34. Berkeley, Los Angeles, and London: University of California Press.

Klama, J.
1988   *Aggression: The Myth of the Beast Within.* New York: John Wiley and Sons.

Knauft, B.
1985   *Good Company and Violence: Sorcery and Social Action in a Lowland New Guinea Society.* Berkeley, Los Angeles, and London: University of California Press.
1987a   Managing Sex and Anger: Tobacco and Kava Use Among the Gebusi of Papua New Guinea. In *Drugs in Western Pacific Societies: Relations of Substance,* ed. L. Lindstrom, 72–98. New York: University Press of America.
1987b   Reconsidering Violence in Simple Human Societies. *Current Anthropology* 28:457–500.

Kohlberg, L.
1966   A Cognitive-Developmental Analysis of Children's Sex-Role Concepts and Attitudes. In *The Development of Sex Differences,* ed. E. Maccoby, 82–172. Stanford: Stanford University Press.

Kondo, D.
1990   *Crafting Selves: Power, Gender, and Discourses of Identity in a Japanese Workplace.* Chicago: University of Chicago Press.

Konner, M.
1982   *The Tangled Wing.* New York: Holt, Rinehart and Winston.

Kopper, B., and D. Epperson
1991   Women and Anger: Sex and Sex-Role Comparisons in the Expression of Anger. *Psychology of Women Quarterly* 15:7–14.

Korbin, J.
1981   Introduction and Conclusion. In *Child Abuse and Neglect: Cross-Cultural Perspectives,* ed. J. Korbin, 1–12, 205–210. Berkeley, Los Angeles, and London: University of California Press.

Kramarae, C.
1982   Gender: How She Speaks. In *Attitudes Towards Language Variation,* ed. E. Ryan and H. Giles, 84–98. London: Edward Arnold.

Lakoff, G., and M. Johnson
1980   *Metaphors We Live By.* Chicago: University of Chicago Press.

Lakoff, G., and Z. Kovecses
1987   The Cognitive Model of Anger Inherent in American English. In *Cultural Models in Language and Thought,* ed. D. Holland and N. Quinn, 195–221. Cambridge: Cambridge University Press.

Lambek, M.
1992   Like Teeth Biting Tongue: The Proscription and Practice of Spouse Abuse in Mayotte. In *Sanctions and Sanctuary: Cultural Perspectives on the Beating of Wives,* ed. D. Counts, J. Brown, and J. Campbell, 157–171. Boulder: Westview Press.

Lamphere, L.
  1974   Strategies, Cooperation and Conflict among Women in Domestic
            Groups. In *Woman, Culture, and Society,* ed. M. Rosaldo and L.
            Lamphere, 97–112. Stanford: Stanford University Press.
  1987   Feminism and Anthropology: The Struggle to Reshape Our
            Thinking about Gender. In *The Impact of Feminist Research in the
            Academy,* ed. C. Farnham, 11–33. Bloomington: Indiana Univer-
            sity Press.

Lancaster, J.
  1989   Women in Biosocial Perspective. In *Gender and Anthropology: Crit-
            ical Reviews for Research and Teaching,* ed. S. Morgen, 95–115.
            Washington D.C.: American Anthropological Association.

Lancaster, J., and C. Lancaster
  1987   The Watershed: Change in Parental-Investment and Family For-
            mation Strategies in the Course of Human Evolution. In *Parenting
            Across the Life Span: Biosocial Dimensions,* ed. J. Lancaster, J. Alt-
            mann, A. Rossi, and L. Sherrod, 187–205. New York: Aldine de
            Gruyter.

Langton, M.
  1988   Medicine Square. In *Being Black: Aboriginal Culture in "Settled"
            Australia,* ed. I. Keen, 201–225. Canberra: Aboriginal Studies
            Press.

Larbalestier, J.
  1991   The Politics of Representation: Australian Aboriginal Women and
            Feminism. *Anthropological Forum* 6:143–157.

Lateef, S.
  1990   Rule by the Danda: Domestic Violence among Indo-Fijians. *Pa-
            cific Studies, Special Issue: Domestic Violence in Oceania,* 13:43–61.
  1992   Wife Abuse among Indo-Fijians. In *Sanctions and Sanctuary: Cul-
            tural Perspectives on the Beating of Wives,* ed. D. Counts, J. Brown,
            and J. Campbell, 185–202. Boulder: Westview Press.

Leacock, E.
  1978   Women's Status in Egalitarian Society: Implications for Social
            Evolution. *Current Anthropology* 19:247–276.

Lee, R.
  1979   *The !Kung San: Men, Women, and Work in a Foraging Society.*
            Cambridge: Cambridge University Press.

Lee, R., and I. DeVore
  1968   *Man the Hunter.* Chicago: Aldine.

Lepowsky, M.
  1990   Gender in an Egalitarian Society: A Case Study from the Coral
            Sea. In *Beyond the Second Sex: New Directions in the Anthropology of
            Gender,* ed. P. Sanday and R. Goodenough, 169–224. Philadel-
            phia: University of Pennsylvania Press.

Lerner, H.
  1985   *The Dance of Anger: A Woman's Guide to Changing the Patterns of
            Intimate Relationships.* New York: Harper and Row.

LeVine, R.
1961   Anthropology and the Study of Conflict: An Introduction. *Journal of Conflict Resolution* 5:3–15.
1962   Witchcraft and Co-Wife Proximity in Southwestern Kenya. *Ethnology* 1:39–45.
1965   Intergenerational Tensions and Extended Family Structures in Africa. In *Social Structure and the Family: Generational Relations,* ed. E. Shanas and G. Streib, 187–204. Englewood Cliffs, N.J.: Prentice-Hall.

Levinson, D.
1989   *Family Violence in Cross-Cultural Perspective.* Beverly Hills: Sage.

Levy, R.
1973   *Tahitians: Mind and Experience in the Society Islands.* Chicago: University of Chicago Press.

Liberman, K.
1985   *Understanding Interaction in Central Australia: An Ethnomethodological Study of Australian Aboriginal People.* Boston: Routledge and Kegan Paul.

Liddle, M.
1989   Feminist Contributions to an Understanding of Violence Against Women—Three Steps Forward, Two Steps Back. *Canadian Review of Sociology and Anthropology* 26:759–775.

Lilley, R.
1989   Gungarakayn Women Speak: Reproduction and the Transformation of Tradition. *Oceania* 60:81–98.

Lorenz, K.
1966   *On Aggression.* New York: Bantam.

Lutz, C.
1985   Ethnopsychology Compared to What? Explaining Behavior and Consciousness among the Ifaluk. In *Person, Self, and Experience: Exploring Pacific Ethnopsychologies,* ed. G. White and J. Kirkpatrick, 35–79. Berkeley, Los Angeles, and London: University of California Press.
1988   *Unnatural Emotions: Everyday Sentiments on a Microneisan Atoll.* Chicago: University of Chicago Press.
1990   Engendered Emotion: Gender, Power, and the Rhetoric of Emotional Control in American Discourse. In *Language and the Politics of Emotion,* ed. C. Lutz and L. Abu-Lughod, 69–91. Cambridge: Cambridge University Press.

Lutz, C., and L. Abu-Lughod (eds.)
1990   *Language and the Politics of Emotion.* Cambridge: Cambridge University Press.

Lutz, C., and G. White
1986   The Anthropology of Emotions. *Annual Review of Anthropology* 15:405–436.

MacAndrew, C., and R. Edgerton
1969   *Drunken Comportment: A Social Explanation.* New York: Aldine.

Macaulay, J.
    1985   Adding Gender to Aggression Research: Incremental or Revolutionary Change? In *Women, Gender, and Social Psychology,* ed. V. O'Leary, R. Unger, and B. Wallston, 191–224. Hillsdale, N.J.: Laurence Erlbaum.

Maccoby, E., and C. Jacklin
    1974   *The Psychology of Sex Differences.* Stanford: Stanford University Press.
    1980   Sex Differences in Aggression: A Rejoinder and Reprise. *Child Development* 51:964–980.

Macdonald, G.
    1988   A Wiradjuri Fight Story. In *Being Black: Aboriginal Cultures in "Settled" Australia,* ed. I. Keen, 179–199. Canberra: Aboriginal Studies Press.

McDowell, N.
    1990   Person, Assertion, and Marriage: On the Nature of Household Violence in Bun. *Pacific Studies, Special Issue: Domestic Violence in Oceania,* 13:171–188.
    1992   Household Violence in a Yuat River Village. In *Sanctions and Sanctuary: Cultural Perspectives on the Beating of Wives,* ed. D. Counts, J. Brown, and J. Campbell, 77–88. Boulder: Westview Press.

McKnight, D.
    1986   Fighting in an Australian Aboriginal Supercamp. In *The Anthropology of Violence,* ed. D. Riches, 136–163. Oxford: Basil Blackwell.

McNeill, S.
    1987   Flashing: Its Effect on Women. In *Women, Violence and Social Control,* ed. J. Hanmer and M. Maynard, 93–109. London: Macmillan.

McNulty, F.
    1980   *The Burning Bed: The True Story of an Abused Wife.* New York: Bantam.

Maddock, K.
    1970   A Structural Interpretation of the *Mirriri. Oceania* 60:165–176.
    1972   *The Australian Aborigines: A Portrait of Their Society.* Ringwood, Victoria: Penguin Books.
    1974   Dangerous Proximities and Their Analogues. *Mankind* 3: 206–217.

Makarius, R.
    1966   Incest and Redemption in Arnhem Land. *Oceania* 37:148–152.

Malinowski, B.
    1913   *The Family among the Australian Aborigines: A Sociological Study.* London: University of London Press.

Marcus, G., and M. Fisher
    1986   *Anthropology as Cultural Critique: An Experimental Moment in the Human Sciences.* Chicago: University of Chicago Press.

Marsh, P., and R. Paton
  1986   Gender, Social Class and Conceptual Schemas of Aggression. In
           Violent Transactions: The Limits of Personality, ed. A. Campbell and
           J. Gibbs, 57–85. Oxford: Basil Blackwell.

Martin, D.
  1976   *Battered Wives.* San Francisco: Glide Publications.

Mascia-Lees, F., P. Sharpe, and C. Cohen
  1989   The Postmodernist Turn in Anthropology: Cautions from a Femi-
           nist Perspective. *Signs: Journal of Women in Culture and Society*
           15:7–33.

Mauss, M.
  1967   *The Gift: Forms and Functions of Exchange in Archaic Societies.* New
           York: W. W. Norton.

Meggitt, M.
  1962   *Desert People.* Melbourne: Angus and Robertson.

Merlan, F.
  1978   Making People Quiet in the Pastoral North: Reminiscences of
           Elsey Station. *Aboriginal History* 2:70–105.
  1986   Australian Aboriginal Conception Beliefs Revisited. *Man* 21:
           474–493.
  1988   Gender in Aboriginal Social Life: A Review. In *Social Anthropology
           and Australian Aboriginal Studies: A Contemporary Overview,* ed. R.
           Berndt and R. Tonkinson, 15–76. Canberra: Aboriginal Studies
           Press.
  1989   On Aboriginal Religion: An Appreciation. Preface in W. Stanner,
           On Aboriginal Religion, i–xviii. Sydney: Oceania Monographs.

Michaels, E.
  1987   The Last of the Nomads, the Last of the Ethnographies or "All
           Anthropologists are Liars." *Mankind* 17:34–46.

Middleton, D.
  1989   Emotional Style: The Cultural Ordering of Emotions. *Ethos*
           17:187–201.

Miller, B.
  1992   Wife-Beating in India: Variations on a Theme. In *Sanctions and
           Sanctuary: Cultural Perspectives on the Beating of Wives,* ed. D.
           Counts, J. Brown, and J. Campbell, 173–184. Boulder: West-
           view Press.

Miller, J.
  1991   The Construction of Anger in Women and Men. In *Women's
           Growth in Connection: Writings from the Stone Center,* ed. J. Jordan,
           A. Kaplan, J. Miller, I. Stiver, and J. Surrey, 181–195. New York:
           Guilford Press.

Miner, V., and H. Longino (eds.)
  1987   *Competition: A Feminist Taboo.* New York: Feminist Press.

Mitchell, J.
  1973   *Woman's Estate.* New York: Vintage Books.

Moore, H.
1988   *Feminism and Anthropology.* Minneapolis: University of Minnesota Press.

Morris, B.
1988   Dhan-gadi Resistance to Assimilation. In *Being Black: Aboriginal Cultures in "Settled" Australia,* ed. I. Keen, 33–63. Canberra: Aboriginal Studies Press.

Moyer, K.
1974   Sex Differences in Aggression. In *Sex Differences in Behavior,* ed. P. Friedman, M. Richart, and R. Van de Wiele, 335–372. Huntington, N.Y.: Robert E. Krieger.

Mukhopadhyay, C., and P. Higgins
1988   Anthropological Studies of Women's Status Revisited: 1977–1987. *Annual Review of Anthropology* 17:461–495.

Murdock, G.
1949   *Social Structure.* New York: Macmillan.

Murphy, R.
1971   *The Dialectics of Social Life.* New York: Basic Books.

Myers, F.
1979   Emotions and the Self: A Theory of Personhood and Political Order among Pintupi Aborigines. *Ethos* 9:343–370.
1980   The Cultural Basis of Politics in Pintupi Life. *Mankind* 12:197–214.
1986   *Pintupi Country, Pintupi Self: Sentiment, Place, and Politics among Western Desert Aborigines.* Washington, D.C.: Smithsonian Institution Press.
1988   The Logic and Meaning of Anger among Pintupi Aborigines. *Man* 23:589–610.

NiCarthy, G.
1987   *The Ones Who Got Away.* Seattle: Seal Press.

Nielsen, J.
1990   Introduction. In *Feminist Research Methods: Exemplary Readings in the Social Sciences,* ed. J. Nielsen, 1–37. Boulder: Westview Press.

Okely, J.
1989   Defiant Moments: Gender, Resistance and Individuals. *Man* 26:3–22.

Ortner, S.
1984   Theory in Anthropology Since the Sixties. *Comparative Studies in Society and History* 26:126–166.
1989   *High Religion: A Cultural and Political History of Sherpa Buddhism.* Princeton: Princeton University Press.

Ortner, S., and H. Whitehead
1981   Introduction: Accounting for Sexual Meanings. In *Sexual Meanings: The Cultural Construction of Gender and Sexuality,* ed. S. Ortner and H. Whitehead, 1–27. Cambridge: Cambridge University Press.

Otterbein, K.
  1986   *The Ultimate Coercive Sanction: A Cross-Cultural Study of Capital Punishment*. New Haven: Human Relations Area Files Press.
Parkes, C., J. Stevenson-Hinde, and P. Marris (eds.)
  1991   *Attachment Across the Life Cycle*. New York: Tavistock-Routledge.
Patai, D.
  1991   U.S. Academics and Third World Women: Is Ethical Research Possible? In *Women's Words: The Feminist Practice of Oral History*, ed. S. Gluck and D. Patai, 137–153. New York: Routledge.
Peacock, J.
  1986   *The Anthropological Lens: Harsh Light, Soft Focus*. Cambridge: Cambridge University Press.
People
  1989   Introduction to "A Love Betrayed, A Brief Life Lost." *People* (February 13):83–84.
Peterson, N.
  1974   The Importance of Women in Determining the Composition of Residential Groups in Aboriginal Australia. In *Women's Role in Aboriginal Society*, ed. F. Gale, 16–27. Canberra: Australian Institute of Aboriginal Studies.
Pilling, A.
  1957   *Law and Feud in an Aboriginal Society of North Australia*. Ph.D. dissertation, University of California, Berkeley.
Price, S.
  1984   *Co-Wives and Calabashes*. Ann Arbor: University of Michigan Press.
Ptacek, J.
  1988   Why Do Men Batter Their Wives? In *Feminist Perspectives on Wife Abuse*, ed. K. Yllo and M. Bograd, 133–157. Beverly Hills: Sage.
Quinn, N.
  1977   Anthropological Studies on Women's Status. *Annual Review of Anthropology* 61:181–225.
  1987   Convergent Evidence for a Cultural Model of American Marriage. In *Cultural Models in Language and Thought*, ed. D. Holland and N. Quinn, 173–192. Cambridge: Cambridge University Press.
Quinn, N., and D. Holland
  1987   Culture and Cognition. In *Cultural Models in Language and Thought*, ed. D. Holland and N. Quinn, 3–40. Cambridge: Cambridge University Press.
Quinn, N., and C. Strauss
  1989   A Cognitive Cultural Anthropology. Paper presented at the American Anthropological Association meetings.
Ramazanoglu, C.
  1987   Sex and Violence in Academic Life or You Can Keep a Good Woman Down. In *Women, Violence and Social Control*, ed. J. Hanmer and M. Maynard, 61–74. London: Macmillan.

Reay, M.
  1970   A Decision as Narrative. In *Australian Aboriginal Anthropology: Modern Studies in the Social Anthropology of the Australian Aborigines,* ed. R. Berndt, 164–173. Nedlands: University of Western Australia Press.

Reid, J.
  1983   *Sorcerers and Healing Spirits: Continuity and Change in an Aboriginal Medical System.* Canberra: Australian National University Press.

Reiter, R. (ed.)
  1975   *Toward an Anthropology of Women.* New York: Monthly Review Press.

Remoff, H.
  1984   *Sexual Choice: A Woman's Decision.* New York: Dutton/Lewis Publishing.

Reser, J.
  1991   The "Socio-Historical" Arguments and Constructions of Aboriginal Violence—A Critical Review of Hunter (1991). *Australian Psychologist* 26:209–214.

Reynolds, V.
  1976   *The Biology of Human Action.* Reading and San Francisco: W. H. Freeman.

Richardson, L.
  1985   *The New Other Woman: Contemporary Single Women in Affairs with Married Men.* New York: Free Press.

Riches, D.
  1986   The Phenomenon of Violence. In *The Anthropology of Violence,* ed. D. Riches, 1–27. Oxford: Basil Blackwell.

Ricks, M.
  1985   The Social Transmission of Parental Behavior: Attachment Across Generations. In *Growing Points of Attachment Theory and Research,* ed. I. Bretherton and E. Waters, 211–227. Monographs of the Society for Research in Child Development.

Robarcheck, C.
  1977   Frustration, Aggression, and the Nonviolent Semai. *American Ethnologist* 4:762–779.

Roheim, G.
  1933   Women and Their Life in Central Australia. *Journal of the Royal Anthropological Institute of Great Britain and Ireland* 63:207–265.

Rohner, R.
  1976   Sex Differences in Aggression: Phylogenetic and Enculturation Perspectives. *Ethos* 4:57–72.

Rosaldo, M.
  1974   Woman, Culture, and Society: A Theoretical Overview. In *Woman, Culture, and Society,* ed. M. Rosaldo and L. Lamphere, 17–42. Stanford: Stanford University Press.

1980*a*   The Use and Abuse of Anthropology: Feminism and Cross-Cultural Understanding. *Signs: Journal of Women in Culture and Society* 5:389–417.

1980*b*   *Knowledge and Passion: Ilongot Notions of Self and Social Life.* Cambridge: Cambridge University Press.

1984   Toward an Anthropology of Self and Feeling. In *Culture Theory: Essays on Mind, Self, and Emotion,* ed. R. Shweder and R. LeVine, 137–157. Cambridge: Cambridge University Press.

Rosaldo, M., and L. Lamphere
1974   *Woman, Culture, and Society.* Stanford: Stanford University Press.

Rose, D.
1986   Passive Violence. *Australian Aboriginal Studies* 1:24–30.

Rose, F.
1960   *Classification of Kin, Age Structure, and Marriage amongst the Groote Eylandt Aborigines.* Berlin: Akademie-Verlag.

1968   Australian Marriage: Land-Owning Groups and Initiations. In *Man the Hunter,* ed. R. Lee and I. DeVore, 200–208. Chicago: Aldine.

Rosenberg, D.
1990   Language in the Discourse of the Emotions. In *Language and the Politics of Emotion,* ed. C. Lutz and L. Abu-Lughod, 162–185. Cambridge: Cambridge University Press.

Rowley, C.
1977   White Settlement and Interaction. In *The Australian Encyclopedia,* 3d ed., 52–61. Sydney: Grolier Society of Australia.

Sackett, L.
1977   Liquor and the Law: Wiluna, Western Australia. In *Aborigines and Change: Australia in the '70s,* ed. R. Berndt, 90–99. Canberra: Australian Institute of Aboriginal Studies.

1978   Punishment as Ritual: "Man-Making" among Western Desert Aborigines. *Oceania* 49:110–127.

1988   Resisting Arrests: Drinking, Development and Discipline in a Desert Context. *Social Analysis* 24:66–77.

Sahlins, M.
1976   *Culture and Practical Reason.* Chicago: University of Chicago Press.

Sanday, P.
1981   *Female Power and Male Dominance: On the Origins of Sexual Inequality.* Cambridge: Cambridge University Press.

Sansom, B.
1980   *The Camp at Wallaby Cross: Aboriginal Fringe Dwellers in Darwin.* Canberra: Australian Institute of Aboriginal Studies.

Saunders, D.
1988   Wife Abuse, Husband Abuse, or Mutual Combat? A Feminist Perspective on the Empirical Findings. In *Feminist Perspectives on Wife Abuse,* ed. K. Yllo and M. Bograd, 90–113. Beverly Hills: Sage.

Schebeck, B.
1978   Names of Body-Parts in North-East Arnhem Land. In *Australian Aboriginal Concepts,* ed. L. Hiatt, 169–177. Canberra: Australian Institute of Aboriginal Studies.

Scheffler, H.
1991   Sexism and Naturalism in the Study of Kinship. In *Gender at the Crossroads of Knowledge: Feminist Anthropology in the Postmodern Era,* ed. M. di Leonardo, 361–382. Berkeley, Los Angeles, and London: University of California Press.

Scheper-Hughes, N.
1987   (ed.). *Child Survival: Anthropological Perspectives on the Treatment and Maltreatment of Children.* Dordrecht: D. Reidel.

Scheper-Hughes, N., and M. Lock
1987   The Mindful Body: A Prolegomenon to Future Work in Medical Anthropology. *Medical Anthropology Quarterly* 1:6–41.

Schieffelin, E.
1985   Anger, Grief, and Shame: Toward a Kaluli Ethnopsychology. In *Person, Self, and Experience: Exploring Pacific Ethnopsychologies,* ed. G. White and J. Kirkpatrick, 168–182. Berkeley, Los Angeles, and London: University of California Press.

Schlegel, A.
1972   *Male Dominance and Female Autonomy: Domestic Authority in Matrilineal Societies.* New Haven: Human Relations Area Files Press.
1977   *Sexual Stratification: A Cross-Cultural View.* New York: Columbia University Press.

Schuster, I. (see also Glazer, I.)
1983   Women's Aggression: An African Case Study. *Aggressive Behavior* 9:319–331.
1985   Female Aggression and Resource Scarcity: A Cross-Cultural Perspective. Unpublished manuscript.

Schuster, I., and J. Hartz-Karp
1986   Kinder, Kueche, Kibbutz: Women's Aggression and Status Quo Maintenance in a Small Scale Community. *Anthropological Quarterly: Culture and Aggression* 59:191–199.

Seligman, M.
1975   *Helplessness: On Depression, Development, and Death.* San Francisco: Freeman.

Seymour, S.
1981   Cooperation and Competition: Some Issues and Problems in Cross-Cultural Analysis. In *Handbook of Cross-Cultural Human Development,* ed. R. Munroe, R. Munroe, and B. Whiting, 717–738. New York: Garland Press.

Shapiro, W.
1977   Structure, Variation and Change in "Balamumu" Social Classification. *Journal of Anthropological Research* 33:16–49.

1979   *Social Organization in Aboriginal Australia.* New York: St. Martins Press.

1981   *Miwuyt Marriage: The Cultural Anthropology of Affinity in Northeast Arnhem Land.* Philadelphia: Institute for the Study of Human Issues.

1990   The Quest for Purity in Anthropological Inquiry. Paper presented at the American Anthropological Association meetings.

Shields, S.
1987   Women, Men, and the Dilemma of Emotion. In *Sex and Gender: Review of Personality and Social Psychology,* vol. 7, ed. P. Shaver and C. Hendrick, 229–250. Beverly Hills: Sage.

1991   Gender in the Psychology of Emotion: A Selective Research Review. In *International Review of Studies of Emotion,* vol. 1, ed. K. Strongman, 227–245. London: John Wiley and Sons.

Shokeid, M.
1982   The Regulation of Aggression in Daily Life: Aggressive Relationships among Moroccan Immigrants in Israel. *Ethnology* 21: 271–281.

Shore, B.
1988   Interpretation Under Fire. *Anthropological Quarterly* 61:161–174.

Shweder, R.
1990   Cultural Psychology—What Is It? In *Cultural Psychology: Essays on Comparative Human Development,* ed. J. Stigler, R. Shweder, and G. Herdt, 1–43. Cambridge: Cambridge University Press.

Shweder, R., and E. Bourne
1984   Does the Concept of the Person Vary Cross-Culturally? In *Culture Theory: Essays on Mind, Self, and Emotions,* ed. R. Shweder and R. LeVine, 158–199. Cambridge: Cambridge University Press.

Simmel, G.
1955   *Conflict.* Glencoe: Free Press.

Smuts, B.
1992   Male Aggression against Women: An Evolutionary Perspective. *Human Nature* 3:1–44.

Stacey, J.
1988   Can There Be a Feminist Ethnography? *Women's Studies International Forum* 11:21–27.

Stanley, L., and S. Wise
1990   Method, Methodology, and Epistemology in Feminist Research Processes. In *Feminist Praxis: Research Theory and Epistemology in Feminist Sociology,* ed. L. Stanley, 20–60. New York: Routledge.

Stanner, W.
1965   The Dreaming. In *Reader in Comparative Religion,* ed. W. Lessa and E. Vogt, 158–167. New York: Harper.

1966   *On Aboriginal Religion.* Oceania Monograph no. 11. Sydney: University of Sydney Press.

1968   *The Boyer Lectures: After the Dreaming.* Sydney: Australian Broadcasting Commission.

Stark, R., and J. McEvoy
1970   Middle Class Violence. *Psychology Today* (November):52–54, 110–112.

Starr, R.
1988   Physical Abuse of Children. In *Handbook of Family Violence,* ed. V. Van Hasselt, R. Morrison, A. Bellack, and M. Hersen, 119–155. New York: Plenum Press.

Steinmetz, S.
1977   The Battered Husband Syndrome. *Victimology* 2:499–509.

Steinmetz, S., and J. Lucca
1988   Husband Battering. In *Handbook of Family Violence,* ed. V. Van Hasselt, R. Morrison, A. Bellack, and M. Hersen, 233–246. New York: Plenum Press.

Stephens, W.
1963   *The Family in Cross-Cultural Perspective.* New York: Holt, Rinehart and Winston.

Stets, J., and M. Straus
1990   Gender Differences in Reporting Marital Violence and Its Medical and Psychological Consequences. In *Physical Violence in American Families,* ed. M. Straus and R. Gelles, 151–165. New Brunswick, N.J.: Transaction Publishers.

Strathern, M.
1980   No Nature, No Culture: The Hagen Case. In *Nature, Culture and Gender,* ed. C. MacCormack and M. Strathern, 174–222. Cambridge: Cambridge University Press.

Straus, M.
1980   Victims and Aggressors in Marital Violence. *American Behavioral Scientist* 23:681–704.

1983   Ordinary Violence, Child Abuse, and Wife-Beating: What Do They Have in Common? In *The Dark Side of Families: Current Family Violence Research,* ed. D. Finkelhor, R. Gelles, G. Hotaling, and M. Straus, 213–234. Beverly Hills: Sage.

Straus, M., and R. Gelles
1986   Societal Change and Change in Family Violence from 1975 to 1985 as Revealed by Two National Surveys. *Journal of Marriage and the Family* 48:465–479.

1990a   (eds.). *Physical Violence in American Families.* New Brunswick, N.J.: Transaction Publishers.

1990b   How Violent Are American Families? Estimates from the National Family Violence Resurvey and Other Studies. In *Physical Violence in American Families,* ed. M. Straus and R. Gelles, 95–112. New Brunswick, N.J.: Transaction Publishers.

Straus, M., R. Gelles, and S. Steinmetz
1980   *Behind Closed Doors: Violence in the American Family.* Garden City, N.Y.: Anchor Press.

Straus, M., and C. Smith
1990   Family Patterns and Child Abuse. In *Physical Violence in American Families,* ed. M. Straus and R. Gelles, 507–523. New Brunswick, N.J.: Transaction Publishers.

Strehlow, T.
1970   Geography and the Totemic Landscape in Central Australia: A Functional Study. In *Australian Aboriginal Anthropology,* ed. R. Berndt, 92–129. Perth: University of Western Australia Press.

Summers, A.
1989   The Hedda Conundrum. *Ms* (April):54.

Swartz, M.
1990   Aggressive Speech, Status, and Cultural Distribution among the Swahili of Mombasa. In *Personality and the Cultural Construction of Society,* ed. D. Jordan and M. Swartz, 116–142. Tuscaloosa: University of Alabama Press.

Switzer, M., and K. Hale
1984   *Called to Account: The Story of One Family's Struggle to Say No to Abuse.* Seattle: Seal Press.

Tavris, C.
1982   *Anger: The Misunderstood Emotion.* New York: Simon and Schuster.

Taylor, C.
1964   *The Explanation of Behavior.* London: Routledge and Kegan Paul.

Tieger, T.
1980   On the Biological Basis of Sex Differences in Aggression. *Child Development* 51:943–963.

Tiger, L.
1970   *Men in Groups.* New York: Vintage Books.

Tiger, L., and R. Fox
1971   *The Imperial Animal.* New York: Holt, Rinehart and Winston.

Tonkinson, M.
1985   Domestic Violence among Aborigines. Paper prepared for the Domestic Violence Task Force.

Tonkinson, R.
1978   *The Mardudjara Aborigines: Living the Dream in Australia's Desert.* New York: Holt, Rinehart and Winston.
1990   The Changing Status of Aboriginal Women: "Free Agents" at Jigalong. In *Going It Alone? Prospects for Aboriginal Autonomy: Essays in Honor of Ronald and Catherine Berndt,* ed. R. Tonkinson and M. Howard, 125–147. Canberra: Aboriginal Studies Press.

Tooby, J., and L. Cosmides
1989   Evolutionary Psychology and the Generation of Culture. Pt. I, Theoretical Considerations. *Ethology and Sociobiology* 10:29–49.

Trivers, R.
1972   Parental Investment and Sexual Selection. In *Sexual Selection and the Descent of Man,* ed. B. Campbell, 136–179. Chicago: Aldine.

Turnbull, C.

1982   The Ritualization of Potential Conflict between the Sexes among the Mbuti. In *Politics and History in Band Society,* ed. E. Leacock and R. Lee, 133–155. Cambridge: Cambridge University Press.

Turner, D.

1974   *Tradition and Transformation: A Study of Aborigines in the Groote Eylandt Area, Northern Australia.* Canberra: Australian Institute of Aboriginal Studies.

1976   Levels of Organization nd Communication in Aboriginal Australia. In *Tribes and Boundaries in Australia,* ed. N. Peterson, 180–191. Canberra: Australian Institute of Aboriginal Studies.

Turner, J.

1984   *A Crying Game: The Diary of a Battered Wife.* Edinburgh: Mainstream Publishing.

Unger, R., B. Raymond, and S. Levine

1974   Are Women a "Minority" Group? Sometimes! *International Journal of Group Tensions* 4:71–81.

Valentine, C.

1963   Men of Anger and Men of Shame: Lakalai Ethnopsychology and Its Implications for Sociopsychological Theory. *Ethnology* 2: 441–477.

Van Allen, J.

1972   Sitting on a Man: Colonialism and the Lost Political Institutions of Igbo Women. *Canadian Journal of African Studies* 6:165–181.

Wagley, C.

1949   *The Social and Religious Life of a Guatemalan Village.* Menasha, Wis.: American Anthropological Association.

Walker, L.

1979   *The Battered Woman.* New York: Harper and Row.

1984   *The Battered Woman Syndrome.* New York: Springer.

1989   *Terrifying Love: Why Battered Women Kill and How Society Responds.* New York: Harper and Row.

Warner, W. L.

1937   *A Black Civilization.* New York: Harper.

Weiss, N.

1989   A Love Betrayed, A Brief Life Lost. *People* (February 13):84–90.

White, G., and J. Kirkpatrick (eds.)

1985   *Person, Self, and Experience: Exploring Pacific Ethnopsychologies.* Berkeley, Los Angeles, and London: University of California Press.

White, G., and K. Watson-Gegeo

1990   Disentangling Discourse. In *Disentangling: Conflict Discourse in Pacific Societies,* ed. K. Watson-Gegeo and G. White, 3–49. Stanford: Stanford University Press.

White, J.
    1983   Sex and Gender Issues in Aggression Research. *Aggression: Theo-
            retical and Empirical Reviews, Vol. 2: Issues in Research,* ed. R. Geen
            and E. Donnerstein, 1–26. New York: Academic Press.

Whiting, B.
    1950   *Paiute Sorcery.* New York: Viking.

Whiting, B., and C. Edwards
    1973   A Cross-Cultural Analysis of Sex Differences in the Behavior of
            Children Aged Three Through Eleven. *Journal of Social Psychology*
            91:171–188.

Whiting, J.
    1969   The Place of Aggression in Social Interaction. In *Collective Vio-
            lence,* ed. J. Short and M. Wolfgang, 192–197. Chicago: Aldine-
            Atherton.

Whyte, M.
    1978   *The Status of Women in Preindustrial Society.* Princeton: Princeton
            University Press.

Williams, N.
    1987   *Two Laws: Managing Disputes in a Contemporary Aboriginal Com-
            munity.* Canberra: Australian Institute of Aboriginal Studies.
    1988   Studies in Australian Aboriginal Law 1961–1986. In *Social An-
            thropology and Australian Aboriginal Studies: A Contemporary Over-
            view,* ed. R. Berndt and R. Tonkinson, 189–237. Canberra: Ab-
            original Studies Press.

Wilson, M., and M. Daly
    1987   Risk of Maltreatment of Children Living with Stepparents. In
            Child Abuse and Neglect: Biosocial Dimensions, ed. R. Gelles and J.
            Lancaster, 215–232. New York: Aldine de Gruyter.

Wilson, P.
    1982   *Black Death, White Hands.* Sydney: Allen and Unwin.

Wolf, M.
    1968   *The House of Lim: A Study of a Chinese Family Farm.* New York:
            Appleton-Century-Crofts.
    1972   *Women and the Family in Rural Taiwan.* Stanford: Stanford Uni-
            versity Press.

Worthman, C.
    1992   Cupid and Psyche: Investigative Syncretism in Biological and Psy-
            chosocial Anthropology. In *The Social Life of Psyche: Debates and
            Directions in Psychological Anthropology,* ed. T. Schwartz, G. White,
            and C. Lutz, 150–178. Cambridge: Cambridge University Press.

Yanagisako, S., and J. Collier
    1987   Toward a Unified Analysis of Gender and Kinship. In *Gender and
            Kinship: Essays Toward a Unified Analysis,* ed. J. Collier and S. Ya-
            nagisako, 14–50. Stanford: Stanford University Press.

Yengoyan, A.
    1990   Cloths of Heaven: Freud, Language, and the Negation in Pitjant-

jatjara Dreams. In *Personality and the Cultural Construction of Society,* ed. D. Jordan and M. Swartz, 201–221. Tuscaloosa: University of Alabama Press.

Yllo, K., and M. Bograd (eds.)
  1988   *Feminist Perspectives on Wife Abuse.* Beverly Hills: Sage.

Young, E.
  1981   *Tribal Communities in Rural Areas.* Canberra: Australian National University Press.

Index

Abbott, S., 194n.5

Abduction, as category of aggression, 198n.6

Aborigines: citizenship status of, 25, 27, 197n.4; control of violence by, 30; population figures, 24; violence against by outsiders, 23–24; violence against outsiders by, 195n.1; Westerners and, 21–28

Abu-Lughod, L., 5, 12, 14, 44, 47, 82, 109, 144

Abu Ras, W., 109, 185

Accusations, shame and, 85

Action: aggression as, 5–6, 193n.2; behavior and, 193n.2; intention vs. consequence and, 6

"Adequate definition of reality," 195n.9

Adolescents: aggression toward, as punishment, 69; fighting by, 130; petrol sniffing by, 39–40

Adultery: as cause for anger, 54; as cause for displaced aggression, 123; as reason for aggression, 104. *See also* Jealousy

Aftermath of fighting, 40, 82–96; healing as expected, 95–96; intention and, 69; reunification, 91–96; revenge, 86–91; shame, 85, 86; in women's vs. men's aggression, 136–137

Agar, M., 8

Aggression: acceptance of, 29, 123–124, 132; aftermath of (*see* Aftermath of fighting); anger and, 55–57, 70–71, 99, 148–149, 156, 179–181, 184; "arguing" vs., 50; associated with head, 64–65; categories of, 198n.6; as cause for anger, 54; children as targets of, 77; competition and, 100–101, 117–118; control of (*see* Control of aggression); cooperation in, 125–129; as counter to aggression, 39; in daily life, 33–43; defined, 4–6; "displaced," 120–125, 153–154; displaced (related cases), 197n.5; domestic vs. public, 129; as dominance attempt, 147–148, 202n.4; drug use and, 63; emotions and, 4; enjoyment of, 96; excluded cases, 197n.5; as expressive behavior, 68, 70–71, 132, 179–181, 183; family as target of, 87, 89–90; as family characteristic, 66–67; family involvement in, 38–39; fear of, 145; female-male (*see* Female-male aggression); feminist views of, 3–4; frequency of, 42–43; friends' views of, 54; functions of, 68–71; gender and (*see* Gender); healing expected from, 95–96; hierarchy and, 109–111; injury prevention (*see* Control of aggression); intensity of, 104–105; in intervention, 80–81; irrational, 65–66; jealousy and, 57–60; lack of fear of, 177-178;

Designer:	U.C. Press Staff
Compositor:	Maple-Vail Book Manufacturing Group
Text:	10/13 Galliard
Display:	Galliard
Printer:	Maple-Vail Book Manufacturing Group
Binder:	Maple-Vail Book Manufacturing Group